DYNAMIC HTML:

A PRIMER

Y0-BDI-155

DYNAMIC HTML: A PRIMER

Simon St. Laurent

A Subsidiary of
Henry Holt and Co., Inc.

MIS:Press
A Subsidiary of Henry Holt and Company, Inc.
115 West 18th Street
New York, New York 10011
http://www.mispress.com

Copyright © 1997 by Simon St. Laurent

Printed in the United States of America

All rights reserved. No part of this book may be reproduced or transmitted in any form or by any means, electronic or mechanical, including photocopying, recording, or by any information storage and retrieval system, without prior written permission from the Publisher. Contact the Publisher for information on foreign rights.

Limits of Liability and Disclaimer of Warranty

The Author and Publisher of this book have used their best efforts in preparing the book and the programs contained in it. These efforts include the development, research, and testing of the theories and programs to determine their effectiveness.

The Author and Publisher make no warranty of any kind, expressed or implied, with regard to these programs or the documentation contained in this book. The Author and Publisher shall not be liable in any event for incidental or consequential damages in connection with, or arising out of, the furnishing, performance, or use of these programs.

All products, names and services are trademarks or registered trademarks of their respective companies.

First Edition—1997

Library of Congress Cataloging-in-Publication Data
St Laurent, Simon
   Dynamic HTML : A Primer / by Simon St. Laurent
      p.   cm.
   ISBN 1-55828-569-5
      1. HTML (Document markup language)
   QA76.76.H94S7   1997
   005.7'2—dc21
97-28076
   CIP

MIS:Press and M&T Books are available at special discounts for bulk purchases for sales promotions, premiums, and fundraising. Special editions or book excerpts can also be created to specification.

For details contact: Special Sales Director
                              MIS:Press and M&T Books
                              Subsidiaries of Henry Holt and Company, Inc.
                              115 West 18th Street
                              New York, New York 10011

10 9 8 7 6 5 4 3 2 1

Associate Publisher: *Paul Farrell*

Managing Editor: *Shari Chappell*   **Production Editor:** *Gay Nichols*
Editor: *Ann C. Lush*   **Technical Editor:** *Bebo White*
Copy Edit Manager: *Karen Tongish*   **Copy Editor:** *Betsy Hardinger*

For Tracey, who makes my sweetest dreams come true

Acknowledgements

I would love to thank Tracey Cranston for being her usual amazing self and helping me stay calm when it didn't seem like anything worked. My parents, who've helped me finance too many of my computing ventures for the last 15 years, provided constant support and encouragement.

Michael Sprague got me started with this book, converting me quite successfully from a Dynamic HTML skeptic to a thorough believer. Ann Lush did a great job of keeping me on track, listening patiently to my complaints and always pointing out the bright side of authoring. Bebo White provided great feedback on the book and the examples, and hopefully some of his comments have taken root in the pages that follow. I'd also like to thank Paul Farrell and Nettie Aljian at MIS:Press for teaching me a lot about the publishing business and the strange but exciting world of computer books.

Contents in Brief

CHAPTER 1: The Problem of Interactivity 1

CHAPTER 2: HTML—The Structures Behind
the Problem 17

CHAPTER 3: Getting Started with Dynamic HTML . . 27

CHAPTER 4: Making the Objects Dance 39

CHAPTER 5: Something's Happening: Events 69

CHAPTER 6: Control or Be Controlled:
Controls and Applets 103

CHAPTER 7: Interactive Documents I:
Letting the User In 127

CHAPTER 8: Interactive Documents II:
Changing Document Content 169

CHAPTER 9: Interactive Documents III:
Communicating with the User 195

CHAPTER 10: Multimedia Effects 221

CHAPTER 11: Binding Data to Your Documents . . . 239

CHAPTER 12: Layers Upon Layers: Netscape
Tools for Dynamic HTML 271

APPENDIX A: The Fine Art of Detecting Browsers . . 317

APPENDIX B: Note on terminology 321

Contents

CHAPTER 1: The Problem of Interactivity 1

Server-Side Includes: Parsing Documents 2

CGI Scripting and Other Server Tools 6

Using JavaScript 10

Using VBScript 13

The Common Problem 15

**CHAPTER 2:HTML—The Structures Behind
the Problem** 17

Documents and Hypertext 17

Structures Break Down into Chaos 19

Making Style Sheets Work 20

Plug-Ins, Applets, and Objects 25

CHAPTER 3:Getting Started with Dynamic HTML . 27

An Object Model for HTML 27

The Old Models 28

All the Objects You Want 31

Trying It Out 35

CHAPTER 4:Making the Objects Dance 39

Every Attribute Is Available 39

The Power of Style 40

Let It <BLINK>........................... 41

Changing Position: HTML in Motion.......... 46

Style Properties You Can Manipulate 55

Changing Document Properties 60

Images: The Old Way, the New Way........... 61

Changing Content: TextRanges, Part 1 66

CHAPTER 5:Something's Happening: Events 69
   Events in VBScript vs Events in JavaScript 70
   The Place of Events in the Object Model:
      Netscape vs. Microsoft 71
   Handling Simple Events 75
     Mouse Events 75
     Loading Events 82
     Form Events 85
     Marquee Events 90
     Data-Binding Events 92
     Other Events 92
     Window Events (Netscape 4.0 Only) 96
   Creating Your Own Events 98
   Inheritance and Event Bubbling 98
CHAPTER 6:Control or Be Controlled:
      Controls and Applets 103
   ActiveX and HTML 104
   Including ActiveX Controls on Your Page 107
   Working with ActiveX Control Properties,
      Methods, and Events 109
   Java 115
   Java and the Web Browser: Applets 117
   LiveConnect and COM: Calling Java
      from JavaScript 118
   LiveConnect: Calling JavaScript from Java 122
CHAPTER 7:Interactive Documents I:
      Letting the User In 127
   Responding to the User 127
   Creating Outlines with Text Ranges 128
   Creating Outlines with Styles 131
   Creating Outlines with Styles and
      Naming Conventions 135

Creating Simple Pop-Up Menus 141
Following Your Every Move 146
Letting the User Move Things Around 148
Moving from Drag to Drag-and-Drop 152
Making Old Interfaces New 155
The Document as Dataset 160

CHAPTER 8:Interactive Documents II:
Changing Document Content 169

textRanges and the Object Model 170
Different Worlds: textRanges vs. Properties 170
Creating textRange Objects From Elements 175
Creating and Manipulating Content-Based
textRange Objects 182
Managing Objects and Elements That Get
Trapped in Your textRange 187

CHAPTER 9:Interactive Documents III:
Communicating with the User 195

Multiframe and Multiwindow Examples 195
Targeting Frames 196
Targeting Windows 199
Hiding Information: The Comic Strip 202
Eliza: Creating an Interface with
textRange Objects 206

CHAPTER 10:Multimedia Effects 221

Transitions 222
Visual Filters 225
Paths 229
Structured Graphics 231
Sequencer 235
Other Controls 238

CHAPTER 11:Binding Data to Your Documents ... 239
  A Quick Introduction to Databases and the Web .. 240
    Tables 241
    Queries 242
    Applications 245
  Old Technology, New Technology 246
    On the Server Side 246
    On the Client Side: HTML Data Binding 253
    Tabular Data Control 255
    An Introduction to Advanced Data Control ... 263
    Events and ADC 267
    Implications of ADC and Data Objects 269
CHAPTER 12:Layers Upon Layers: Netscape
        Tools for Dynamic HTML 271
    Layers: An Introduction 272
    Client-Side includes Made Real 276
    Hiding Information with Layers 280
    Hidden Information: The Comic Strip 288
    Animation with Layers 292
    Drag and Drop with Layers 294
    Clipping: Windows On Layers 301
APPENDIX A: The Fine Art of Detecting Browsers . 317
APPENDIX B: Note on terminology 321
Index 323

Break It Down to Make It Stronger

When HTML was created in 1991, it dramatically changed the way people access information. By providing an intelligible, easy-to-learn standard for hypertext documents, HTML and the other World Wide Web standards made it possible for ordinary people to create complicated hypertext documents and distribute them easily. Although HTML tags were often cryptic, learning HTML wasn't much harder than learning a word processor, at least at first. The structures are simple, even elegant, and it's not difficult to create readable documents that provide a lot of information. Over time, HTML documents acquired new design frills and a measure of interactivity, but the underlying structure didn't change very much.

It's time for a second revolution. Although HTML gives designers a basic set of structures, the structures lack flexibility. Once an HTML document is loaded, it can't be changed. Applets and plug-ins provide interactivity, but the basic HTML code can't change its appearance in response to user needs. Although HTML has come a long way in designability, it's time for it to move forward in programmability.

The Web is on the verge of a change nearly as dramatic as the appearance of the first graphical browsers. One of its fundamental elements is about to be broken and rebuilt to be stronger, better, and faster. The browser will finally achieve full status as an interface, much as Netscape has hyped it recently. Interactive documents—documents that easily transform parts of themselves in "live" ways that seem as transparent as the traditional desktop GUI—are on the way. Best of all, you don't have to be a Java expert or C++ guru to work with them.

The source of all this promise is Dynamic HTML. A proposed standard developed by the W3 committee (http://www.w3.org), Dynamic HTML was first implemented in Microsoft Internet Explorer 4. The basic concept is simple: break the document into containers of information that can be separately addressed and modified—live. The document is no longer static, because Dynamic HTML allows scripts, applets, and ActiveX objects to modify the HTML code directly. The browser will keep up with changes to the HTML and will redisplay the document without having to go back to the server or rebuild the page from scratch. HTML is no longer just a way to present information; instead, it has become an interface that gives users a much more powerful way to interact with the information. HTML developers will be able to build powerful interfaces without needing to resort to heavy-duty Java or ActiveX programming, although both kinds of programming will have their uses in conjunction with Dynamic HTML.

Like every other Web standard, Dynamic HTML is affected by the browser wars. After Netscape and Microsoft began submitting their varying standards to open committees, including members of both sides, a few false prophets predicted the end of the browser wars. But the companies will probably always find new things to fight about. In this battle, I think Microsoft has much more to offer, but I hope to give you a fair perspective on the advantages and disadvantages of the models and tools offered by both sides. Revolutions have a way of fragmenting, and computing revolutions have proven to be no purer than any other. Despite the tumult, new tools are emerging that will give developers (including ordinary Web creators) an easy way to create rich documents with much more depth and programmability. One word of warning: taking advantage of these tools will require some knowledge of scripting. I've tried to write this book to benefit HTML developers as well as programmers and scripters, but advanced techniques inevitably require advanced knowledge. I've included information along the way to help non-scripters make immediate use of the power of Dynamic HTML, but as the book progresses there's simply too much to explain. If you've programmed in anything resembling C (for JavaScript) or Basic (for VBScript), you'll probably be fine and can skip some of the sections devoted to elementary programming concepts. If you have no programming experience, read this book as far as you can. Try the examples and make small changes. Then visit your local bookstore (or the Netscape and Microsoft Web sites) for a good tutorial on scripting. I suspect you'll be better off learning JavaScript. Most of this book uses JavaScript for the scripting, although I've also provided some illustrations in VBScript as well as one long project that's based on a previously developed Basic program. I have serious doubts about the viability of Visual Basic, but if you're working in a Microsoft shop you may be able to ignore them.

CHAPTER 1

The Problem of Interactivity

At the inception, it was possible to learn HTML and Web page design in an hour. It wasn't really programming, just a collection of mark-up tags that produced approximately the same output every time a page was opened. Almost as soon as the Web sprang into existence, users demanded a more sophisticated type of interactivity. They wanted documents capable of changing every time a page opened. To meet this need, a succession of techniques were developed for creating live pages, first on the server and eventually on the client. These approaches demand a much more sophisticated level of programming than HTML does. Some of them work on the server and others on the reader's browser, but all of them have drawbacks, primarily in ease of use and performance.

Because of the limitations of browsers, most of these solutions work on the Web server. Using them requires more than simple HTML; you need a thorough understanding of the process of retrieving Web documents. Because you'll probably need to use these techniques in conjunction with HTML, it's worthwhile to understand the process. The examples in this chapter barely begin to take advantage of the power of these techniques but should give you a grounding to help you understand how Dynamic HTML goes well beyond their capabilities.

Normally, a browser on a computer attached to the Internet sends a request to a server. The URL for a document contains three key pieces of information: the protocol to use to transfer data, the server where the data is stored, and a path to the document. If that document is a static file, the process is simple and looks like Figure 1.1. The browser interprets the URL, figures out which server to contact, and sends a request with some simple information. The server processes the request, finds the file, and sends it to the browser. If the document needs more files to display (such as graphics), the browser issues new requests for each needed file and displays the document as the files arrive.

Server-Side Includes: Parsing Documents

If a document needs to include information that changes, the situation is a little more complicated. If the changes are simple, a server-side include might do the trick. Instead of pulling up the file and transmitting it, the server pauses to examine the document and make additions as requested by tags in the document. The overall process is similar to a standard HTTP request, but the server takes a few more steps (see Figure 1.2)

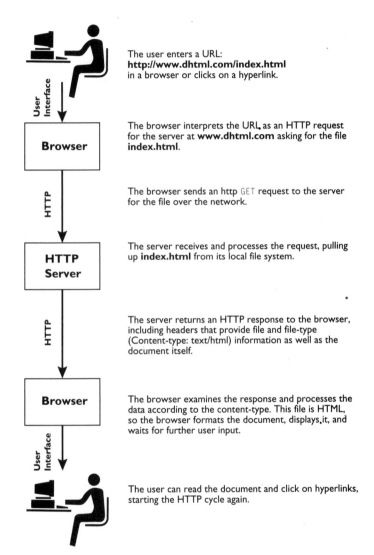

The user enters a URL:
http://www.dhtml.com/index.html
in a browser or clicks on a hyperlink.

The browser interprets the URL as an HTTP request
for the server at **www.dhtml.com** asking for the file
index.html.

The browser sends an http GET request to the server
for the file over the network.

The server receives and processes the request, pulling
up **index.html** from its local file system.

The server returns an HTTP response to the browser,
including headers that provide file and file-type
(Content-type: text/html) information as well as the
document itself.

The browser examines the response and processes the
data according to the content-type. This file is HTML,
so the browser formats the document, displays it, and
waits for further user input.

The user can read the document and click on hyperlinks,
starting the HTTP cycle again.

Figure 1.1 Retrieving an HTML document using HTTP.

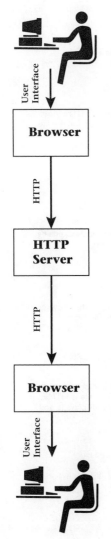

The user sees a URL:
http://www.dhtml.com/test.shtml
in a browser or clicks on a hyperlink.

The browser interprets the URL as an HTTP request
for the server at **www.dhtml.com** asking for the file
test.shtml.

The browser sends an http GET request to that server
for that file over the network.

The server receives and processes the request, pulling
up **test, shtml** from its local file system. Because of the
.shtml file extension, the server knows it has to read
through the document to find <#!--INCLUDE-->
statements. It finds the tags and replaces them with the
contents of the files or information to which they refer.

The server returns an HTTP response to the browser,
including headers that provide file and file-type
(Content-type: text/html) information as well as the
newly built document.

The browser examines the response and processes the
data according to the content-type. This file is HTML,
so the browser formats the document, displays it, and
waits for further user input.

The user can read the document and click on hyperlinks,
starting the HTTP cycle again.

Figure 1.2 Retrieving an HTML document using server-side
includes.

Using this technique takes a bit more knowledge about your server, because the rules for includes vary more than with most HTML. Generally, the rules are simple. The include tags look like HTML comments. **Include.shtml** (or **Include.stm** on Microsoft's InternetInformation Server) looks like this:

```
<HTML>
<HEAD><TITLE>Server include</TITLE></HEAD>
<BODY>
<!-#INCLUDE FILE="test.html"->
<P>This line is from the original file.</P>
</BODY>
</HTML>
```

test.html contains this line:

```
<H1>This is the included text</H1>
```

The result is shown in Figure 1.3.

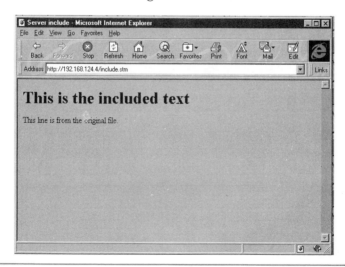

Figure 1.3 Include results.

This approach is useful for simple tasks, such as links to the latest headlines on a site that changes slowly, but it's limited. It places a burden on the server, requiring the machine to parse the entire file every time it serves it. This technique offers other options, such as the ability to include file information—such as the last date a file was modified or its size in bytes—but unfortunately the options can vary from server to server.

CGI Scripting and Other Server Tools

CGI (Common Gateway Interface) scripting gives you far more power than you get with server-side includes. CGI links the HTTP server to programs running (usually) on the same machine. You can create pages for users as individual requests come in, and you can customize pages to match that information. Depending on the kind of server on which the site resides, you can write CGI programs in languages from C++ to Perl to AppleScript to Python. Given the right system, you can use almost any language. As usual, some languages are better than others for particular tasks.

CGI adds another layer to the HTTP transaction (see Figure 1.4). Instead of receiving requests and sending back files, CGI lets you receive information with those requests and respond dynamically. Its most common application is in forms processing. The user fills out a form and clicks the **Submit** button. The user's browser sends to the server a request that includes the information the user entered into the form. The server passes the information to another program for processing and then sends the output of that program to the user's browser.

The user enters a URL
(**http://www.dhtml.com/cgi-bin/test.pl**)
in a browser, clicks on a hyperlink, or clicks
the **Submit** button on a form.

Browser

The browser interprets the URL as an HTTP
request for the server at **www.dhtml.com** asking
for the file at **cgi-bin/test.pl.**

The browser sends an HTTP GET or POST (if there is form
data to send) request to the server for the file over the network.

HTTP Server

The server receives the request. Because **test.pl** is in a directory reserved
for programs, the server determines that it should execute the **test.pl**
program and not just return its content (the program) to the browser.

The server starts test.pl, passing it all of the information the browser
sent with the request.

CGI Program

The CGI program executes, using the data given it by the server. It may
run other programs, acces databases, use the file system, or do whatever
it's been programmed to do to process the request.

The program returns an HTTP response to the server, including headers
that provide file and file-type (Content-type: text/html) information as
well as the document.

HTTP Server

The server receives the information from the program and packages the
response to indicate successful completion of the program as well as
returns the contents of the CGI program's results.

The HTTP response is relayed to the client.

Client

The browser examines the response, and processes the data according
to the Content-type. This file is HTML, so the browser formats the
document, displays it, and waits for further user input.

The user can read the document and click on hyperlinks, starting
the HTTP cycle again.

Figure 1.4 HTTP transaction with CGI processing.

Perl is still the most common language used for scripting CGI. It combines the syntax of C with the power of UNIX regular expressions and adds strange magic all its own. Originally created to perform administrative tasks, Perl has moved well beyond its base in the UNIX world. Although Perl programs can be indecipherable, it is possible to write simple programs in Perl with a minimum of effort. The example we'll show here is especially simple. For the sake of demonstration (this is a book about dynamic HTML and not CGI), we'll show a readable program that sends a message to the user without demanding or processing any input.

```
#!/usr/local/bin/perl

print "Content-type: text/html\n\n";
print "<HTML>\n";
print "<HEAD><TITLE>Very Simple CGI</TITLE></HEAD>";
print "<BODY>\n";
print "<H1>CGI Sample</H1>\n";
print "This is a demonstration of what you can do
with simple Perl.<BR>";
print "You'll need another whole book to make it
interactive.";
print "But this is a start.\n";
print "</BODY>\n";
print "</HTML>\n";
```

Note that you must include the "Content-type" line. The server won't look at this file once it's created, so the normal responsibilities of the server (such as indicating what type of file it is) fall to the programmer. The "\n" code is short for *newline*, a line break to keep the resulting code readable. If all goes well—all the files are placed in the right directory, and all the permissions are set correctly—the results should look like Figure 1.5.

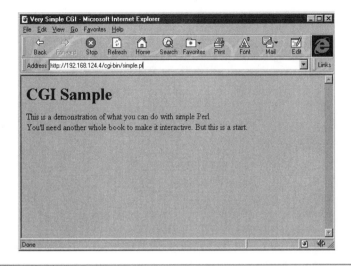

Figure 1.5 CGI results.

The results of this program aren't very exciting, but they illustrate how to create a simple HTML file using some programming. You can create flexible programs that produce a wide range of responses to user input or store that input (perhaps in a database) for later use. Most of the interactive pages available on the Web use CGI to some extent. For a more detailed explanation, I recommend *Introduction to CGI/Perl: Getting Started with Web Scripts*, by Steven Brenner and Edwin Aoki (MIS:Press, 1996).

If you don't want to go to the trouble of writing complex programs to create pages with server-side interaction, you can check out FrontPage 2.0, Microsoft's Web site editing program. It includes *bots*, small programs that attach to the host server and provide lots of functionality for very little work. They can process forms, provide timestamps on pages, and even give users a friendly way to search your site.

Using JavaScript

Netscape introduced JavaScript with Netscape 2.0, and Microsoft responded with JScript in Internet Explorer 3.0 as well as VBScript, a scripting language based on the flagship Visual Basic. JavaScript and JScript are converging, but it's not always easy to tell what will work on a particular browser. Still, these languages have provided HTML developers with powerful new tools to make the browser do new and different things. Not everything has to take place on the server; the client takes a more active part (see Figure 1.6).

In this example, we'll include a small dynamic element: the date. This script isn't very useful, but it provides one bit of updated information.

```
<HTML>
<HEAD><TITLE>Simple
JavaScript/JScript</TITLE></HEAD>
<BODY>
<CENTER><H1>JavaScript/JScript Dynamic
Pages</H1></CENTER>
<HR>
<SCRIPT LANGUAGE="JavaScript">
<!- Hide This Code From Non-JS Browsers
document.writeln("<P>See?  This was created today!
</P>");
var today = new Date();   // Use today's date
var text= "Today is " + (today.getMonth() + 1) + "/"
+ today.getDate() + "/" +today.getYear()+".";
document.writeln(text);
//->
</SCRIPT>
</BODY>
</HTML>
```

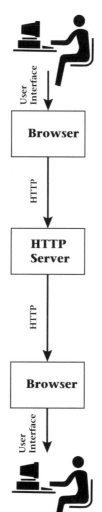

The user enters a URL
(http://www.dhtml.com/index.html)
in a browser or clicks on a hyperlink.

The browser interprets the URL as an HTTP request
for the server at **www.dhtml.com** asking for the file
index.html.

The browser sends an http GET request to that server
for the file over the network.

The server receives and processes the request, pulling
up **index.html** from its local file system.

The server returns an HTTP response to the browser,
including headers that provide file and file-type
(Content-type: text/html) information as well as the
document itself.

The browser examines the response and processes the
data according to the content-type. This file is HTML,
so the browser parses it, looking for scripts to compile
and possibly run. In the initial laoding process, the script
can actively create a document. Then it formats the docum
displays it, and waits for further user input.

The user can read the document and click on hyperlinks,
starting the HTTP cycle again. Clicks and other actions
may also activate scripts.

Figure 1.6 HTTP transaction with script processing.

As you can see, most of the page is written in HTML. The only parts that are written by the program are two lines of text, one of which includes the date. The SCRIPT tags tell script-aware browsers (primarily those from Microsoft and Netscape) that a script will follow. Within those tags are HTML comment tags (to keep old browsers from pouring out unreadable script) along with a simple program that writes a few lines of HTML code and then goes away. The document is created dynamically, and then the program ends, leaving you with a screen like the one in Figure 1.7.

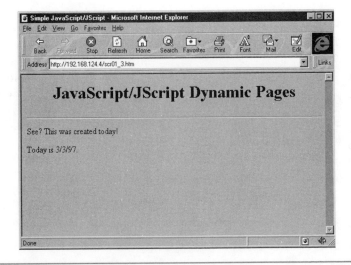

Figure 1.7 JavaScript results.

This approach can be extended to do far more complex things. You can create *cookies*, which store small amounts of information about a user's preferences on a user's machine and use that information to create customized pages on subsequent visits. You can customize most aspects of Web pages and even the browsers. There's still one problem, though. If I were to load the example page at 11:59 PM and take a coffee break, when I got back the page would still display the previous date. The page doesn't change once the script finishes running. Until the user reloads the page to run the program again, the page will never change the date.

Using VBScript

Microsoft introduced VBScript with Internet Explorer 3.0, offering Visual Basic developers a Web scripting language they were already familiar with. Although JavaScript and JScript are based on a C- and Java-style syntax, VBScript offers similar features in a friendlier dialect of Basic. As part of Microsoft's move to allow developers to use familiar (Microsoft) tools to create ActiveX controls, the company created VBScript to make it easy for developers to implement ActiveX in a Web environment. For the most part, because it's far more likely to become accepted as a common standard, we'll stick to using JavaScript and JScript, but VBScript will allow you to do similar things using a different programming language.

The program we created in JavaScript looks like this in VBScript:

```
<HTML>
<HEAD><TITLE>Simple VBScript</TITLE></HEAD>
<BODY>
<CENTER><H1>VBScript Dynamic Page</H1></CENTER>
<HR>
<SCRIPT LANGUAGE="VBScript">
<!- Hide This Code From Non-Scripting Browsers
document.write ("<P>See?  This was created today!
</P>")
Dim today, text
today = Date() 'set the date
```

```
text= "Today is " & Month(today) & "/" & Day(today)
& "/" & Year(today) & "."
document.write (text)
-->
</SCRIPT>
</BODY>
</HTML>
```

As you can see, the syntax is quite different, although both versions are readable. VBScript doesn't have semicolons at the end of each line, and it uses an apostrophe to begin a comment instead of a double slash. It also concatenates strings with an ampersand instead of a plus sign and generally looks a little more readable. This program does the same thing as its JavaScript equivalent: it writes a few lines of code and then goes away, never to run again. The results are similar (see Figure 1.8)

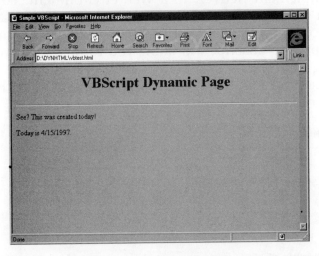

Figure 1.8 VBScript results.

The date may change when you go out for a midnight coffee break, but the display on your screen will sit there until you reload the page. VBScript is as static as the others.

The Common Problem

With Dynamic HTML, we can fix the date problem—and much more. By making a slight change to the structure of the mark-up language, we'll be able to keep the date in sync with a real clock. And that's only the beginning!

Solving that problem, however, requires more than a change in our scripting languages; it requires a change in the underlying framework that governs what we see in a browser. (We could switch all our development to Java or ActiveX controls, but both techniques raise dramatic performance and security issues, not to mention learning curves, that HTML can easily avoid.) We'll look at what HTML has given us so far and what needs to change before we can make the leap to a more interactive browsing experience.

CHAPTER 2

HTML—The Structures Behind the Problem

As we saw in Chapter 1, trying to program in HTML is much like fitting a square peg in a round hole. The structure of browsers and the Web conspire to make it very difficult to change much with this simple mark-up language at the base level of document formatting. The load-once, never-refresh mentality of current browsers has made programming a difficult matter best reserved for experts.

Still, HTML's explosive growth would never have occurred if HTML really were the straitjacket Microsoft's and Netscape's press releases have sometimes made it out to be. For its time (it was created in 1991), it was a liberating form of communication. Its simplicity and extensibility guarantee it a long life, and some form of HTML will undoubtedly persist in the world of computing for years to come.

Documents and Hypertext

HTML was born at CERN, the high-energy physics laboratory in Geneva, Switzerland. Scientists there had a simple problem: they needed to share papers and other documents more quickly than traditional paper distribution would allow. Although a centralized document-handling system might have solved some of their problems, the scientists also needed to share documents with colleagues all over the world. Tim Berners-Lee, who continues to have an important influence over Web standards, led the development of a system that would allow scientists to share fairly complex materials easily using a simple set of protocols over the Internet.

His system consisted of two major protocols. HTTP, the Hypertext Transfer Protocol, provided a simple way for users to request and receive files over the Internet. (Although HTTP hasn't received as much attention as HTML has, it recently received its first major overhaul with HTTP 1.1.) The second protocol, HTML, was the mark-up language that provided a standard way to format documents.

At that point, no one was planning to send live stock quotes over the Web, nor was anyone planning to create wild multimedia sites that incorporated graphics and animation. The Web was seen more as a library than as a playground or billboard, and the original HTML specifications provided for as much formatting as a typical scientific journal might allow.

Still, HTML was the first popular implementation of hypertext. As static as HTML may now seem, these early documents were extremely exciting to researchers, who were glad to move beyond footnotes and create complex documents in which connections were as important as content. An electronic Web by its nature has much more life than a printout of the same pages might suggest. A few commentators were impressed (or confused) enough by HTML's ability to create links that they called it a *programming language*. In fact, many programmers were horrified by the <A HREF="goto.html> tag's similarity to the GOTO statement and its potential for "spaghetti programming," lacking as it did any kind of structure and connected only by forward links. They called it an abomination. (I was one of the skeptics until I realized it's better to use something that works than to wait for something perfect.)

Structures Break Down into Chaos

The developers at CERN began by creating a simple subset of a far more complex mark-up language, SGML (Standard Generalized Mark-up Language). SGML is used primarily for technical and legal documentation, and it is most commonly used by large organizations that maintain libraries of documents that are worked on by large numbers of people. The U.S. government, for example, keeps many of its documents in SGML. Unfortunately for programmers, SGML is huge and unwieldy. Learning all of SGML can take years, and developing a browser that can deal with all of it is probably not a worthwhile project.

SGML's influence lingers on in HTML's insistence on document structures, the seperation of content from formatting, and logical tags. This doesn't mean *logical* as in "can be interpreted by a browser" but rather the use of, for example, <EM> for emphasis instead of <B> for bold. Although these tags do the same thing on most browsers, bold is font-specific, whereas emphasis gives the interpreter much more freedom in formatting the document. The most obvious holdover from SGML is the <H1> through <H6> tags, which make it easy to create an outline from the headline levels in a document. Designers now use these tags for varying degrees of emphasis (or ignore them and use <FONT> tags).

Although logical tags can make some aspects of programming easier, their main purpose is to make it easy to create tables of contents and indices automatically. They've been largely buried in the blizzard of tags introduced since the browser market exploded in 1995, but they still exist, and they make Dynamic HTML development a good deal easier.

Throughout 1995 and 1996, a large number of tags were created, most of them by Netscape and Microsoft, so that designers could make pages look precisely the way they wanted without regard to underlying structure. After the academics at the W3 Consortium (which oversees HTML—at least, in theory) had been overwhelmed by the demand for design control, they arrived at some compromises that promise to combine the designers' demand for precise placement and specification with the academics' and developers' demand for structure. Cascading style sheets, introduced late last year, make it possible to specify particular fonts, sizes, and even placement (in an additional standard) for a wide variety of HTML elements. Suddenly, <H1> is useful again.

NOTE   An emerging technology, XML (Extensible Mark-up Language), promises to make it easy to extend HTML without creating the kinds of incompatibilities that have appeared in the last few years. Unfortunately, it is still on the horizon and will probably not be available until the release of Internet Explorer 5.0 and Netscape 5.0. It offers many of the advantages of style sheets but goes well beyond their limitations making it possible to create new tags and define their meanings easily.

Making Style Sheets Work

Style sheets give designers control over the way tags work. Until recently, this functionality was controlled by the browser developers. Using a simple syntax, designers can specify a level 1 header, for example, as 20-point Arial, boldface, red. Style sheets can be built into a document, or they can be loaded as separate files, making it easy to centralize the style information for an entire site. Style sheets do a lot for HTML, and, as we'll see later, they make it easy to handle many different projects in Dynamic HTML.

Cascading style sheets are "cascading" because a document can draw on a large number of sheets, some in separate files elsewhere on a server, others included in the HEAD section of an HTML document, and still others inside HTML tags and included as an attribute. In the examples used in this book, we'll be working primarily with the last two uses of styles. For more information on Cascading style sheets, be sure to check out *Cascading Style Sheets: A Primer* (MIS:Press, 1997).

A style sheet might look like this:

```
<STYLE TYPE="text/css"><—
H1 {font-family: Arial, Helvetica; font-weight:
bold; font-size: x-large; color: red}
H2 {font-family: Arial, Helvetica; font-weight:
bold; font-size: large; color: blue}
H3 {font-family: Arial, Helvetica; font-weight:
bold; color: green}

A :link {color: red}
A:visited {color:lime}
A:active {color:yellow}

H1 B {color:purple}
H1.black {font-family: serif; color: black}
H3#freaky {font-family: serif; color: aqua}
—></STYLE>
```

This style sheet does many different things. First, the type of style sheet specifies that it is a cascading style sheet and not, for instance, a JavaScript style sheet. Internet Explorer will work only with cascading style sheets, and Netscape Communicator works with both types. A comment opening follows the STYLE tag to hide the style information from browsers that can't handle style information. If it weren't there, many users of America Online and older browsers who visited your site would see pages prefaced by miles of style information, because the built-in browser doesn't support styles and doesn't ignore the contents of the style tags.

JavaScript style sheets are part of Netscape's own version of "dynamic HTML," and we'll come back to it in Chapter 11 when we take a side-by-side look at what Netscape and Microsoft are offering.

NOTE

The next three entries in the style sheet are more typical. They tell the browser how you want to display H1, H2, and H3. The entries are self-explanatory, but you may want to check out the official W3C recommendation at http://www.w3.org/pub/WWW/TR/REC-CSS1, because there are many more possibilities. You can use any of the standard HTML colors or specify colors in hex format (e.g., #FFFFFF.) You can specify the font size as a number if you prefer, and you can also specify the font family as a generic entry (e.g., serif or sans-serif). One of the nicest features of style sheets is that you can list multiple font families; the browser will use the first match it finds, making it much easier to develop pages for multiple platforms.

The next three items indicate the link colors. They're an easy alternative to including the colors in the BODY tag, and they are very useful if you plan to implement centralized style sheet management.

The next three lines start to take advantage of the power of style sheets. The first one indicates that all bold text within an H1 heading will be purple. The next two lines take advantage of subclasses and IDs, two powerful features that you'll learn more about later when we put Dynamic HTML to work. First, all H1 tags with the attribute CLASS=black are specified to be displayed in black (instead of purple) and in a serif font. The last tag will apply only to the *one* tag that has the attribute ID=freaky, making it aqua in a serif font. IDs make it particularly easy to manipulate a document.

Now we'll demonstrate how style sheets can transform a document. Our initial code looks like this:

```
<HTML>
<HEAD> <TITLE>Page without style sheets</TITLE>
<BODY BACKGROUND=#FFFFFF>
<H1>This is heading 1.  This is <B>bold</B> heading
1.</H1>
<H1>This is heading 1 in black.</H1>
<H2> This is heading 2.</H2>
<H3>This is heading 3.</H3><H3>This is freaky
heading 3.</H3>
<A HREF="http://nevervisited.com">unvisited
link</A><BR>
<A HREF="http://www.microsoft.com">visited link</A>
</BODY>
</HTML>
```

The result is shown in Figure 2.1.

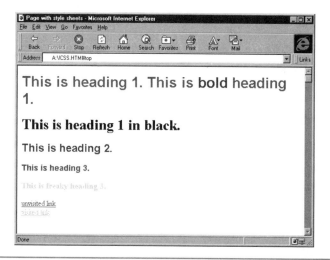

Figure 2.1 Document without styles.

Adding the style sheet is simple. It requires only the contents of the STYLE tag and a few ID and class attributes where we want them to take effect:

```
<HTML>
<HEAD> <TITLE>Page with style sheets</TITLE>

<STYLE TYPE="text/css"><-
H1 {font-family: Arial, Helvetica; font-weight:
bold; font-size: x-large; color: red}
H2 {font-family: Arial, Helvetica; font-weight:
bold; font-size: large; color: blue}
H3 {font-family: Arial, Helvetica; font-weight:
bold; color: green}

A:link {color: red}
A:visited {color:lime}
A:active {color:yellow}

H1 B {color:purple}
H1.black {font-family: serif; color: black}
H3#freaky {font-family: serif; color: aqua}
-></STYLE>
</HEAD>
<BODY BACKGROUND=#FFFFFF>
<H1>This is heading 1.  This is <B>bold</B> heading
1.</H1>
<H1 class="black">This is heading 1 in black.</H1>
<H2> This is heading 2.</H2>
<H3>This is heading 3.</H3><H3 ID="freaky">This is
freaky heading 3.</H3>
<A HREF="http://nevervisited.com">unvisited
link</A><BR>
<A HREF="http://www.microsoft.com">visited link</A>
</BODY>
</HTML>
```

Figure 2.2 shows what the page looks like afterward (unless the user has never visited www.microsoft.com, in which case the last link will still be unvisited).

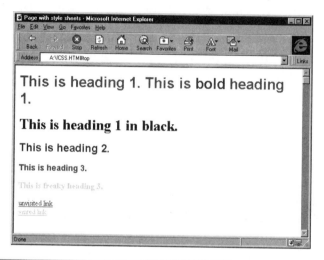

Figure 2.2 Document with styles.

We'll be dealing with styles and style sheets throughout the rest of this book as we examine Dynamic HTML. Later, we'll see how to use styles to place graphics and text on a page precisely, and we'll learn how to layer graphics and text. For now, keep in mind that styles are a powerful tool that combines the original structured presentation of HTML with the ability to make your pages look exactly the way you want them to look.

Plug-Ins, Applets, and Objects

Even if HTML becomes perfectly dynamic and easily programmable, there will still be many things it isn't very good at, such as animation, database manipulation, and terminal emulation, to name a few examples. Java,

ActiveX, and plug-ins address these and a wide variety of other tasks far more efficiently and more flexibly. Of course, these approaches have their inefficiencies and incompatibilities. Even the standard for including these kinds of Web objects is in dispute, although the OBJECT tag supported by Microsoft and the W3 seems likely to take over the EMBED, APPLET, and perhaps even the IMG tags.

Java doesn't execute very quickly, although it's undoubtedly the most powerful cross-platform standard ever to appear in computing. ActiveX works well on Windows 95 machines, but its ability to do anything a Windows 95 program can do creates a serious security flaw that Microsoft's digital signature program doesn't completely address. Because it was developed for Windows 95, ActiveX doesn't work on other platforms, and the ports Microsoft is creating are likely to suffer from the same performance problems that plague Java. Plug-ins can be convenient, especially for handling multimedia, but if they aren't ported to the particular browser on the particular platform you're using, they may as well not exist. Although a few key plug-ins have achieved widespread acceptance, developers can't count on every user having particular plug-ins installed.

All these technologies work with Dynamic HTML. It may require some effort to establish communications between an ActiveX object and HTML, but once you've set it up, you can ease the interface burden of your ActiveX objects and allow the browser to handle many mundane tasks. What's more, the latest changes to HTML will make it possible for many users to avoid having to resort to using more-advanced technologies.

CHAPTER 3

Getting Started with Dynamic HTML

The old HTML served developers well, but now it's time to take it apart and rebuild it. The changes will appear to be cosmetic, but the new model will be more tightly ordered than the previous one. The foundations are being replaced by a much stronger base that will support many years of HTML development.

An Object Model for HTML

Until recently, the concept of object orientation was confined to the realm of high-powered programming. It rarely bothered users except for the occasional bug caused by programmers who thought—wrongly—that they knew what objects were about. Over the past 30 years, object orientation has percolated down from academic computer science programs to the Web pages created by sixth-graders. Fortunately, objects in the context of HTML aren't nearly as complex as objects in C++ or even Java. Most of the time Web objects will be a selection of HTML between a few tags, but every now and then a Java applet or ActiveX control will creep in, so it's probably best to use the computer science terminology.

Objects in this context refers to the different pieces of a Web page that your browser juggles: the headers, images, paragraphs, applets, tables, and everything else that's been crammed into the Web. The problem with HTML is that pages get loaded as single pieces that can't be manipulated as they're loaded. It's as if a developer built a huge project from Legos and then welded it together before sending it to the kids who want to play with it. They can admire it—maybe a few motors will be whirring and lights blinking—but they can't take it apart and use its components to rebuild it in a different way. Even the motors are glued into place and can't be used to change the overall structure of this unwieldy piece of plastic.

Dynamic HTML lets you take the project apart. Replacing red bricks with green bricks is easy, and adding a motor to energize the graphics isn't much more difficult. Developers who have been working with JavaScript and JScript have been able to do a little bit of this, mostly by working with frames. Netscape developers have had a taste of what's possible with Navigator 3.0's images array, which allows you to change the appearance of a graphic. This capability makes it easy to create buttons that highlight when the mouse rolls over them or graphics that change cyclically. Microsoft developers who felt left out of that bit of magic can celebrate. Dynamic HTML will let them do that and much more.

The Old Models

The first step is to divide the document into its objects. If HTML had stayed a purely logical language, this process might have been easier. Still, the logical tools provided by the originators of HTML give us a good place to start. The object models developed by Netscape and Microsoft for their competing browsers have formed the terms of the debate and have given us the scripting languages with which to work.

The document itself is an object that exists in a layer below the window object, the browser window that frames the document. The hierarchy above the document level is fairly well agreed upon by Microsoft and Netscape. It looks roughly like Figure 3.1.

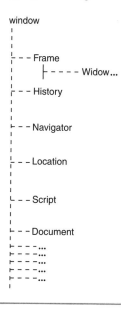

Figure 3.1 The upper levels of the document model.

The Window object is the uppermost box, although it is possible to make calls across different windows if you know their names. The Window object can contain Frame objects, which in turn can contain all the information a window can hold. The History object keeps the **Forward** and **Back** buttons working; the browser is simply keeping a list of where the user has been. The Navigator object contains information about the user's browser, and Location contains the current URL. The History list is protected from scripts, so you can't read where the user has been lurking, although you can send the user backward and forward along the list.

Microsoft and Netscape disagree about the location of the Navigator object; Netscape places it on the same level as the Window object, and Microsoft places it one level lower. Fortunately, the location makes no difference when you're programming. The Navigator object is a read-only convenience. A script can find out what browser you're looking at, but, despite the best efforts of Microsoft and Netscape, they can't change it. (You can change the location directly, something that's especially useful if you need to change several frames at the same time.)

The Script object contains all the scripts that are kept in the main document of a window. This object is especially important when there are frames within the window, because the scripts in the Window object are easily accessible to scripts in the frames below.

A few built-in objects don't fall under the Window object. The Date, Math, and String objects are the three main "rogue" objects.

N O T E

The Document object is where most of the battles are taking place. The object model in Figure 3.1 was created primarily by Netscape (hence the Navigator object), but the Document object is in flux. Internet Explorer 3.0 supported only three objects below the Document object: the Link array, which included all the links on a page, the Anchor array, which included all the <A> anchors on a page, and the Form array, which included all the <FORM> elements. None of these objects is especially exciting, although the Form array is useful for figuring out what a user has done on a form before sending it to be processed on a server; it's also useful for processing the results locally. Netscape 3.0 added the Images array, which let scripters change the graphic that appears in a particular IMG tag. Microsoft was pummeled by developers for not supporting the Images array in

Internet Explorer 3.0, but version 4.0 supports it and provides much more.

Still, even with the Images array, most of the page remained unavailable to scripting. Nothing in the text could be changed, so any highlighting (such as rollovers) had to be done with graphics. Many developers who had spent a lot of time coding suddenly found themselves learning the finer points of Photoshop, all because they couldn't change the color of a headline without reloading a page. Now it's possible.

All the Objects You Want

Internet Explorer 4.0 introduces a new object that inherits from the Document object: the "all" collection. It includes all the objects contained in the document, addressable by name (the NAME attribute used in Netscape 3.0) or ID (the CSS attribute we discussed earlier.) You can reference any tag in the document and change any of its attributes. If changing the color, the font, the image source, and the position isn't good enough for you, you can use another set of functions to change the HTML contained in that tag. Not only that, but the browser will refresh itself to keep up with any and all changes. Suddenly, you can make changes on-the-fly. If you're an experienced scripter and know how to reference objects, you can skip to the section titled "Trying It Out." Otherwise, stay here for a more detailed explanation of the mechanics of making the all collection work.

Our first simple examples will modify styles and a bit of text, so don't panic if you don't understand scripting. As your understanding increases, the examples will get more complicated. If you need more information about how the scripting languages work, look at the scripting tutorials available at http://www.microsoft.com/jscript or http://www.microsoft.com/vbscript.

First, we'll take a quick look at the syntax of dealing with objects. Fortunately, most of the simple property and method manipulation will be the same whether you're working in JavaScript, JScript, or VBScript. All of them use a simple syntax, somewhat like the syntax for identifying domain names on the Internet except that you read them left-to-right instead of right-to-left. For example, in www.w3.org, "org" is the top-level domain, indicating an organization as opposed to a company (com) or an educational institution (edu). "w3," the next level down, identifies which organization (in this case, the W3 organization, which sets standards and makes recommendations for the Web). "www," the next level down, takes you to a specific computer within the network.

When you're scripting a browser, it works similarly except that you read it the other direction. Here's an example written out in full:

```
window.document.all.myobject.style.fontStyle
```

window is the top-level object, document is the document displayed in that window, all is the collection of objects within that document, and myobject is an object created within that document by using the attribute ID=myobject within a tag. style is a property of myobject, and fontStyle is a property yet another layer down from style. It's much like a giant, collapsible outline that you must navigate.

N O T E   Sometimes you'll see another layer before the Window object. It's usually either the name of a window, the word *top*, or the word *this*. When you're working with multiple windows, this extra layer makes life much easier. This same kind of expansion can happen with frames, especially when you nest frames inside frames. The full object name can get unwieldy, but don't worry—you'll rarely use it.

Fortunately, unless you're manipulating multiple windows you won't have to write the full object syntax very often. A script in a document "knows" which document it's in, so you can make all your calls relative to that and omit the window.document call. The full names are usually used only when you're manipulating multiple documents, usually with frames.

You can also omit the document.all. object reference. As long as you don't assign object IDs that conflict with the names of other objects, you can refer to your objects directly by name. It would be easy to make this mistake with Date, for example, but generally you won't need to worry about it. Remember never to give your objects the same name as a built-in object, and never give two objects in a document the same name.

Objects can have two things lurking beneath their name: properties and methods. Properties are like variables. You can read them and sometimes write them with a simple statement:

```
myobject.style.fontStyle="italic";
```

This code would set in italics the text included in the element with the ID myobject. With Dynamic HTML, the font would actually change on screen. You can manipulate properties to do much more than change a font. As we'll see later, the style sheet standard includes a system for positioning objects on the screen. This means that you can use simple commands to tell the browser to move things around the screen.

N O T E

The use of style sheets will be critical to making these functions work. However useful the <FONT> tag may have been in the past, you'll want to use styles within other structure tags in the future. This technique makes it much easier to manipulate your objects, because all the display properties of your object are contained within the style object instead of floating around all over the page.

Methods are more like little programs, or even functions. The history object won't let you read where the user has been, but it has methods to send the user backward and forward through the list:

```
<A HREF="javascript:history.back()">Click here to go
back</A>
```

When the user clicks on the text, the script calls the back method of the history object for this document. That makes the browser take users to the previous page exactly as if they had pressed the **Back** button in the toolbar. We'll use some methods Microsoft has added to the document object to make changes to HTML after it has been loaded.

JavaScript, JScript, and VBScript

Unfortunately (or fortunately, depending on how many choices you like to have) the scripting world is fragmented. JavaScript and JScript are similar, and drawing closer together, but VBScript remains something of an orphan. Netscape has demonstrated no interest in using VBScript in its browsers, and it will probably remain a tool used only by Internet Explorer shops. For intranets, that's fine, because you can control the browser your employees use. On the Internet, you'll be much happier if you stick with the variations on JavaScript.

There are a few differences beginning scripters need to know about, although they don't affect the object model. First, you can't call VBScript directly from an HREF as you can JavaScript. You must call a function. Functions are also called a little bit differently. If a function has no arguments, you don't need the parentheses after the function name. Within a function, VBScript code doesn't need a semicolon at the end of each line; using one will generate a syntax error. The control structures also differ, as we'll see later, although both languages can be made to do the same things. I recommend that you use JavaScript for most of the examples, but keep in mind that all the structures we discuss throughout the book are accessible in VBScript with a little bit of rewriting.

Now that we know a bit about the objects we'll be working with, it's time to put them to work.

Trying It Out

For our first example we'll keep things simple:

```
<HTML>
<HEAD><TITLE>Dynamic HTML Experiment</TITLE>
</HEAD>
<BODY BGCOLOR=#FFFFFF>
<P ID="test1"
onmouseover="javascript:document.all.test1.style.fon
tStyle='italic'"
onmouseout="javascript:document.all.test1.style.font
Style='normal'" >This is a test</P>
</BODY></HTML>
```

It doesn't take much code to make this work, and we didn't need to create any functions. In the future, we'll create functions and find ways to make things work in a more general way, but this example is really simple. When you roll over the text with the mouse, the preceding tiny piece of code sets the style of the text (as with style sheets) to italic. When the mouse rolls away, the text is set back to normal. It's all keyed to the ID attribute of the paragraph element.

There's a reason to use opening and closing paragraph tags. Plug in the code and try it out. At first you'll see the text shown in Figure 3.2.

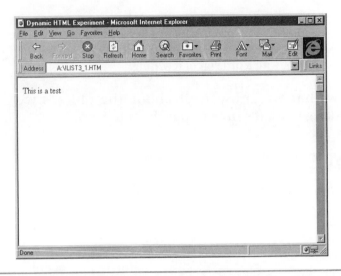

Figure 3.2 Before you roll the mouse over the text.

Roll the mouse over the text, and you'll see the italicized text shown in Figure 3.3.

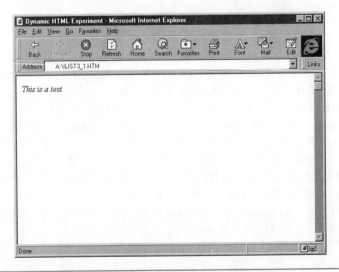

Figure 3.3 The text with the cursor over it.

When you roll the mouse away, the text returns to the original font.

This example may not seem like much, but the ability to change live text is the beginning of many powerful coding possibilities. (You might also notice that I included the document.all reference for clarity. It works, but it isn't necessary. From now on, I'll omit it.)

CHAPTER 4

Making the Objects Dance

Now that we know how to address the objects of our document, it's time to make them react. This chapter will focus on techniques for changing the objects' appearance and content. We'll leave the more interactive, event-driven possibilities for Chapter 5.

Styles will be crucial to these projects, as will a new kind of object called the textRange. If you ever wanted to create your own alternative to the <BLINK> tag, felt bored with a page's background graphic, wanted to change a headline, or wanted to see your company logo dance around a Web page, you've come to the right place.

Every Attribute Is Available

Microsoft's listing of all the properties available in a document is available at http://www.microsoft.com/workshop/author/dynhtml/dhtm0449.htm. The list is enormous and includes hundreds of properties that cover every attribute available in an Internet Explorer-compatible HTML tag. If you need to print out all the properties (Internet Explorer 4 will let you print all the pages linked from a page), be sure to do it on a high-speed office printer or it will take hours.

The best thing about these properties is that most of them have read-write permissions, so you can examine them and change them. The browser will adjust its display to accommodate your changes, whether you changed the color of some text, the image in a graphic, the background image of a page, or the position of an image. Almost every piece of HTML is available at your command.

The Power of Style

In the example in Chapter 3, we used a simple bit of style manipulation to change the font of some text. Now we'll take that style manipulation to new levels, demonstrating along the way a few of the style properties at your disposal. Although style manipulation isn't as dramatic as some of the other features, it's a good place to get started. It's easy to do and, with any luck, will encourage you to use cascading style sheet commands in your future documents whether or not you plan to script them.

One danger to watch for is the name difference between cascading style sheet properties and the properties of the style object in Internet Explorer 4.0. In cascading style sheet, it's font-family; in Internet Explorer 4.0, it's fontFamily. A simple rule should get you through this minefield: all multiword properties in a style sheets are connected by hyphens. All multiword properties in Internet Explorer 4.0 use the same name for the property, but the hyphens are dropped and the words are closed up. The first word is not capitalized, but each subsequent word is capitalized. So font-size becomes fontSize, and border-right-width becomes borderRightWidth. It's annoying, but at least it's consistent. The values for the properties (such as aliceblue, red, green, and aqua for color) remain the same in both systems.

NOTE An ongoing debate between Netscape and Microsoft concerns the programmability of style sheets and not just of styles. Netscape's JavaScript style sheets are programmable but take effect immediately after they're loaded without allowing change. Microsoft doesn't let you program the style sheet itself but will let you change the style attributes of a document without requiring a reload. Later, we'll explore how to change the class of an object and thereby bounce it from style to style.

Let It <BLINK>

Probably the one design element most Web developers can agree to hate is the <BLINK> tag. I've complained about it myself, although it serves a purpose once in a while: emulating older, text-based systems that have no other way to get the user's attention. Microsoft hasn't seen fit to implement this blot on Netscape's reputation, but Dynamic HTML gives us all the tools we need to remedy that. Along the way, we'll see how to use styles to make text do all kinds of things.

First, we need a simple framework, including some text to blink and a simple loop to bounce back and forth between styles. For this application, we'll use a timer created with the setTimeout() method of the window object. The method requires two arguments. The first is a function to call when the timer goes off, and the second is the duration of the timer in milliseconds. The timer is a little strange, because it's really a function, returning a value you can use to turn off the timer (with clearTimeout()) if your code needs that. As a result, you don't call it directly; instead, assign it to a variable.

We'll set up two functions. The first one sets the style of the target object its way and then sets up a timer to call the other function, which changes the style of the target option to something else. The second function then sets a timer for the first one. It isn't very sophisticated, but it's effective. If you wanted to add a third or fourth state to your object, you could extend the chain, making the second timer call the third function and then having that function loop back to the first one. You can even create several separate chains, although at some point you'd probably need to reorganize your code to keep it comprehensible.

Functions and Subroutines in JavaScript and VBScript

If you've come up through the ranks of HTML designers and don't understand much about programming, the concept of a function may seem alien. Basically, it's a convenient way to organize a series of commands. Technically, a function is supposed to return a value, although this requirement isn't enforced in either JavaScript or VBScript. Although you can do a lot just by setting properties, it usually takes a series of commands to create exciting effects. Executing JavaScript directly from an HREF (as we did in the Chapter 3 example) is messy, especially if you need to do the same thing in several places in a document. Calling functions is much easier and guarantees cleaner, more maintainable code. All functions in either language must be defined between <SCRIPT> tags.

Functions are fairly simple in both JavaScript and VBScript, but the syntax differs slightly. At first, we'll call functions that neither need parameters provided to them nor return values to the code that called them. These functions are self-contained programs, but they aren't very flexible, as we'll see. Defining a function in VBScript this way is simple:

```
function name_of_function
[commands go here]
end function
```

You can use the sub keyword instead of the function keyword for bits of code that won't be returning a value.

This is proper Visual Basic construction, but in VBScript the browser doesn't care. JavaScript functions are a little more complex:

```
function name_of_function () {
[commands go here]
}
```

JavaScript requires the empty parentheses even when there aren't any parameters to pass. The opening brace, { ,marks the start of the function code, and the closing brace, } ,marks the end. You'll also see braces for smaller command structures, such as if statements and while and for loops. Keep in mind that there have to be as many closing braces as opening braces, and you can usually put the sets together. If the function returns a value, you'll also see the return keyword at the end of the function.

From this point on, the scripting will get more complicated. Much of the material will still be useful to developers who don't need to know the ins and outs of scripting, but powerful capabilities demand powerful tools. You may want to visit your local bookstore and find a good reference on JavaScript or VBScript.

The basic framework looks like this in JavaScript:

```
<HTML>
<HEAD><TITLE>Dynamic HTML BLINK Testing
Ground</TITLE></HEAD>
<BODY BGCOLOR=#FFFFFF>
<P ID=blinker STYLE="color: black">This is ground
zero!</P>

<SCRIPT LANGUAGE="JavaScript">
function blink_on() {
blinker.style.color="black";
timerOne=setTimeout("blink_off()", 1000);
}
```

```
function blink_off() {
blinker.style.color="white";
timerTwo=setTimeout("blink_on()", 1000);
}

blink_off();
</SCRIPT>
</BODY>
</HTML>
```

The same thing looks like this in VBScript:

```
<HTML>
<HEAD><TITLE>Dynamic HTML BLINK Testing
Ground</TITLE></HEAD>
<BODY BGCOLOR=#FFFFFF>
<P ID=blinker STYLE="color: black">This is ground
zero!</P>

<SCRIPT LANGUAGE="VBScript">
function blink_on
blinker.style.color="black"
timerOne=setTimeout("blink_off()", 1000, "VBScript")
end function

function blink_off
blinker.style.color="white"
timerTwo=setTimeout("blink_on()", 1000, "VBScript")
end function

blink_off
</SCRIPT>
</BODY>
</HTML>
```

The only significant difference between the two versions
is that the setTimeout function needs a third parameter

to warn it that VBScript will be coming up instead of JavaScript.

NOTE   In both languages, you must put the script *after* the main body of the HTML. Because we're calling the blink_off function immediately, the script won't be able to find the blinker object when it runs the first time, because it won't have been created by the browser yet. You can place your scripts before the HTML if they get called only after the document has loaded.

You can use either version, and your results should be the same: blinking text in the top left proclaiming, "This is ground zero!" Unfortunately, print can't convey the magic of this blink, but your screen should look something like the one in Figure 4.1.

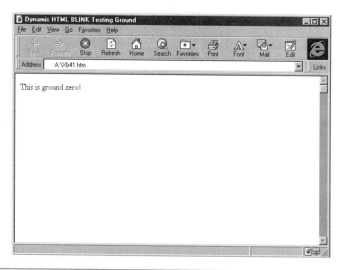

Figure 4.1 Results of the initial <BLINK> experiment.

We have just re-created in Internet Explorer one of the worst features to appear in Netscape. On the bright side, we now have a convenient laboratory to test a wide variety of style tags. The first thing you might want to try is to change the colors. Blinking isn't so bad when you turn down the contrast and alternate between, say, blue and purple.

To get a sense of how to change styles, you can experiment with the following replacements for the key lines in the blink_on and blink_off routines. Leave the rest of the code alone. (For VBScript, omit the semicolon at the end of the line.)

To change the font family, use these lines:

| blink_on | `blinker.style.fontFamily="serif";` |
| blink_off | `blinker.style.fontFamily="sans-serif";` |

To change the font size, use this:

| blink_on | `blinker.style.fontSize="12pt";` |
| blink_off | `blinker.style.fontSize="20pt";` |

To change the font style, use this:

| blink_on | `blinker.style.fontStyle="italic";` |
| blink_off | `blinker.style.fontStyle="normal";` |

To change the font weight, use this:

| blink_on | `blinker.style.fontWeight="bold";` |
| blink_off | `blinker.style.fontWeight="normal";` |

Changing Position: HTML In Motion

Styles can be used to change many properties in addition to the simple text properties we've seen so far. The W3C's Cascading Style Sheet specifications provide the top, left, and zIndex style properties, which let you position objects anywhere on the page. The left property provides an x-coordinate for the left edge of the object, and top provides a y-coordinate for the top edge. zIndex specifies the layer occupied by the object: whether it rests on top of other objects, behind them, or between them. Internet Explorer

4.0 can handle all those possibilities, although at this point it seems capable of working only with graphics and not text.

Now we'll take our BLINK framework and make it bounce a graphic around the screen. Unfortunately, because Internet Explorer won't presently let us position text objects, we must change our blinker object to an image. Most of the program remains the same, but it addresses some new style properties:

```
<HTML>
<HEAD><TITLE>Dynamic HTML Motion Testing
Ground</TITLE></HEAD>
<BODY BGCOLOR=#FFFFFF>

<IMG SRC="ms.gif" ID=blinker
STYLE="container:positioned; position:absolute;
top:10; left:10; height:76; width:349;">

<SCRIPT LANGUAGE="JavaScript">
function blink_on() {
blinker.style.top=10;
blinker.style.left=10;
timerOne=setTimeout("blink_off()", 1000);
}

function blink_off() {
blinker.style.top=100;
blinker.style.left=100;
timerTwo=setTimeout("blink_on()", 1000);
}

blink_on();
</SCRIPT>
</BODY>
</HTML>
```

The most important changes are in the IMG tag. You'll notice some additional style attributes that aren't in the

W3C Recommendations. container:positioned and position:absolute tell the browser that this graphic doesn't just float in the text like a normal graphic: it will have a hard-wired position given in pixels by the top, left, and zIndex tags. The top and left are specified to give the graphic an initial position, and height and width should also be provided. You can still use the traditional HEIGHT and WIDTH attributes if you prefer, although I find it easier to put everything I can into the style. (zIndex is optional; with only one graphic on the screen it wouldn't make much sense. We'll get to it in a moment.)

You can use any graphic you like. Make sure to set the height and width attributes appropriately.

When you open this file in Internet Explorer 4, you'll first see the image shown in Figure 4.2.

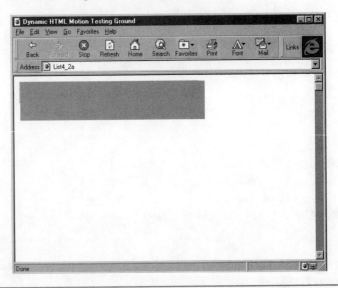

Figure 4.2 Image in first (on. position).

After a second, it'll change to the image shown in Figure 4.3.

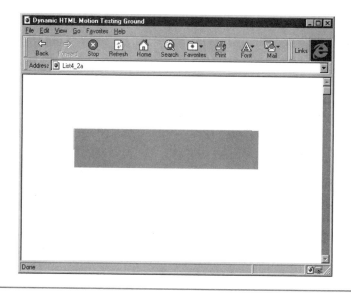

Figure 4.3 Image in second (off. position).

The next example will demonstrate a serious limitation of our blink example. Layers make possible all kinds of graphic explorations; graphics can overlap and slide over one another. Transparent GIFs also work, making it easy to create sophisticated graphical interfaces. First, we'll try to flip two boxes back and forth between layers. All we'll change is the zIndex property.

```
<HTML>
<HEAD><TITLE>Dynamic HTML Layers Testing
Ground</TITLE></HEAD>
<BODY BGCOLOR=#FFFFFF>
<IMG SRC="graphic1.gif" ID=graphic1
STYLE="container:positioned; position:absolute;
top:10; left:10; height:50; width:50; zIndex:1">
<IMG SRC="graphic2.gif" ID=graphic2
STYLE="container:positioned; position:absolute;
top:30; left:30; height:50; width:50; zIndex:2">
<SCRIPT LANGUAGE="JavaScript">
```

```
function blink_on() { //we'll put graphic1 on top
graphic1.style.zIndex=1;
graphic2.style.zIndex=2;
timerOne=setTimeout("blink_off()", 1000);
}
function blink_off() { //we'll put graphic2 on top
graphic2.style.zIndex=1;
graphic1.style.zIndex=2;
timerTwo=setTimeout("blink_on()", 1000);
}
blink_on();
</SCRIPT>
</BODY>
</HTML>
```

In theory, the two layers should bounce back and forth, sometimes showing the gray box (graphic1) on top, sometimes showing the black. Unfortunately, changing the zIndex doesn't always force Internet Explorer 4.0 to redraw the page, so nothing will happen and your screen will remain looking like Figure 4.4.

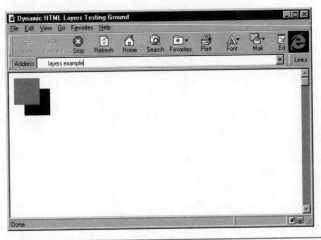

Figure 4.4 The failed layer blink.

There are ways to make it redraw, although few of them are pretty and none appears to be programmable (yet). If you start dragging other windows on top of Internet Explorer 4.0, dropping them, and then moving them away, and if you catch the blink at the right point, you'll be rewarded by the boxes changing position. Minimizing the window and reopening it also works. Experience will be your best guide to determine what works, because none of this information is publicly documented. Over time, I suspect Microsoft will catch up with the remaining pieces and make them work, too.

The blink example isn't enough, so we'll combine motion with layering to demonstrate the power of layers. This demonstration creates a loop that makes the squares move toward each other and back again. When they come back, they'll have changed layers, and the graphic that previously slid across on top will now slide underneath.

```
<HTML>
<HEAD><TITLE>Dynamic HTML Motion and Layers Testing
Ground</TITLE></HEAD>
<BODY BGCOLOR=#FFFFFF>
<IMG SRC="graphic1.gif" ID=graphic1
STYLE="container:positioned; position:absolute;
top:10; left:0; height:50; width:50; zIndex:1">
<IMG SRC="graphic2.gif" ID=graphic2
STYLE="container:positioned; position:absolute;
top:10; left:200; height:50; width:50; zIndex:2">
<SCRIPT LANGUAGE="JavaScript">
function slide_em() {
where++; //increases the value of where by 1
if (where<400) { //this keeps it from going too long
place=where; //we use place so where stays a clean
counter
if (place>200) {place=(400-where);} //this bounces
it back
graphic1.style.left=place;
```

```
graphic2.style.left=(200-place); //this one's going
backward
if (where==200) { //did we hit the edge?
graphic2.style.zIndex=1; //moves it back a layer
graphic1.style.zIndex=2; //moves it up a layer
}
timer=setTimeout("slide_em()", 20); //let Internet
Explorer catch up
}
}
var where=0; //creates the variable where and sets
it to zero
slide_em(); //calls the main routine
</SCRIPT>
</BODY>
</HTML>
```

You should get results like those shown in Figures 4.5. and 4.6.

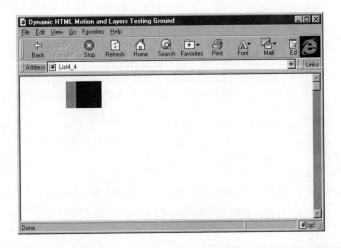

Figure 4.5 The first time crossing, black on top.

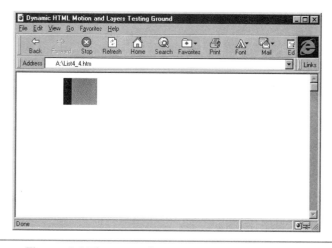

Figure 4.6 The second time crossing, gray on top.

Notice that lower numbers in the zIndex place the graphic further back in line. Higher numbers bring it closer to viewers. I had to write this script using setTimeout and a series of if statements to make it work. All I wanted to do was to make the left property of one of the graphics move from 0 to 200 and back to 0, with the other graphic doing the opposite. I first wrote the script for slide_em as a for loop:

```
function slide_em() {//won't work—no refresh!
for (where=0; where<200; where++) { //loop going up
graphic1.style.left=where;
graphic2.style.left=200-where;
}
//zIndexes switch
graphic2.style.zIndex=1;
graphic1.style.zIndex=2;
for (where=200; where=0; where-) { //loop going down
graphic1.style.left=where;
graphic2.style.left=200-where;
}
}
```

Unfortunately, as long as you stay within the function, Internet Explorer won't update the screen. For this function, the final positions of both graphics are the same as at the start, so the computer sits there for a minute and it doesn't look as if anything happened. The setTimeout call gives the computer time to realize that it needs to redraw the graphics properly. As messy as it is to manage counters and timers, it has the advantage of working.

Layers and Positioning— Netscape vs. Microsoft

The good news is that some of the positioning information is usable in both the Netscape and the Microsoft browser. Both browsers have their roots in a W3C working draft, "Positioning HTML Elements with Cascading Style Sheets." All the style tags work with both browsers. Unfortunately, each browser provides features that the other one doesn't. The direct scriptability of objects through the document.all collection, is at this point strictly a Microsoft feature. If you load these examples into a Netscape browser (for now, at least), they'll just sit there. What I've been calling *layers*, in reference to the zIndex tag, is a modest technique compared with the plans Netscape has for its version of layers, which includes a full (and scriptable) <LAYER> tag.

Layers in Netscape Communicator are like small, positionable documents, each with its own content. They can be hidden and displayed to create simple animations as well as complex effects. Their biggest advantage is that they provide a way to display and move groups of objects instead of individual items. As we'll see in Chapter 12 this can be a significant advantage at times. With any luck, the two vendors will come to an agreement, giving Netscape Communicator users the power of the Dynamic HTML features described here, and Internet Explorer users the convenience of layers.

Figuring Out the Size of Your Playground— The Visual Object

It's wonderful to be able to position graphics pixel by pixel and move them around the screen, but at times you need to know exactly what kind of screen you're working with. Fortunately, Internet Explorer 4 added the Visual object, whose properties can tell you the dimensions and color depth of the screen. You can even create a page that will send viewers to different pages depending on their screen resolution.

Visual is below window on the object hierarchy, at the same level as document. The hres and vres properties give you the horizontal and vertical screen resolutions, respectively, in pixels. The colorDepth property gives you the number of bits used per pixel. Eight bits gives you 256 colors, 16 bits gives you 65,536 colors, and 24 bits gives you 16.7 million colors. Like hres and vres, Color Depth is read-only, but if you need to claim additional resources for your multimedia extravaganzas, Internet Explorer also offers the bufferDepth property. If you set it to 1, 4, 8, 15, 16, 24, or 32, Internet Explorer will do its best to buffer your graphic rendering off-screen. Higher values provide additional buffering power, but at the cost of memory. Unless you have a good reason to use it, leave bufferDepth alone.

Style Properties You Can Manipulate

Not all style properties are applicable to every HTML element. As we've seen, text can't be moved and positioned the way graphics can, although it's easy to change what text looks like. Making a graphic italic isn't likely to have much effect, either. Table 4.1 should help you figure out which style characteristics are available to the tags you need to program.

Table 4.1 HTML Style Properties

Property	Applies to	Notes (Sample Values in Parentheses)
background	All elements in cascading style sheet; may not be fully implemented in Internet Explorer	Sets all the background properties at once.
background Attachment	All elements	Whether the background scrolls or remains fixed (cssScroll, cssFixed).
backgroundColor	All elements	Background color of an element.
backgroundImage	All elements	Background image URL of an element.
backgroundRepeat	All elements	Whether the background should repeat (repeat, repeatx, repeaty, norepeat).
border	All elements in cascading style sheet; may not be fully implemented in Internet Explorer	Sets all border values for an element at once.
borderBottomColor	All elements	Takes color value.
borderBottomStyle	All elements	None by default; may also be dotted, dashed, solid, double, groove, ridge, inset, outset (not all implemented).
borderBottomWidth	All elements	May be thin, medium, thick, or a number specifying points.
borderLeftColor	All elements	Takes color value.

Property	Applies to	Notes (Sample Values in Parentheses)
borderLeftStyle	All elements	See borderBottomStyle.
borderLeftWidth	All elements	See borderBottomWidth.
borderRightColor	All elements	Takes color value.
borderRightStyle	All elements	See borderBottomStyle.
borderRightWidth	All elements	See borderBottomWidth.
borderTopColor	All elements	Takes color value.
borderTopStyle	All elements	See borderBottomStyle.
borderTopWidth	All elements	See borderBottomWidth.
clear	All elements	Specifies whether floating images are allowed on the sides of an object. May be none, left, right, or both.
color	Text, horizontal rules	Takes color value.
cssText	Special	Sets or returns the persisted representation of the style rule.
display	All elements	Sets the way an object is displayed by the browser. May be block, inline, listItem, or none. None should make objects disappear.
font	Text	Sets all font values for an element at once.
fontFamily	Text	Sets the font for an element. Helvetica, Arial, serif, sans-serif are common.
fontSize	Text	Sets the font size for an element. May use small, medium, or large as well as point sizes.

continued on next page

Property	Applies to	Notes (Sample Values in Parentheses)
fontStyle	Text	Sets the font to normal, italic, or oblique.
fontVariant	Text	Sets the font to normal or small-caps.
fontWeight	Text	Sets the font to a weight from 100 to 900 (if supported) or to normal, bold, bolder, or lighter.
height	Images*	Specifies the height in pixels.
left	Images*	Specifies the position of the left edge in pixels from the left edge of the window.
letterSpacing	Text	Allows you to specify additional spacing between letters and text. May not be supported.
lineHeight	Text	Specifies distance between text baselines. May be normal, number to multiply by point size, absolute measurement, or percentage.
margin	All elements	Sets all margin values for an element at once.
marginBottom	All elements	Specifies space below bottom margin.
marginLeft	All elements	Specifies space below left margin.
marginRight	All elements	Specifies space below right margin.
marginTop	All elements	Specifies space below top margin.

Property	Applies to	Notes (Sample Values in Parentheses)
overflow	Images*	Declares what to do if an element's contents are too large for height and width. May be none, clip, or scroll.
posHeight	Images*	Same as height but returns a number and not a string.
posLeft	Images*	Same as left, but returns a number and not a string.
posTop	Images*	Same as top but returns a number and not a string.
posWidth	Images*	Same as width but returns a number and not a string.
textAlign	Text	May be left, right, center, or justify.
textDecoration	Text	May be none, underline, overline, line-through, or blink.
textDecoration LineThrough	Text	true or false.
textDecoration Overline	Text	true or false.
textDecoration Underline	Text	true or false.
textIndent	Text	May be a measurement or percentage; indents the first line.
textTransform	Text	none is default; may also be capitalize, uppercase, or lowercase.
top	Images*	Specifies the position of the top edge in pixels from the top edge of the window.

continued on next page

Property	Applies to	Notes (Sample Values in Parentheses)
verticalAlign	Text	May be baseline (default), sub, super, top, text-top, middle, bottom, text-bottom, or a percentage above the baseline.
visibility	Images*	Whether to render an object transparently. Values are inherit, visible, and hidden. (Inherit takes its cue from tag layers surrounding the IMG.)
width	Images*	Specifies width of an image in pixels.
zIndex	Images*	Integer specifying layer of a positioned graphic; lower values are displayed behind higher values.

* CSS Specification says it should apply to all elements, but currently Internet Explorer applies it only to text.

The list is subject to change at the whims of the browser developers, but most of these properties (except the positioning properties) come directly from the cascading style sheet specification and should be fairly stable.

Changing Document Properties

Styles are wonderful, but there were many HTML tags out there before anyone thought of styles. Many tags are scriptable, as demonstrated by the pages that assault visitors with flashing background colors courtesy of JavaScript. Internet Explorer 4 opens up new possibilities, some of which may be useful for tasteful projects.

The document object contains all the tags included in your HTML document. In theory, it's built on the <HTML> tag that appears at the start of the document. It includes every piece of information generated by a page. We've been working through the all collection, which lets us reach every named object easily, but several other collections, properties, and methods also deserve attention. We'll deal with most of the collections individually in their own sections, but the properties of the document and the body objects have much to offer.

Images: The Old Way, the New Way

Netscape Navigator 3.0 introduced the images collection to the document object, giving developers the power to create animated pages with simple scripting. Internet Explorer 4.0 has caught up with the images collection, but to a large extent Dynamic HTML has made it obsolete. We'll walk through a few examples to demonstrate the images collection as well as your alternatives using Dynamic HTML. Each approach has advantages in particular situations, and the images collection has the advantage of additional compatibility.

To begin, we'll use a simple set of images connected by an easy-to-remember naming convention. If you aren't using naming conventions for your graphics, you should consider it, because it makes programming much easier. We'll be working with a group of pictures of marshmallow rabbits. For convenience, I've named them **bunny1.gif** through **bunny4.gif**. All we'll do for now is to cycle them through the same image position, addressing the graphic through the images collection. Our results will be viewable on both Internet Explorer and Netscape.

```
<HTML>
<HEAD><TITLE>Images Collection Demo</TITLE></HEAD>
<BODY>
<IMG NAME="bunny" SRC="bunny1.gif" HEIGHT=106
WIDTH=75>
<SCRIPT language="JavaScript">
function rabbit (img_name, width, height) {
   this.picture=new Image(width, height);
   this.picture.src=img_name;
}

function new_rabbit (img_name, width, height) {
   rabbit [img_name] = new rabbit (img_name, width,
height);
}

function change_rabbit (img_name) {
    var fileplace=rabbit[img_name].picture.src;
//NS-Mac
    document.images["bunny"].src= fileplace;
}

function run () {
   which++; //increases the value of which by 1
   if (which>4) {which=1} //keeps it cycling
   change_rabbit(("bunny" + which + ".gif"));
   timer=setTimeout("run()", 2000); //let browser
catch up
}

function initialize_rabbits() {
   for (count=1; count<5; count++) {
       new_rabbit(("bunny" + count + ".gif"), 75,
106);
   }
}
```

```
initialize_rabbits();
var which=1;
run();
</SCRIPT>
</BODY>
</HTML>
```

If you run this code on Netscape for the Mac, you'll see marshmallow rabbits cycling through the top left of your browser window (see Figure 4.7).

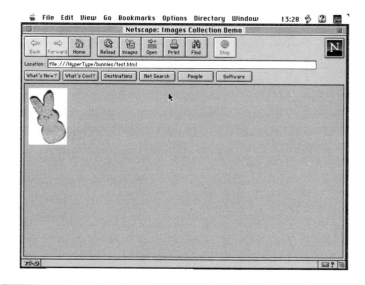

Figure 4.7 Netscape/Mac showing rabbits demonstration.

On Internet Explorer 4 for Windows, the same code works quite well (see Figure 4.8).

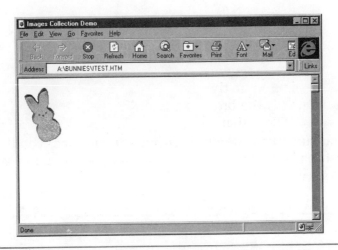

Figure 4.8 Internet Explorer for Windows 95 showing rabbits demonstration.

This code is a little complicated. The run() function uses the same setTimeout() mechanism we used before. Before we start cycling the rabbits, though, we initialize the list of files using the new_rabbit() and rabbit() functions, which create a list of graphics and download the image files. Although we could get away without doing it in this example, it's always a good idea to preload your images if it will affect the response time the user perceives. Graphics that highlight selections, for example, should pop up instantly and not require another trip to the server.

A few other capabilities built into this program illustrate features—such as height and width attributes—that you don't need yet but will want in the future. If you're working with graphics of different sizes, it pays to store this information where you can get to it easily. In this case, the images were all the same size, but it's worth building it right the first time. The other function that might not seem necessary is change_rabbit, because all we're changing here is the image source. But once we start changing other attributes, such as position, you'll want to separate the action from the main body of the program.

The program is simple. It uses the document.images collection to reference the IMG element named bunny that is created at the start of the document. Then the program tells the browser that the source of that image is changing. Note that we're not replacing the image object with the rabbit object; instead, we're replacing the image objects property with the appropriate rabbit objects property. The creation of the rabbit object during initialization has already downloaded the bunny graphics, so the user won't have to wait for a transition between the graphics. Changing graphics is close to the limit of what you can do with the images collection, but it's enough to make possible many highlights as well as animation.

Accessing the graphic through the images collection has one other advantage. If you have many images on a page, you can create a naming convention for them that's similar to the one we used for the rabbits. For example, you could use place1, place2, and place3. If you needed to change them all at once, you could use a loop to create a string (such as placename) containing their names and then refer to the image source as document.images[placename].src. (Similarly, document.all[placename] would also work, but it isn't the usual way to access the all collection and isn't as compatible.)

Using the document.all collection makes accessing images a bit easier. The main change in our program is in the change_rabbit function:

```
function change_rabbit (img_name) {
document.bunny.src= rabbit[img_name].picture.src;
}
```

If you write it this way, you won't be able to run it with Netscape. On the other hand, it will be consistent with the way you access other properties, such as style.top and style.left to put the graphic in motion.

Changing Content: TextRanges, Part I

I've saved the most powerful new feature of Dynamic HTML for last. This part gives Dynamic HTML the power to move the HTML interface well beyond animated presentations and a few forms. These latest additions make it possible to create full-fledged desktop applications that combine HTML with applets or ActiveX controls. It's extremely simple. Dynamic HTML gives you the power to change the attributes of an object and to change the content of an object.

We'll start with another example using our BLINK demonstration.

```
<HTML>
<HEAD><TITLE>Dynamic HTML BLINK Testing
Ground</TITLE></HEAD>
<BODY BGCOLOR=#FFFFFF>
<P ID=blinker STYLE="color: black"
onClick="blink_off()">This is ground zero!</P>
<SCRIPT LANGUAGE="JavaScript">
function blink_on() {
 var r;
 r = document.rangeFromElement(blinker);
 r.pasteHTML("This is ground zero!");
 timerOne=setTimeout("blink_off()", 1000);
}
function blink_off() {
 var r;
 r = document.rangeFromElement(blinker);
 r.pasteHTML("Ground zero just got <EM
style='color:red'>hit!</EM>");
 timerTwo=setTimeout("blink_on()", 1000);
```

```
}
</SCRIPT>
</BODY>
</HTML>
```

You'll have to click on the text to make it start blinking (Internet Explorer has a few unexplainable glitches that produce an error 800000a if we call it directly as we did the previous ones.) The text should alternate between the "This is ground zero!" screen and the one in Figure 4.9.

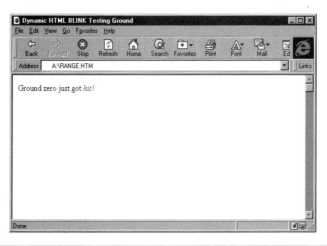

Figure 4.9 Flip side of blinking text.

It's a small start. We'll see much more of textRange objects in Chapter 9, where we'll cover them in depth. Pasting in new HTML is only one of the many possibilities provided by Microsoft's new textRange object.

CHAPTER 5

Something's Happening: Events

Although some of the effects we saw in Chapter 4 were impressive, blinking pages are rarely crowd-pleasers. In this chapter, we'll bring users in on the action, making their actions determine what happens to the document. Technically, this chapter leaves behind dynamic HTML for the world of scripting. Microsoft refers to the objects we worked with in Chapter 4 as HTML objects, whereas the event object is considered a scripting object. Although this chapter may seem like a refugee from a book on scripting, it's necessary. Creating interesting pages using Dynamic HTML requires events, and Internet Explorer 4.0 and Netscape Communicator have provided a new set of tools for managing events.

Some of the techniques are simple, but others require a sophisticated understanding of the object model. As we did in the Chapter 4, we'll start with the simplest tasks and then tackle more complicated ones toward the end of the chapter. These examples are not necessarily the most powerful way to use events, but they should give you a fair idea of how to harness events and use them for complex, interesting, tasks.

Events in VBScript vs Events in JavaScript

When Microsoft introduced VBScript, it sought to retain as much of Visual Basic's flavor as possible in a stripped down environment. Although some concessions have been made to the object model Netscape pioneered, Microsoft has developed its own method for dealing with events. As a result, the calls to JavaScript/JScript and VBScript event handlers are often made differently.

In Internet Explorer's JScript, the call is usually made in the tag that will receive the event initially:

```
<IMG SRC="graphic.gif" NAME="test"
onClick="doSomething()">
```

When this graphic receives a click, the doSomething() function will be called. VBScript can also work this way, although it introduces some complications:

```
<IMG SRC="graphic.gif" NAME="test"
onClick="doSomething" LANGUAGE="VBScript">
```

This call becomes complicated when developers mix JavaScript and VBScript. By default, the browser expects functions called this way to be in JavaScript. The LANGUAGE attribute changes this to VBScript, but the browser will remain in VBScript unless it leaves the page or encounters a tag that specifies LANGUAGE="JavaScript". This arrangement isn't a problem unless you mix and match scripting languages.

VBScript also offers a different style that doesn't have this problem. It uses a naming convention rather than a direct call.

```
<IMG SRC="graphic.gif" NAME="test">
<SCRIPT LANGUAGE="VBScript">
sub test_onClick
commands go here
end sub
</SCRIPT>
```

Programmers can argue over which approach they prefer. VBScript's naming convention approach tends to produce much more organized code, and the JavaScript approach provides more flexibility and can reduce the number of duplicate functions.

One other approach works only in Internet Explorer: using the SCRIPT tag's FOR, EVENT, and LANGUAGE attributes. Our example would look like this:

```
<IMG SRC="graphic.gif" NAME="test">
<SCRIPT FOR="test" EVENT="onclick"
LANGUAGE="JavaScript">
alert("You clicked?");
</SCRIPT>
```

The Place of Events in the Object Model: Netscape vs. Microsoft

Although most of the JavaScript approaches just listed work for both Netscape and Internet Explorer, it appears that events are one of the next major battlegrounds in the battle of the browsers. Microsoft and Netscape have staked out different turf in the battle over what the event object will look like. This has impact on the ways we can call functions as well as an interesting side effect you may want to use in your scripts. able 5.1 shows the shared elements of the Microsoft and Netscape objects.

Table 5.1 Microsoft and Netscape event properties

Microsoft	Netscape	Notes
event.x	event.x (or event.layerX)	x-coordinate of mouse cursor at event
event.y	event.y (or event.layerY)	y-coordinate of mouse cursor at event
event.button	event.which	Indicates which button was pressed
event.shiftkey event.ctrlkey event.altkey	event.modifiers	Indicates modifier keys pressed when event happened.
event.srcElement	event.target	Announces which object initially received the event.

Most of the remaining information handled by the Microsoft and Netscape objects differs so much that the table would be filled with "no equivalent" if it continued. The information differs in both what is available and how it gets passed. The following pieces of code use a method of calling event handlers that isn't recommended by Microsoft, although it seems to work well once you figure out how to collect the extra event data. The first piece of code looks like this:

```
<HTML>
<HEAD>
<TITLE>Event Tester 2 MS11.23</TITLE>
</HEAD>
<BODY BGCOLOR=#FFFFFF>
<SCRIPT>
function MSresults(button1, shift1,x1,y1) {
```

```
alert('Document got an event .  Y-position is '+y1
+'. '+'X-position is '+x1 + '. '+'Shift key is ' +
shift1 + '. '+ 'Button used is ' + button1 +'.');
}
document.onmousedown=MSresults;
</SCRIPT>
This shouldn't work, eh?  It does!
</BODY>
</HTML>
```

When you click anywhere in the window, you'll get an alert box listing the location of the click (see Figure 5.1):

Figure 5.1 Dialog box from Internet Explorer.

Note the different way we assigned this function to handle the onmousedown event. Instead of calling the code from a tag or using a SCRIPT FOR construction, we assigned MSresults to document.onmousedown. In theory, onmousedown is a property of the document object just as if it has been placed in the BODY tag. This technique works, and you may want to use it later, especially because it lets you change dynamically the function that gets called by an event. It's just like changing the color of text but involves a little more programming. Note that the sequence of parameters (button1, shift1, x1, and y1) is in reverse order from that shown in the Microsoft documentation.

The code for Netscape Navigator looks like this:

```
<HTML>
<HEAD>
```

```
<TITLE>
Event Tester 2 NS 11.23
</TITLE>
</HEAD>
<BODY BGCOLOR=#FFFFFF>
<SCRIPT>
function NSresults(e) {
alert('Document got an event: ' + e.type); alert ('x
position is ' + e.layerX); alert ('y position is ' +
e.layerY);
if (e.modifiers & Event.ALT_MASK) {
        alert('Alt key was down for event!'); }
return true;
}
document.onmousedown=NSresults;
</SCRIPT>
This works, eh?
</BODY>
</HTML>
```

This sample came from the Netscape JavaScript 1.2 documentation but it doesn't work with Internet Explorer at all. The first few messages alert you that everything was undefined, followed by the script crashing when it reaches the incomprehensible (to Explorer) Event.ALT_MASK constant Netscape uses to make sense of its modifiers property. Netscape also passes the event as object, whereas Internet Explorer passes the event's properties as parameters. One advantage of Netscape's version is that all of the properties of the event object are (technically) available whatever the event, but whether that will prove to be useful has yet to be determined.

Perhaps eventually both versions will work somewhere. In the meantime, these clashes of style can produce interesting results (such as document.onmousedown) that you may find useful if you're not writing to multiple browsers. In the meantime, unless you can control which browser your readers are using, you may want to limit yourself to events that only flash the event (such as onclick) and don't require extra parameters. Users may not notice if a color fails to appear when the cursor rolls over text, but angry alert boxes about JavaScript errors are sure to get their attention.

Handling Simple Events

Internet Explorer provides a wide range of events, from simple mouse clicks to events indicating that an image didn't load properly to a final "we're leaving this page now!" event. Although you probably don't need to handle every event, it's good to know which options are available. The following discussion starts with mouse events—the ones most programmers need immediately—and eventually covers all the events available in Internet Explorer 4.0 and Netscape Communicator 4.0.

Mouse Events

The number of mouse events has grown with each release of the browsers, making the Web interface behave more like the GUI interfaces with which most users are working. The current round of browsers has made it possible to handle nearly as many different kinds of mouse interaction as other programs handle, making it easier to create fine-grained interfaces that can handle a wide variety of user interactions.

onclick

The onclick event is the simplest and most frequent event in the Web world. HTML has its own click handlers; every <A HREF> tag is waiting for a click to load the target document. That was enough power to get HTML started, but developers needed a more responsive interface once the revolution began. Onclick makes it easy, offering the power to make most elements of HTML into live (though unmarked) buttons waiting for a user's mouse click. Using onclick is simple:

```
<HTML><BODY>
<IMG SRC="hithere.gif" NAME=clicker
onclick="javascript:clicker.src='goaway.gif'>
</BODY></HTML>
```

This little routine changes the image from one graphic to another when the user clicks on it. It won't go back to its original state when you're finished, although you could implement that with another simple function. The onclick event works with all recent versions of Internet Explorer and Netscape. Netscape developers will often find that <A HREF="javascript:*functionCall()*"> works better with many elements.

ondblclick

Double-clicking lets you create a slightly more complicated interface. HTML users frequently click from place to place, always using single clicks, but there are times when it's useful to have a double click available. The single-click bias of HTML has made it difficult to, for example, create Web training packages for software, because most software responds to double clicks. Using ondblclick is as easy as using onclick.

```
<HTML><BODY>
<P ID="target">If this is green, you  clicked only
once. If red, you double-clicked.</P>
<IMG SRC="button.gif"
onclick="javascript:target.style.color='#00FF00'"
```

```
ondblclick="javascript:target.style.color='#FF0000'"
>
</BODY></HTML>
```

This code changes the color of the target paragraph. If you watch closely (or if you have a slow machine), you can watch the green appear before the red as an onclick event goes off for the first click of the double click. Ondblclick is available only on Internet Explorer 4.0.

onmousedown

If you want to implement a click-and-drag routine, you have to know when (and where) the user pushed the mouse button before it is released. The onmousedown event takes place as soon as the button clicks, unlike onclick, which waits for the button to come up again. (An onclick event is a combination of an onmousedown and an onmouseup event in the same location.)

The following sample code uses Dynamic HTML to tell you where you pressed the mouse button. (Note that the left button returns 1, the right button 2, and the middle button 4.)

```
<HTML><BODY>
<B>X:</B> <SPAN ID=xcoord> ? </SPAN><BR>
<B>Y:</B> <SPAN ID=ycoord> ? </SPAN><BR>
<B>Button:</B> <SPAN ID=button> ? </SPAN><BR>
<SCRIPT LANGUAGE="JavaScript">
//this is only for Internet Explorer 4.0
function MSresults(button1, shift1,x1,y1) {
var r;
r=document.rangeFromElement(xcoord);
r.pasteHTML(x1);
r=document.rangeFromElement(ycoord);
r.pasteHTML(y1);
r=document.rangeFromElement(button);
```

```
r.pasteHTML(button1);
}
document.onmousedown=MSresults;
</SCRIPT>
</BODY></HTML>
```

This event is supported by Internet Explorer 4 and Netscape Communicator 4, although the incompatibilities between object models means that code will work only for one of the two browsers. (The preceding code is for Internet Explorer.)

onmousemove

Onmousemove is much like onmousedown, but onmousemove doesn't wait for the user to click. In effect, onmousemove fires continually whenever the mouse is in motion. This makes it easy to create drag-and-drop routines and also lets you create graphics that follow the user's cursor all over the active window. (We'll try that later.) The following sample code tells you where you've moved the mouse as you move it and also lets you know if any buttons are down. Note the way that x and y can go negative if you're holding down the mouse button and move outside the document window.

```
<HTML>
<BODY>
<B>X:</B> <SPAN ID=xcoord> ? </SPAN><BR>
<B>Y:</B> <SPAN ID=ycoord> ? </SPAN><BR>
<B>Button:</B> <SPAN ID=button> ? </SPAN><BR>
<SCRIPT>
//this is only for Internet Explorer 4.0
function MSresults(button1, shift1,x1,y1) {
var r;
r=document.rangeFromElement(xcoord);
r.pasteHTML(x1);
```

```
r=document.rangeFromElement(ycoord);
r.pasteHTML(y1);
r=document.rangeFromElement(button);
r.pasteHTML(button1);
}
document.onmousemove=MSresults;
</SCRIPT>
</BODY></HTML>
```

Because onmousemove returns parameters, it has the same problems as onmousedown with Internet Explorer and Netscape Communicator. You can make it work with either browser, but the code will be different and incompatible. (The preceding code is for Internet Explorer.)

onmouseout

The onmouseout event tells you when the user has left the area. For the most part, you'll use it with onmouseover to remove the highlight from objects when an onmouseover has highlighted them. It's also good for creating objects that want to say good-bye to users leaving your page.

```
<HTML><BODY>
<H3 ID=hello onmouseout="farewell()"> Hello? </H3>
<SCRIPT>
//this is only for Internet Explorer 4.0
function farewell() {
var r;
r=document.rangeFromElement(hello);
r.pasteHTML("Goodbye!");
}
</SCRIPT>
</BODY></HTML>
```

Onmouseout is another simple event that's supported by and compatible with Netscape browsers. (Because of its use of Dynamic HTML the preceding example is for Internet Explorer 4 only.)

onmouseover

Onmouseover is most useful for highlighting places you'd want the user to click but don't want to highlight with the usual link colors or borders around a graphic. You can also use it to create new interfaces that appear only when the user is rolling through the area. We'll combine it with our previous onmouseout code to create an element that changes when the mouse rolls over it and when the mouse leaves the area.

```
<HTML><BODY>
<H3 ID="hello" onMouseOver="welcome()"
onMouseOut="farewell()"> Hello? </H3>
<SCRIPT>
//this is only for Internet Explorer 4.0
function welcome() {
var r;
r=document.rangeFromElement(hello);
r.pasteHTML("Welcome to my element!");
}
function farewell() {
var r;
r=document.rangeFromElement(hello);
r.pasteHTML("Goodbye!");
}
</SCRIPT>
</BODY></HTML>
```

Onmouseover is another simple event that's supported by and compatible with Netscape browsers. (Because of its use of Dynamic HTML, the preceding example is for

Internet Explorer 4 only. Using the images() collection would be a good way to implement this functionality across both browser platforms.)

onmouseup

Onmouseup is like onmousedown except that onmouseup gets fired when the user releases the mouse button. It uses the same parameters and is frequently used in combination with onmousedown. We'll use it later to demonstrate drag and drop.

```
<HTML>
<BODY>
<B>X:</B> <SPAN ID=xcoord> ? </SPAN><BR>
<B>Y:</B> <SPAN ID=ycoord> ? </SPAN><BR>
<B>Button:</B> <SPAN ID=button> ? </SPAN><BR>
<SCRIPT>
//this is only for Internet Explorer 4.0
function MSresults(button1, shift1,x1,y1) {
var r;
r=document.rangeFromElement(xcoord);
r.pasteHTML(x1);
r=document.rangeFromElement(ycoord);
r.pasteHTML(y1);
r=document.rangeFromElement(button);
r.pasteHTML(button1);
}
document.onmouseup=MSresults;
</SCRIPT>
</BODY></HTML>
```

Because onmouseup returns parameters, it has the same problems as onmousedown with Internet Explorer and Netscape Communicator. You can make it work with either browser, but the code will be different and incompatible. (The preceding code is for Internet Explorer.)

Loading Events

These handlers are most useful for taking various kinds of corrective and supplementary action as your page and its objects load. The onunload event lets you clean up as the user leaves the page.

onabort

The onabort event is most useful when your page is dependent on the loading of a particular graphic. You could throw in a quick replacement for an image map with Dynamic HTML, for example, to keep your site navigable even if impatient users are giving your site problems. You could also use it simply to complain.

```
<HTML><BODY>
<SCRIPT>
function whine() {
  alert("Why couldn't you let me finish?  It won't
take more than an hour, promise.");
}
</SCRIPT>
<IMG SRC="hugepic.gif" onAbort="whine()">
</BODY></HTML>
```

The onabort event works just as well in Netscape as in Internet Explorer, although in Netscape you can't replace an image map with text if you want to.

onerror

The onerror event is much like onabort, but it means that network traffic is being difficult or something else is breaking your image. You can use it in the same way, keeping your users from cursing too much when things don't go as they should.

```
<HTML><BODY>
<SCRIPT>
function oops() {
  alert("I can't seem to find that graphic.  Oh
well.");
}
</SCRIPT>
<IMG SRC="nonexist.gif" onerror="oops()">
</BODY></HTML>
```

The onerror event also works with Netscape in the same way.

onload

The onload event is useful when you want to execute code immediately after your page has loaded. It's handy if you need to create extra windows (such as remote controls) that go with a page. You might also want to use it when you need all the elements of your page present before you launch a critical task, or you might use it just to say hello:

```
<HTML><BODY onLoad="hello()">
<SCRIPT>
function hello(){
alert ("hello there!  We've just loaded!");
}
</SCRIPT>
<P>This page is a little too enthusiastic.</P>
</BODY></HTML>
```

You can use onload with the window object (in which case you call it in the BODY element) or with the FRAME, APPLET, EMBED, IMG, or OBJECT element in Internet Explorer 4. The onload event can also be used in the same way with Netscape browsers, but only within the BODY, FRAME, and IMG tags.

onreadystatechange

The onreadystatechange event is an Internet Explorer-only tag that's most useful for monitoring ActiveX objects. This event doesn't return a parameter directly, but you can find out the current state of an object by checking its strReadyState property.

```
<HTML><BODY>
<SCRIPT>
//this code is for Internet Explorer only
function state() {
    var s;
    s=imagetest.strReadyState;
    alert("The image is at state " + s);
}
<IMG ID=imagetest SRC="test.gif"
onreadystate="state()">
</BODY></HTML>
```

Four states are available: complete(4) means the control is loaded and ready to go; interactive(3) means that although the object isn't completely loaded, you can begin to work with what's there; loading(2) means the control is coming in but isn't yet ready; uninitialized(1) means that the object isn't yet officially created and is still loading. This tag applies to the APPLET, IMG, OBJECT, and SCRIPT elements as well as the document object. Not all objects will return every state.

onunload

The onunload event occurs when a window or frame is unloading a page to load a new one. You can use it to clean up any mess your page may have left with floating windows, but there isn't much else to do with it except wish users a fond farewell.

```
<HTML><BODY onUnload="growl()">
<SCRIPT>
function growl(){
alert ("I warned you not to leave!");
}
</SCRIPT>
<P>Don't even think about leaving.</P>
</BODY></HTML>
```

You can use onunload with the window object (in which case you call it in the BODY element) or with the FRAME, APPLET, EMBED, IMG, or OBJECT element in Internet Explorer 4. The onunload event can also be used in the same way with Netscape browsers, but only within the BODY, FRAME, and IMG tags.

Form Events

When JavaScript first appeared in Netscape 2.0, it was primarily a tool for validating user input into forms before sending them for server-side processing. The form events haven't seen the kind of dramatic growth of some of the other sections, but they still provide powerful tools for directing users through forms. Form events make it easy to protect your server from mis-typed data and other hassles created by users who don't read the directions.

onblur

The onblur event occurs when a form element loses focus. This means that the user was typing something into a control and clicked elsewhere or pressed the **Tab** key to move to another field. It could also mean that the user exited one open window or frame and entered another, because onblur has been expanded to include the frame and window objects. Here, we'll use it to pester the user about leaving a text box:

```
<HTML><BODY>
<SCRIPT>
function pester(){
alert("C'mon!  I'm better than the other text
boxes!");
}
</SCRIPT>
<H3>Useless form</H3>
<FORM>
<INPUT TYPE="text" VALUE="Don't leave!"
onBlur="pester()">
</FORM>
</BODY></HTML>
```

The onblur event is available in both Internet Explorer and Netscape Communicator. Internet Explorer 4 also supports onblur for additional elements, including anchors (the A tag), APPLETs, AREAs (in image maps), DIV tags, EMBED objects, IMG images, and OBJECTs.

onchange

The onchange event is more useful than onblur for form validation, primarily because onchange happens only when the data in the form element has actually changed. In this way, the user need not wait for your code to run when it's pointless. On the other hand, it's still possible for the user to get by without changing the (wrong) information in the form field. For this reason, you'll want to combine the validation from onchange with a final onsubmit validation before sending the form to a server. The easiest way is to create separate validation routines for each of your elements. In that way, onchange can call the appropriate routine for its element, and onsubmit can call all of them in sequence before submitting the form to the browser.

```
<HTML><BODY>
<P>What's your favorite kind of HTML?</P>
<FORM><INPUT TYPE=text ID="kind"
onchange="validate()"></FORM>
<SCRIPT>
function validate(){
  var check;
  check=document.forms[0].kind.value;
  if (check !="Dynamic") {
   alert("Don't you mean you like Dynamic HTML?");
  }
}
</SCRIPT>
</BODY></HTML>
```

The onchange event is available in the Internet Explorer and Netscape browsers and behaves the same way in either environment.

onfocus

Before Dynamic HTML, the most you could do with onfocus was to add help text to the status bar by changing the window.defaultStatus property. Using an alert box would create an endless loop as the form object gave up focus to the alert box, got it back when the user clicked the OK button, and gave it back to the alert box immediately. Now you can use onfocus to change the surrounding text and provide more interesting context-sensitive help than that of the status bar.

```
<HTML><BODY>
<SCRIPT>
```

```
//this code is for Internet Explorer only
function callIt(){
var r;
r=document.rangeFromElement(announce);
r.pasteHTML("Enter something!");
}
</SCRIPT>
<P ID=announce>This is a text box:</P>
<FORM><INPUT TYPE=text onFocus="callIt()"></FORM>
</BODY></HTML>
```

The code for using this event with the status bar would have been similar, changing window.defaultState instead of using the textRange method. You can do similar things either way, but the status bar isn't as dramatic a place to offer your users help. The onfocus event is available in both Internet Explorer and Netscape. Internet Explorer 4 also supports onfocus for additional elements, including anchors (the A tag), APPLETs, AREAs (in image maps), DIV tags, EMBED objects, IMG images, and OBJECTs.

onreset

Onreset isn't good for much. Because the form data is being reset to its default values anyway and you can't do anything to stop the reset, you'll use this function primarily to post a message alerting that values are being reset. If you're using forms that are getting filled in by objects that reside in a different frame, onreset would also let you notify users that they should reenter their data.

```
<HTML><BODY>
<FORM onReset="javascript:alert('Defaults have been
restored')">
<P>Default Value: <INPUT TYPE=text VALUE="Dull
Default"></P>
```

```
<INPUT TYPE=reset VALUE="Reset Form">
<FORM>
</BODY></HTML>
```

The onreset event is available in the Internet Explorer and Netscape browsers and behaves the same way in either environment.

onselect

The onselect tag has been troublesome ever since its appearance in Netscape 2.0. It doesn't return any information about the text selected. It just alerts you that the user has selected or unselected some text. It's useful only with TEXT and TEXTAREA controls, and barely useful at that.

```
<HTML><BODY>
<FORM>
<P>Select Me: <INPUT TYPE=text VALUE="Select some
text!" onSelect="javascript:alert('Congratulations.
You know how to select text.')"></P>
<INPUT TYPE=reset VALUE="Reset Form">
<FORM>
</BODY></HTML>
```

The onselect event works the same way in the Netscape and Microsoft browsers.

onsubmit

The onsubmit event gives you control over the validation of your forms. Unlike onreset, the onsubmit event lets you stop the form submission if you don't like the looks of the data. All you have to do is return the value false. We'll use the same routine we used with onchange for validation and combine it with onsubmit to make sure the user gets the right answer.

```
<HTML><BODY>
<SCRIPT>
function validate(){
  var check;
  check=document.forms[0].kind.value;
  if (check !="Dynamic") {
    alert("Don't you mean you like Dynamic HTML?");
    return false;
  }
}
function formvalid() {
    checkvalid=validate();
    return checkvalid;
}
</SCRIPT>
<P>What's your favorite kind of HTML?</P>
<FORM onSubmit="formvalid()"><INPUT TYPE=text
ID=kind onchange="validate()">
<INPUT TYPE=submit VALUE="Submit data">
</FORM>
</BODY></HTML>
```

For a form such as this one, with only one value, we could have called validate() directly. The advantage of creating the checkvalid() function is that we can use it to check more than one INPUT value. Also note that we're finally taking advantage of the fact that functions have return values. In this case, if the data isn't what we want, the return value is false, preventing the submission. (Because no ACTION is listed in the FORM tag, nothing would happen anyway, but it's a good way to test it.) The onsubmit event works the same way in the Netscape and Microsoft browsers.

Marquee Events

When Microsoft shipped Internet Explorer 2.0, the company needed something to differentiate its product from Netscape's browsers. Taking notice of all the text scrollers and stock tickers that were decorating Web pages, Microsoft decided to create a Marquee object that would provide that functionality without additional programming. The HTML coder need provide only text and options to control the color, speed, and direction of the text. Marquees can be useful, but they remain an Internet Explorer—only feature. The events they provide are useful primarily for coordinating other happenings with the comings and goings of the marquee. (Don't confuse the Marquee object generated by the MARQUEE tag with the Marquee ActiveX control, which lets you scroll entire HTML pages across the screen.)

onbounce

The onbounce event occurs only in marquees whose behavior is set to alternate. Onbounce provides a way to respond when the marquee bounces off the sides of its space. You could play a sound, flash a color, or send an alert. Onbounce returns one parameter, side, which lets you know which side the contents collided with.

```
<HTML><BODY>
<MARQUEE BEHAVIOR=alternate DIRECTION=right
HEIGHT=160 WIDTH=160
onBounce="javascript:alert('This is
bouncing!')">Bouncy Text </MARQUEE>
</BODY></HTML>
```

The onbounce event is available only in Internet Explorer.

onfinish

The onfinish event takes place when the marquee completes the number of loops specified. You can use this event to open a page with a marquee and then change to other, less showy methods of presenting information, or you could launch a multimedia extravaganza if the marquee wasn't enough for you.

```
<HTML><BODY>
<MARQUEE LOOP=3 onfinish="javascript:alert('This is
finished!')">This is the marquee we're testing.
</MARQUEE>
</BODY></HTML>
```

The onfinish event is available only in Internet Explorer.

onstart

The onstart event, another simple marquee event, happens when the marquee begins the display of every loop after the first. Onstart is also fired at the start of a bounce cycle when the behavior of the marquee is set to alternate.

```
<HTML><BODY>
<MARQUEE LOOP=3 onstart="javascript:alert('This
marquee is getting started!')">This is the marquee
we're testing. </MARQUEE>
</BODY></HTML>
```

The onstart event is available only in Internet Explorer.

Data-Binding Events

Perhaps the most revolutionary events available to date, the data-binding objects will be discussed as a group in Chapter 11. As exciting as they are, you need to understand the full context of Internet Explorer 4's new data-binding system and its associated ActiveX objects to make any sense of them.

Other Events

If you want to create a complete interface, it's useful to be able to detect the user's typing, and most of the following events let you do that. The only nonkeyboard event here, onscroll, gives you the additional advantage of knowing when the user is scrolling the window, making it possible to respond.

onhelp

The onhelp event lets developers provide the classic online help functions that have existed since the days of DOS. If the user presses the **F1** key, the onhelp event takes place:

```
<HTML><BODY onhelp="informkey()">
<SCRIPT>
function informkey() {
alert("You pushed the help key.");
}
</SCRIPT>
<P> Try asking for help!  (F1)</P>
</BODY></HTML>
```

The onhelp event is available only in Internet Explorer 4.0.

onkeydown

The onkeydown event takes place, like the onmousedown event, as soon as the user has pressed the key and before it bounces back up. The onkeydown event is available in the Netscape Communicator 4.0 and Microsoft Internet Explorer 4.0 browsers, and the ASCII code of the key pressed comes through the event object in both cases, but the implementation differs in other ways. For Netscape, onkeydown appears in event.which; for Microsoft, in event.keycode. Internet Explorer also passes modifier key information as a parameter, whereas Netscape puts it in the event.modifiers property. Internet Explorer 4 also lets you return a different ASCII value and thereby override the keycode the user entered. The following code will work in Internet Explorer 4.0:

```
<HTML><BODY onkeydown="informkey()">
<SCRIPT>
function informkey() {
keypushed=(event.keyCode);
alert("You pushed the " + keypushed + " key.");
}
</SCRIPT>
<P> Try pushing some keys!</P>
</BODY></HTML>
```

VBScript coders have a distinct advantage here, because they have a function, Chr(), that converts these codes to characters. Until Microsoft and Netscape improve on the unescape() function, JavaScripters will be stuck working with numbers. Although the onkeydown event is supported by both browsers, you'll have trouble using the same code to handle it in both Microsoft and Netscape browsers.

onkeypress

An onkeypress event is a combination of an onkeydown and an onkeyup event, or it can happen when a user holds down a key longer than the operating system considers necessary for the key to repeat. Internet Explorer 4 will also let you return a different ASCII value and thereby override the keycode the user entered. You can use onkeypress pretty much as you would the onkeydown event:

```
<HTML><BODY onkeypress="informkey()">
<SCRIPT>
function informkey() {
keypushed=event.keyCode;
alert("You pushed the " + keypushed + " key.");
}
</SCRIPT>
<P> Try pushing some keys!</P>
```

```
</BODY></HTML>
```

Although onkeypress is supported by both browsers, you'll have trouble using the same code to handle it in the Microsoft and Netscape browsers. In this way it is similiar to onkeydown.

onkeyup

The onkeyup event occurs only when the user releases a key, making this event useful for avoiding repeats caused by an impatient user holding down a key. Internet Explorer 4 also lets you return a different ASCII value to override the keycode the user entered. The code for Internet Explorer 4.0 is similiar to that of the previous two events:

```
<HTML><BODY onkeyup="informkey()">
<SCRIPT>
function informkey() {
keypushed=(event.keyCode);
alert("You pushed the " + keypushed + " key.");
}
</SCRIPT>
<P> Try pushing some keys!</P>
</BODY></HTML>
```

Although onkeyup is supported by both browsers, you'll have trouble using the same code to handle it in the Microsoft and Netscape browsers.

onscroll

The onscroll event occurs when the user moves the scroll bar. This event was created by Microsoft but uses a Netscape-like way to pass the scrolling information to the function handling onscroll. It comes in as a scrollObject, with parameters actualX and actualY that identify how far the scroll bar traveled.

```
<HTML><BODY onScroll="scrollAlert()">
<SCRIPT>
function scrollAlert(scrInfo) {
    alert('You scrolled ' + scrInfo.actualX + ' x-
pixels and ' + scrInfo.actualY + 'y-pixels');
}
</SCRIPT>
<H1>This is just some random text to scroll through.
Nothing exciting at all.  This is just some random
text to scroll through.  Nothing exciting at all.
This is just some random text to scroll through.
Nothing exciting at all.  This is just some random
text to scroll through.  Nothing exciting at all.
This is just some random text to scroll through.
Nothing exciting at all.  This is just some random
text to scroll through.  Nothing exciting at all.
This is just some random text to scroll through.
Nothing exciting at all.  This is just some random
text to scroll through.  Nothing exciting at all.
This is just some random text to scroll through.
Nothing exciting at all.  This is just some random
text to scroll through.  Nothing exciting at all.
</H1>
</BODY></HTML>
```

The onscroll event is available only in Internet Explorer 4.0.

Window Events (Netscape 4.0 Only)

The following events are available only for Netscape 4.0, although they may at some point appear in Internet Explorer 4. Ondragdrop is fired when a user drops a file into the browser. If you return false to the event handler, Netscape will stop handling the event (it would open the document) and let you take control. In Preview Release 5, however, Netscape still hadn't implemented the data portion of the event object, which returns the URL of the file being dropped. To handle ondragdrop, you'd write code such as this:

```
<HTML>
<HEAD><TITLE>DragDrop Event</TITLE></HEAD>
<BODY>
<SCRIPT LANGUAGE="JavaScript">
function dragHandle(e){
  alert(e.data);
}
window.ondragdrop=dragHandle;
</SCRIPT>
<H3>Drop a file here!</H3>
</BODY>
</HTML>
```

Onmove happens when the user moves a window or frame, and onresize takes place when the user resizes a window or a frame. Onmove returns the coordinates of the upper-left corner of the window:

```
<HTML>
<HEAD><TITLE>Onmove Event</TITLE></HEAD>
<BODY>
<SCRIPT LANGUAGE="JavaScript">
function moveHandle(e){
  alert(e.screenX+" " +e.screenY);
}
window.onmove=moveHandle;
</SCRIPT>
<H3>Move this window!</H3>
</BODY>
</HTML>
```

Onresize works in the same way except that it returns the height and width of the window after it's been resized:

```
<HTML>
<HEAD><TITLE>Onresize Event</TITLE></HEAD>
<BODY>
<SCRIPT LANGUAGE="JavaScript">
function resizeHandle(e){
   alert(e.width+" " +e.height);
}
window.onresize=resizeHandle;
</SCRIPT>
<H3>Resize this window!</H3>
</BODY>
</HTML>
```

All these events seem useful, and perhaps soon they'll make an appearance in Internet Explorer. For now, even if Internet Explorer supported them, the differences in the object model would render them incompatible.

Creating Your Own Events

If you use applets and ActiveX objects, you can call JavaScript and VBScript functions using techniques similar to those used to handle browser-generated events. Chapter 6 will explore these possibilities in greater depth.

Inheritance and Event Bubbling

One of the most exciting features of Internet Explorer 4 is known as *event bubbling*. The bubbles may not be champagne, but they offer cause for celebration. In event bubbling, events that start on one element can emanate through other elements until they find an element that wants to handle them. If nothing handles the event, it disappears. This simple, powerful feature lets you create groups of objects easily. For example, consider the following code:

```
<HTML>
<BODY>
<SPAN>
<P>See this image?<A HREF="nowhere.html"><IMG
SRC="picture.gif">
</A></P></SPAN></BODY></HTML>
```

If an event occurs in the IMG tag here, it could be handled by the IMG tag. If it's not, the A element gets its chance, followed by the P, the SPAN, and the BODY (see Figure 5.2). All those elements can handle events for the objects contained within their boundaries.

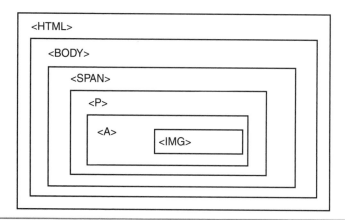

Figure 5.2 Event bubbling architecture

This means that you can group elements and then write the code to handle them only once. The document object is a logical place to do this, although you could also create SPANs or DIVs to separate groups of objects that need to be handled differently. Internet Explorer also provides a srcElement property in its event object that lets you determine which object fired the event in the first place.

Event bubbling can be used with Dynamic HTML to create simple handlers for highlighting text and graphics and managing many objects easily. In this example, we'll use it to highlight and unhighlight text as the onmouseover and onmouseout events occur:

```
<HTML><BODY onmouseover="highlight()">
<SCRIPT>
function highlight() {
hilite=window.event.srcElement;
hilite.style.color="red";
}
function dim() {
dimmer=window.event.srcElement;
dimmer.style.color="blue";
}
function dim2() {
dimmer=window.event.srcElement;
dimmer.style.color="gray";
}
</SCRIPT>
<SPAN ID=text1 onmouseout="dim()">
<P ID=p1>This is text piece 1. </P>
<P ID=p2>This is text piece 2.  </P>
<P ID=p3>This is text piece 3.  </P>
</SPAN>
<HR>
<SPAN ID=text2 onmouseout="dim2()">
<P ID=p4>This is text piece 4.  </P>
<P ID=p5>This is text piece 5.  </P>
<P ID=p6>This is text piece 6.  </P>
<SPAN>
</BODY></HTML>
```

All the text in this example starts black, turns red as the mouse rolls over it, and then turns blue or green depending on which SPAN it belongs to. This element of Microsoft's event model will make it easy for developers to create generic interfaces that work with a wide variety of interface pieces. Although it may not be useful in every situation, this feature makes it simple to combine similar actions with common code.

Events bubble up through the object model whether or not they've been handled. If you want to stop an event from bubbling further through the hierarchy, you need to 'sink' the bubble: set event.cancelBubble to true. The event will stop at your handler and go no further. The next event will come through as before and continue past your handler unless you reset cancelBubble to false. This technique makes it easy to create conditional handlers that can decide whether to allow events to continue up the object model.

You can also take advantage of events to override default handlers. The most obvious and most useful way is by using the <A> tag. If you return false to an onClick handler, your code will be executed but the link to the HREF will not be made. With this broad new power, you can create hyperlinks that go (or don't go) depending on what else the user has done in your document.

Netscape's Event Capturing Model

Netscape's competing model works in the opposite direction. Instead of letting events flow from ground zero to the edges of the document, Netscape asks that you explicitly declare the objects to handle an event. This approach has its uses, although it may seem more complicated than Internet Explorer at first. The window and document objects get four new methods: captureEvents, releaseEvents, routeEvents, and handleEvent. To make a window handle all mouse clicks, for example, you'd specify this inside a SCRIPT tag:

```
window.captureEvents(Event.CLICK);
```

This code would set up the window to control all click events, whatever the original recipient might have been. (The releaseEvents method turns this event off.) To make the window object control multiple events, you separate them with a | character:

```
window.captureEvents(Event.CLICK |
Event.MOUSEDOWN);
```

After this code executes, the window will manage the onclick and onmousedown events. Once the window manages events, it must provide routines to handle them (otherwise, they disappear). The routine must do one of four things to handle the event, whatever else it may do in the course of its execution. The simplest possibilities are to return true or false, which (if the event cares, as onsubmit might) can cancel the event. The other two options involve the remaining two methods. Calling the routeEvent method lets you send the event to other, nonspecified handlers, effectively sending it down the object and element hierarchies until it finds another event handler. Calling the handleEvent method sends the event to another specific element. For instance, the following would send the event down to the third image in the document to be handled as it sees fit:

```
window.document.images[2].handleEvent(e);
```

You'll need to use the target property of the event object to figure out which element sent the event in the first place.

Whether the W3 committee and the warring browser developers can find a way to integrate the two object models is a difficult question. Until this battle is resolved, developers building pages for the two different browsers will find themselves facing major challenges in event handling.

CHAPTER 6

Control or Be Controlled: Controls and Applets

Applets and ActiveX controls haven't yet transformed the Web, but they promise to make many tasks possible and many tasks easier. In the long term, applets and ActiveX controls will probably decide the outcome or outcomes of the browser wars, because lightweight interpreted browser scripts have their limits when it comes to writing heavy-duty code. The initial appearance of the Netscape plug-in model set the stage for a long line of contenders, including Java applets, ActiveX controls, and a few other interfaces that claim the potential to transform the Web.

For our purposes, programming objects will remain largely black boxes. As much as I'd like to create powerful programs using ActiveX or Java, it's not appropriate in a primer on Dynamic HTML. This chapter will cover what you need to know when you integrate Java applets and ActiveX controls into your Web pages but provides only a basic discussion of how to create simple objects. To give you a peek inside the black boxes you'll be manipulating, both sections include brief descriptions of ActiveX and Java development. Like it or not, harnessing the power of Dynamic HTML for business applications often means working with applets and controls, and the more you understand about the structure of that communication, the better. (If you'd rather wait, you can skip this chapter and come back to it when you need it.)

Object technology is another area of conflict between Microsoft and Netscape even when both companies claim to support the same standard (for example, Java). Unfortunately, the worst of the land mines are placed at the juncture between objects and scripting languages, a critical point for making Dynamic HTML work. By the end of this chapter, we'll see what to avoid and what to use for specific browsers and development situations.

ActiveX and HTML

ActiveX is Microsoft's contender in the object wars. Microsoft has been ahead of the pack in breaking programs into smaller components that are reusable, shareable between programs, and interchangeable, but it has always done it in its own way. Dynamic link libraries (DLLs) made it possible for programs to share code and link to other files at runtime, providing an easy way for programmers and programs to share code. The object linking and embedding (OLE) standard let programs share data and functionality, making it possible to run one program within the confines of another. COM, the Component Object Model, extends general OLE by creating standards for components to interconnect and communicate. (Distributed COM, or DCOM, the latest update, extends COM to let the components communicate among computers on a network.) This progression has culminated in the ActiveX control, a small program that can communicate with and be a part of other programs seamlessly. Originally developed to let Visual Basic programmers use objects developed in Visual C++, ActiveX has grown into a full-blown component standard that is integrated with the Internet.

An ActiveX control can do anything a regular Windows 95 application can. ActiveX has amazing powers to provide a full-blown interface with all the controls Windows users are accustomed to seeing. It also lets you communicate with other machines, interact with databases, and present multimedia extravaganzas. On the other hand, an ActiveX control can also shut down your machine, erase your hard drive, infect your computer with viruses, transmit your files to unknown parties elsewhere on the Internet, and generally crash your computer. With great power comes great risk.

Microsoft has tried to address these issues with a system of verification whereby an ActiveX control can carry a digital signature that states the original source of the object. Internet Explorer is set up not to allow you to download ActiveX controls, signed or otherwise. The security settings allow you to selectively accept ActiveX components or open your machine and accept everything the Internet throws in your direction.

If users take the trouble to inspect the digital signatures, which include links to the originator of the file and the "bank" that maintains the list of signatures, this system can work fairly well. Unfortunately, users on slow links who visit Microsoft sites will quickly find themselves turning off the security. The new Microsoft Network, for example, ships with a browser whose security is set to high, but MSN requires ActiveX controls. You can't really use it until you've relaxed the security. After visiting a few pages with multiple ActiveX elements, I gave up and turned off security, thereby endangering my machine's health in a radical way. Still, given the level of hassle (and the lack of important material on that machine), it seemed like the best—if not the safest—way to get work done.

The other problem with ActiveX is its strong connection with the Win32 (Windows 95) application programming interface (API) and the Intel x86 microprocessor architecture. Microsoft offers Internet Explorer for the Macintosh and for Windows NT running on the DEC Alpha, MIPS, and PowerPC architectures, but none of those versions can handle ActiveX controls in their current form. There has been talk of porting ActiveX to other platforms, but so far no implementation has appeared. Making ActiveX work on another architecture would probably take a huge amount of interpretation, bogging down performance and complicating development. Because of these limitations, you should use ActiveX only when your audience uses only Intel (or compatible) machines running Windows 95 or NT. If that isn't the case, you must provide alternatives if you want your users to reach your content. It is possible to use ActiveX controls in Netscape Communicator for Windows 95 and NT with the NCompass plug-in, but this solution isn't always reliable or complete.

You can develop ActiveX controls with the Visual Basic 5.0 Control Creation Edition, which Microsoft offers as a free download at http://www.microsoft.com/vbasic. If you need a higher horsepower development environment, you can get Visual Basic Professional Edition (which has a wizard to make ActiveX controls easier to develop), Visual C++ 5.0, or even the Microsoft Visual Studio, which includes both Visual C++ and Visual Basic and a host of other tools for programming and Web development. Third-party developers also offer some great tools, such as Borland's Delphi 3. If you have programming skills in any of these areas, ActiveX is the easiest way to transfer them directly to the Web, and it also lets you plug your components into other Windows 95 and NT programs.

For our purposes, however, we're more concerned with connecting ActiveX controls to Dynamic HTML pages. You can control ActiveX controls from Web pages by calling their methods, and ActiveX controls can call scripts in your page by triggering events. From the Web developer's perspective, the ActiveX control is a black box that takes certain parameters, provides certain functions, and produces certain events. It's a little more complicated than the average Web element, but it isn't dramatically different when it comes to developing pages.

Including ActiveX Controls on Your Page

Much of the appeal of ActiveX controls is that other people have programmed lots of them, potentially sparing Web developers the onerous task of reinventing the programming wheel. (You may have to pay for them, of course.) Including ActiveX controls in your pages is reasonably simple, although the notation for identifying them was definitely created for computers and not for people. We'll be doing a lot of this work later in the book when we examine the ActiveX controls that Microsoft has included with Internet Explorer.

ActiveX controls arrive through the <OBJECT> tag, which identifies the object you'll be using, supplies it parameters, and downloads it if necessary. The OBJECT tag has many parameters, which are listed in Table 6.1.

Table 6.1 Parameters of the OBJECT Tag

Attribute	Notes
ACCESSKEY	Specifies an accelerator key for the element; takes a string.
ALIGN	Works as for the IMG tag: BOTTOM, LEFT, MIDDLE, and so on.
CLASSID	The class identifier for an ActiveX control.
CODE	Names the file of the Java class when OBJECT is used for Java instead of APPLET.
CODEBASE	Gives a URL where the browser can find the object if it isn't installed already.
CODETYPE	A reserved attribute.

continued on next page

Attribute	Notes
DATA	Specifies a URL for the object's data.
DATAFLD	See Chapter 11 on data binding.
DATASRC	See Chapter 11 on data binding.
DISABLED	Turns off the object. Great for debugging pages.
HEIGHT	Same as IMG: specifies height in pixels.
ID	Identifies the object for cascading style sheets and Dynamic HTML.
NAME	Identifies the object; can be used with Dynamic HTML.
STYLE	A style sheet for the tag.
TABINDEX	Specifies the order in which the object will receive focus when the user presses the **Tab** key.
TITLE	Used to provide advisory information."
TYPE	Specifies the MIME type, if any, of the scripting engine.
WIDTH	Same as IMG: the width of the object in pixels.
event	Lets you attach handlers for any of the events listed in Chapter 5.

You'll use only a few of these parameters most of the time. You should always include an ID attribute if you want to refer to the object from scripts. The CLASSID value will be a long hexadecimal value produced by the compiler of your ActiveX control. You'll need to include the CODEBASE attribute whenever you're providing a control over a network, and that will be most of the time unless you're using the controls provided with Internet Explorer 4.0. As with images, it's a good idea to use the HEIGHT and WIDTH attributes to help the browser at load time even if you aren't concerned about the way the control looks.

A simple OBJECT tag might look like this:

```
<OBJECT ID=demo
CLASSID="FFFFFFFF-FFFF-FFFF-FFFF-FFFFFFFFFFFF"
CODEBASE="http://www.demosinc.com/demo.ocx"
HEIGHT=100 WIDTH=50>
```

```
<PARAM NAME="demoName" VALUE="Easy Demo">
<PARAM NAME="authenticateUser" VALUE="No">
</OBJECT>
```

This object doesn't really exist, so don't try using it. One important thing to remember is that your CLASSID attribute must always be on one line. If you're using an editor that adds line breaks to your code, you may find that your controls won't load. Find the offending extra character and remove it, and your code should work again. The preceding object specifies a CODEBASE attribute, because it refers to a demonstration that few users will have on their computers. (If they already have the demonstration, Internet Explorer can figure that out and won't make them download it again.) Because this demonstration needs a bit of screen space, it also declares a HEIGHT and WIDTH.

The PARAM tags are the other important part of this declaration. Some ActiveX controls are fairly flexible about the parameters they can accept, but others need specific NAME and VALUE sets. Generally speaking, each PARAM for an ActiveX control will contain only one NAME and one VALUE. Named parameters make programming much simpler, because you don't have to worry about getting parameters backward and producing strange, untraceable errors.

Working with ActiveX Control Properties, Methods, and Events

ActiveX controls fit smoothly into Internet Explorer 4.0's document object model, and it's easy to script most controls. You need to know which methods and properties are exposed to your scripts and which events the object fires. With that information, you're ready to use the control in the same way you use any other element of your HTML code. You'll most likely want to use VBScript to handle your ActiveX controls, because it provides easier handling of control events.

For the following demonstrations, we'll use the ActiveMovie control, one of the ActiveX controls Microsoft has included with Internet Explorer 4.0. ActiveMovie is scriptable, although most developers just let it present a movie without their having to do much. You'll find that ActiveMovie offers a wide variety of properties and methods that give you more control over the presentation of video. You should substitute the name of your own AVI (or other format) file in the FileName parameter of the object tag.

```
<HTML>
<HEAD><TITLE>ActiveMovie Demo</TITLE></HEAD>
<BODY>
<SCRIPT LANGUAGE="JavaScript">
function FrameIt(){
     if (player.DisplayMode==0){ //0 means time is
displayed
          player.DisplayMode=1;
          FrameButton.value="Time"}
     else {
          player.DisplayMode=0;
          FrameButton.value="Frames"
     }
}
function PlayIt(){
     if (player.CurrentState==2) {//2 means movie is
playing
     PlayButton.value="Play";
```

```
      player.Pause();
      }
      else { //other values mean movie is stopped or
paused
      PlayButton.value="Pause";
      player.Run();
      }
}
function StopIt(){ //stop stops and restarts movie
      player.Stop();
      PlayButton.value="Play";
}
</SCRIPT>
<OBJECT CLASSID="CLSID:05589FA1-C356-11CE-BF01-
00AA0055595A" ID=player HEIGHT=300 WIDTH=300>
<PARAM NAME="FileName"
VALUE="F:\dynhtml\actmov\mail2.avi">
</OBJECT>
<BR>
<INPUT TYPE=BUTTON VALUE="Play" onclick="PlayIt()"
ID=PlayButton>
<INPUT TYPE=BUTTON VALUE="Stop" onclick="StopIt()"
ID=StopButton>
<INPUT TYPE=BUTTON VALUE="Frames"
onClick="FrameIt()" ID=FrameButton>

</BODY>
</HTML>
```

When you first load this code, you'll see something like
Figure 6.1 (except that your movie will be the one
displayed).

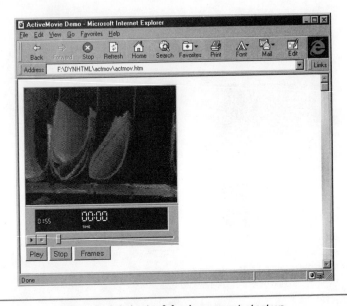

Figure 6.1 ActiveMovie page at startup.

This code depends on several properties and methods to get its work done. Switching between the time display (minutes:seconds) and the frame count requires only that we change the DisplayMode property of our ActiveMovie player. The default value of zero makes the player show a time display; changing it to 1 makes it show a frame count. The FrameIt() routine manages this flip-flop and also changes the content of the button to reflect the current option (see Figure 6.2).

If you want to change the play state of the movie (playing, paused, or stopped), use one of the control's methods: Run(), Pause(), or Stop(). (Run() just means play; I'm not sure why they didn't call it that.) There is also a property, CurrentState, that can tell you whether the movie is playing, paused, or stopped. Our little scripts

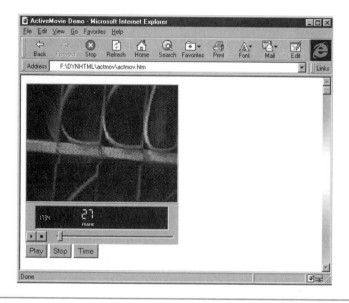

Figure 6.2 Movie with frames displayed.

provide an alternative interface to the basic controller that comes as part of ActiveMovie. You probably won't use this script with its ugly buttons, but you could create a more elaborate player for a page and then use these functions instead of depending on the utilitarian built-in controller. Much like the Play/Pause button on many VCRs, the PlayIt() function does two things. If the video clip is playing, the function pauses it; if it's paused, it plays it. The function changes the button text to indicate what it can do for you next (see Figure 6.3).

The StopIt() function has a simpler task. It doesn't care whether the clip is playing or paused. It just resets the clip to its first frame, stops the action, and resets the PlayButton to Play.

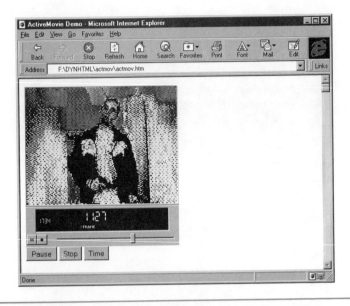

Figure 6.3 Player paused part way into the movie.

Our little player has a small problem. If the movie goes all the way through to the end, the movie will stop and reset, but the PlayButton will still say **Pause**. To make it change, we need to capture the StateChange event. To do this in JavaScript, we use the <SCRIPT FOR= EVENT=> syntax:

```
<SCRIPT FOR="player" EVENT="StateChange"
LANGUAGE="JavaScript">
    if (player.CurrentState==0)
{PlayButton.value="Play";}
</SCRIPT>
```

Alternatively, if we had used VBScript, we could use the Sub object_event syntax and pick up the parameters the event passes:

```
<SCRIPT LANGUAGE="VBScript">
```

```
Sub player_StateChange(oldState, newState)
 if newState=0 then PlayButton.value="Play"
 end sub
</SCRIPT>
```

We didn't have to find out the player.CurrentState value, because the event passed us both the original state and the new resulting state. Either approach will work in Internet Explorer, and you can add the VBScript code to your JavaScript document without causing a stir.

Most ActiveX controls are no more difficult than this, although some of them (as we'll see in Chapter 10) can get much more complicated, with parameters and even additional CLASSIDs piling up inside the OBJECT tag. Once you get past the CLASSID attribute, ActiveX controls can make advanced Web development easy.

Java

Java is ActiveX's main competition. When Sun debuted Java in August 1995, it was the fruit of a long development process that had been aimed at programming consumer appliances, such as cable TV boxes and handheld organizers. Java's target audience was unusual for a programming language, and it freed the Sun developers from the constraints of using an established programming package with established calls, setting them on the road to creating as flexible a language as possible. With the explosive growth of the Web, Sun changed the focus of the project and the designers set about creating the most powerful, secure cross-platform system they could.

Java is a language, but it's also much more. The Java language is based on C and C++, with some of the more dangerous (crash-prone) features of those languages removed. Java has a cleaner syntax and less ambiguity than C++ and offers built-in tools to manage many of the basic tasks of creating programs. If Java were just a variant of C, though, it wouldn't have received the press coverage and accolades it has.

Java programs (and applets—secure microprograms) aren't written for a particular operating system. Instead, they're written for an abstracted machine: the Java Virtual Machine. The JVM is just a standard for creating Java-compatible environments on any machine capable of managing the Java environment. Unlike ActiveX controls, Java programs aren't compiled into machine-specific, API-specific code. Instead, they compile to generic bytecodes, which are then interpreted (or recompiled) to fit the machine on which they're run. For developers, this means that one piece of code can run on Windows 95, NT, OS/2, Macintosh, Sun Solaris, IBM AIX, Linux, HP-UX, DEC Unix, and a multitude of other operating systems and architectures, regardless of the underlying platform. Other developers have the task of creating JVM environments for each platform, but once that's been set up, it's easy to run Java applications in any environment. The growing list of compatible systems includes almost every PC and workstation and most of the server machines on the market. The JVM environment still isn't as rich as the Windows 95, Macintosh, or X Window GUI, but development tools are becoming friendlier and the implementations are improving slowly.

Netscape was the first licensee, immediately touting Java as the best way to break free of the platform-specific barriers that limited communications on the Internet. IBM has joined the Java revolution enthusiastically, building a complete Java implementation into OS/2 Warp 4.0 and moving it quickly to servers and network computers. Even Microsoft, which derided Java at first as merely a language, and not a very good one, has come around to supporting Java. Microsoft is a Sun licensee, as are all the other vendors, although Java may eventually move away from Sun and into the world of open standards ruled by committee. In an interesting related development, the Java Virtual Machine is branching out, as developers in other languages have figured out how to compile their code to Java bytecodes, making it possible to use the JVM even through older languages such as COBOL and Smalltalk. The JVM imposes the same security restrictions on bytecodes created with these applications as it does on native Java code.

Java and the Web Browser: Applets

Although it is possible to create full-fledged applications in Java, most of the programs created in Java so far are *applets*: programs with limited privileges that are designed to work in a Web browser window. Although a few holes have been discovered in the Java security model, it is much stricter than that of ActiveX. Applets have no right to store or read data on the user's local machine, making it difficult to create "Trojan horse" applications that download from the Web to create great damage. (The user has some flexibility on this issue, but developers are warned not to expect these privileges.) Applets can't start other programs, nor are they allowed to communicate with servers except the one from which they were served originally. The interpreter (or just-in-time compiler) on the Web browser side is required to check bytecodes for bad, missing, corrupt, or dangerous code and will prohibit such code from executing. In addition, the cross-platform nature of Java makes it much harder to create programs that take advantage of loopholes in a particular operating system. A signature system for Java applets—much like the one described earlier for ActiveX—will also be available with Netscape 4.0, although for now it remains an option.

Most of the initial Java development focused on multimedia. Applets that bounced heads around a box, let users simulate running (and destroying) a nuclear reactor, and spun planets around in a galaxy competed for attention with animated stock tickers that could present nearly live data. More recently, developers have turned to Java to create front ends for databases in Web-based client-server applications. As long as the applet lived in its own little box in the window, managing this kind of application was easy for a Web browser to handle. Connecting Java applications to HTML, however, has proven more difficult and more controversial. We'll look at the Netscape and Microsoft approaches, with simple applets written for both in Java. As we'll see, Netscape lets your script and the applet call each other's methods, whereas Microsoft only allows scripting methods to call applets: applets still can't call scripting methods. There are ways around this limitation, but it will probably remain a headache for developers.

LiveConnect and COM: Calling Java from JavaScript

LiveConnect is Netscape's means of connecting JavaScript in your Web page with the Java code in your applets. (You can also use LiveConnect to control plug-ins from both JavaScript and Java, a feature we won't cover here.) Calling Java methods from JavaScript is simple, but calling JavaScript from Java takes a bit more work.

We'll start with an easy example that connects the input in a text box to the text displayed in a Java applet box. You need two pieces to make this work. First, you need the Java applet, and you need to know what its declared methods are. If you don't have the source code, you can make this example work if you know the available methods and their parameters. Our Java applet has three methods and a few variables. If you don't know Java and don't want to know Java, you can skip this listing and move to the next one, which covers the HTML side. If you're feeling undaunted, however, following is the Java source code. (You'll need a Java compiler such as Sun's Java Development Kit, Symantec's Café, or Microsoft's Visual J++ to make this work.)

```
import java.applet.Applet;
import java.awt.Graphics;
//LiveConnect Demonstration
public class strtest extends Applet
{
     String showString;
     public void init(){
     showString= new String("LiveConnect Demo");
}
     public void paint(Graphics g){
     g.drawString(showString, 20, 20);
}
     public void setString(String yourString) {
     showString=yourString;
     repaint();
}
}
```

The applet will use (and therefore imports) routines from the Applet and Abstract Windowing Toolkit (AWT) libraries. Its one class, strtest, has one variable, showString, a string containing the text the applet displays. At applet startup, the init() routine is called and sets the string to "LiveConnect Demo." The paint routine is called next. It draws the showString variable on the applet's window. The setString routine is the method we'll be calling from the HTML to change the text. Knowledge of the details of the rest of the applet isn't necessary from the HTML developer's perspective. The setString routine takes a string as a parameter, sets the display text to that string, and orders the applet to repaint itself, changing the string.

The second part, the HTML is simple:

```
<HTML>
<HEAD><TITLE>LiveConnect Test</TITLE></HEAD>
<BODY>
<APPLET CODE="strtest.class" NAME="strtest"
WIDTH=150 HEIGHT=25>
</APPLET><BR>
<FORM NAME="inputPlace">
<INPUT TYPE="text" SIZE=30 NAME="words"><BR>
<INPUT TYPE="button" VALUE="SetString"
onClick="document.strtest.setString(document.inputPl
ace.words.value)">
</FORM>
</BODY>
</HTML>
```

This code sets up the applet (in much the same way as we did the OBJECT, but without the CLASSID) and provides a text input box to accept a string entered by the user. When the user clicks on the SetString button, the JavaScript calls the Java applet's setString method, changing the text and repainting the applet. Try this in Netscape, and you'll see the screen shown in Figure 6.4.

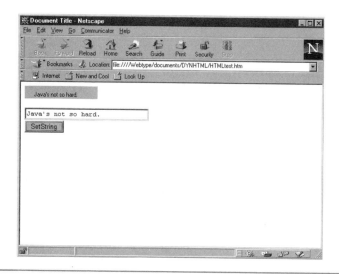

Figure 6.4 Simple LiveConnect demo in Netscape 4.0.

Try it in Internet Explorer, and it will also work (see Figure 6.5).

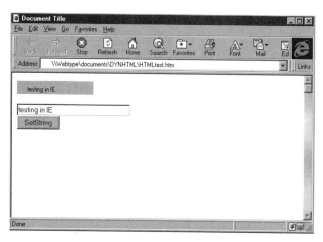

Figure 6.5 Simple JScript/JavaScript demo in Internet Explorer 4.0.

Microsoft doesn't call its technology LiveConnect, but up to this point it works in exactly the same way. As long as you're passing code only *from* the script to the applet and not passing it from the applet *to* the script, you can write code for both browsers without any difficulty. That side of the equation works. On the other hand, Microsoft's COM technology isn't yet up to the task of letting Java talk back to your scripts except through simple returned values. Java is not allowed to return events to the browser or call scripted functions. It can talk to other ActiveX controls and COM objects, but the complexity of setting up an arrangement with another object to forward events is more than most programmers care to deal with. It requires that you create an additional new COM object every time you create a new applet.

LiveConnect: Calling JavaScript from Java

Perhaps sometime soon Microsoft will catch up to Netscape and let us call scripts from Java applets. In the meantime, let's see how the Netscape LiveConnect solution works. It isn't seamless, but it isn't much harder if you know Java. The remainder of this chapter will demand a basic knowledge of Java, and nonprogrammers are welcome to skip to the next chapter. The examples are simple, but Java syntax is rather strange for beginners, even beginners experienced with JavaScript.

N O T E   If you run this example in Internet Explorer, you will get errors when the Java tries to call the script. You should implement browser detection and make sure that this code is run only on Netscape 3.0 and 4.0 browsers, or you should at least warn your users.

We'll add Netscape's LiveConnect solution to our current applet and have it send an alert via JavaScript when the text changes. It imports routines from a Netscape library:

```
import java.applet.Applet;
import java.awt.Graphics;
import netscape.javascript.*;
// HelloWorld
public class strtest2 extends Applet
{
     String showString;
     public void init(){
     showString= new String("LiveConnect Demo"); }
public void paint(Graphics g){
     g.drawString(showString, 20, 20);
     }
public void setString(String yourString) {
     String args[]={yourString, showString};
     showString=yourString;
     repaint();
     JSObject win= JSObject.getWindow(this);
     win.call("tester",args);
     }
}
```

The most important line is the addition of

```
import netscape.javascript.*;
```

This line tells the Java compiler that it needs to find additional Netscape-specific classes so that Java can interact with JavaScript. (It may be difficult to set things up so that your compiler can find these classes. Check Netscape's latest documentation and your compiler's instructions for adding packages to the class library.) The setString method receives three new lines. The first one creates an array that contains the arguments we'll pass to the JavaScript function. The next two lines are the same as before. The following line gets a window object reference from the browser that it can use to communicate JavaScript calls.

```
JSObject win= JSObject.getWindow(this);
```

The final line uses the window object's call method to call a function and pass some arguments. If you're not passing any arguments, you can use instead the win.eval function, which interprets a string as JavaScript. Generally, though, you'll find that you need to use the win.call syntax, complete with the arguments array, if you plan to do substantive work. Netscape also provides exception handlers that you should use to create more robust code if you plan to distribute these applets.

The HTML doesn't change much except for one additional attribute in the APPLET tag and the extra function that we'll call from Java:

```
<HTML>
<HEAD><TITLE>Java-to-JavaScript
Communication</TITLE></HEAD>
<BODY>
<APPLET CODE="strtest2.class" NAME="strtest2"
WIDTH=150 HEIGHT=25 MAYSCRIPT>
</APPLET><BR>
<FORM NAME="inputPlace">
<INPUT TYPE="text" SIZE=30 NAME="words"><BR>
<INPUT TYPE="button" VALUE="SetString" onClick=
"document.strtest2.setString(document.inputPlace.wor
ds.value)">
<SCRIPT LANGUAGE="JavaScript">
function tester(replacement, original) {
alert("You changed from " + original + " to " +
replacement + ".");
}
</SCRIPT></FORM>
</BODY></HTML>
```

Note the new MAYSCRIPT attribute in the APPLET tag. If you don't include it, your applet will generate errors when it tries to call scripts. It's basically a simple security system that makes sure Web developers don't have to contend with Java applets taking control of their pages. The tester function is a JavaScript function that accepts two arguments and displays the results.

The results are promising (see Figure 6.6).

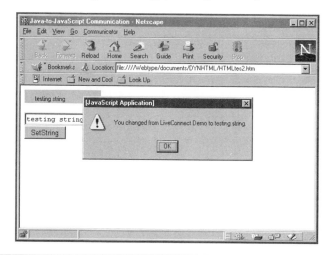

Figure 6.6 Java to JavaScript with LiveConnect.

I can't say that this approach is easy, but if you're interested in Java, you should give LiveConnect a try. It makes it easy for your Java applets to take real control of your Web pages and lets you enhance Java's minimal set of Web browsing tools with the window and targeting control you get with JavaScript. I'd love to be able to combine this technology with the full features of the Microsoft implementation of Dynamic HTML, but for now I can't combine the strengths of the two browsers. With any luck, that situation will change soon. A new standard from Sun for creating Java Beans arrived with the new Java Development Kit, and it promises to make it easy for developers to mix and mingle Java components.

Netscape will support it; Microsoft has announced some support and I hope will soon deliver a simpler way to connect Java to scripting in its browsers.

CHAPTER 7

Interactive Documents I: Letting the User In

It's time to put all the parts together and start building real applications. Dynamic HTML has given the browser enough flexibility to be a useful interface, the event handlers make it possible to respond to much more than clicks on links, and objects give us tools for handling more-powerful processing than we can accomplish with scripting. In this chapter and the two that follow, we'll build a series of small applications you can modify and use in a wide variety of situations. We'll also tackle some more complex programs.

N O T E

Unless explicitly stated otherwise, examples from this point on are guaranteed to work only in Internet Explorer 4.0. If you want to use some of these techniques in mixed-browser environments, you should implement the kind of browser detection code explained in Appendix A. I hope that Netscape is developing a document object model that follows the same lines, but I expect the same kinds of browser incompatibilities that have existed for the past few years to be with us for a long time.

Responding to the User

One of the easiest things to do with Dynamic HTML is to create expandable outlines. Instead of forcing your users to navigate multiple pages to move down a level or two in an outline, you can impress them with a nearly instant response to their request. There are several ways to create outlines and similar interfaces, and we'll examine a few of them. Techniques that are appropriate for small outlines can be unwieldy for large ones, but you may eventually find other uses for them.

Creating Outlines with Text Ranges

When I first heard that Dynamic HTML would allow me to replace the HTML code in a document, I thought it would be a great way to create outlines and other expanding objects. I created a simple JavaScript demo, and it worked, although not very elegantly:

```
<HTML>
<HEAD>
<TITLE>Outlines - the very hard way</TITLE>
</HEAD>
<BODY BGCOLOR=#FFFFFF>
<SCRIPT LANGUAGE="JavaScript">
function Expand1(){
var r,newHTML;
newHTML='<H2 id="Number1"
onClick="Collapse1()">Clickable Outline, Heading
1</H2><H3 id=Element1><A HREF="click1.html">Click to
go!</A></H3>';
r=document.rangeFromElement(Number1);
r.pasteHTML(newHTML);
}
function Collapse1(){
var r,newHTML;
newHTML='<H2 id="Number1"
onClick="Expand1()">Clickable Outline, Heading
1</H2>';
```

```
r=document.rangeFromElement(Number1);
r.pasteHTML(newHTML);
newHTML='';
r=document.rangeFromElement(Element1);
r.pasteHTML(newHTML);
}
function Expand2(){
var r,newHTML;
newHTML='<H2 id="Number2"
onClick="Collapse2()">Clickable Outline, Heading
2</H2><H3 id=Element2><A HREF="click2.html">Click to
go somewhere else!</A></H3>';
r=document.rangeFromElement(Number2);
r.pasteHTML(newHTML);
}
function Collapse2(){
var r,newHTML;
newHTML='<H2 id="Number2"
onClick="Expand2()">Clickable Outline, Heading
2</H2>';
r=document.rangeFromElement(Number2);
r.pasteHTML(newHTML);
newHTML='';
r=document.rangeFromElement(Element2);
r.pasteHTML(newHTML);
}
</SCRIPT>
<H2 id="Number1" onClick="Expand1()">Clickable
Outline, Heading 1</H2>
<H2 id="Number2" onClick="Expand2()">Clickable
Outline, Heading 2</H2> <P>There's no end to the
crazy things you can do with Dynamic HTML!</P>
</BODY>
</HTML>
```

This approach works (see Figures 7.1 and 7.2).

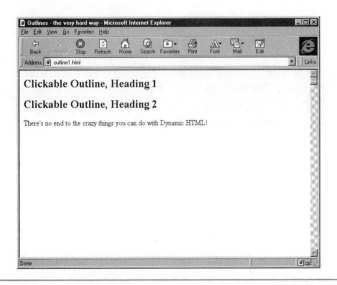

Figure 7.1 Outline before a click.

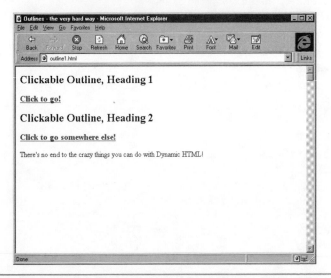

Figure 7.2 Outline after both headings have been clicked.

Unfortunately, the code is ugly, and it's tolerable only when there's only one level below the headers. The basic mechanism (pasteHTML) is simple, but the code it produces is not. If you have many headlines to deal with, you'll find yourself managing two functions per headline, each of which contains a lot of HTML. It's easy to screw up with quotation marks inside the HTML and mess up your code, and generally there are too many parts flying around. What's more, users who open this script in browsers other than Internet Explorer IE 4 will have no way to get to the lower layers.

Creating Outlines with Styles

Fortunately, there's a better way. *Styles* make it possible to hide and display elements as well as change their font and position. Using DIV tags and the display style property, you can create a simple and workable outline with a minimum of effort. (This may work in Netscape 4.0 PR2; watch for more details.)

```
<HTML>
<HEAD>
<TITLE>Outlines - a better way</TITLE>
</HEAD>
<BODY BGCOLOR=#FFFFFF>
<SCRIPT LANGUAGE="JavaScript">
function OpenerX(){
    if (outlineBody.style.display=="none") {
    outlineBody.style.display="";
}
    else {outlineBody.style.display="none";}
}

function headline1X(){
    if (headline2.style.display=="none") {
```

```
     headline2.style.display="";
}
     else {headline2.style.display="none";}
window.event.cancelBubble=true;
}

function headline2X(){
     if (Blurb.style.display=="none") {
     Blurb.style.display="";
}
     else {Blurb.style.display="none";}
window.event.cancelBubble=true;
}

function BlurbX(){
window.event.cancelBubble=true;
}
</SCRIPT>
<DIV ID="Opener" onclick="OpenerX()" style="font-
family:sans-serif; font-size:20pt">
Outline here!
</DIV>
<DIV ID="outlineBody" style="display:none">
<DIV ID="headline1" onclick="headline1X()"
style="font-family:sans-serif; font-size: 16pt">
This is the first headline!
<DIV ID="headline2" onclick="headline2X()"
style="font-family:sans-serif; font-size: 14pt;
display:none"> This is the second headline!
<DIV ID="Blurb" onclick="BlurbX()" style="font-
family:sans-serif; font-size: 12pt; display:none">
This is a blurb, your friendly bottom level element.
</DIV> </DIV> </DIV>
<DIV ID="headline3" style="font-family:sans-serif;
font-size: 16pt">
This header doesn't go anywhere.
```

```
</DIV>
</DIV>
</BODY>
</HTML>
```

The greatest advantage of this version is that it appears fully opened on older browsers. It may not collapse, but at least users will be able to reach the information in the outline and connect to any links inside it without having to break open your source code to figure out where you wanted them to go.

Your visitors who use Internet Explorer 4.0 will see the screen in Figure 7.3 when they open this file.

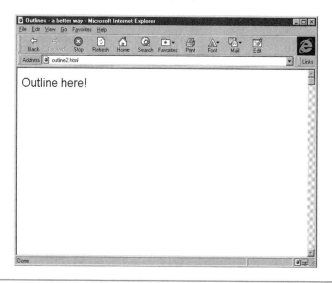

Figure 7.3 Unopened outline.

Visitors with older browsers, and visitors who have clicked open the entire outline will see the screen in Figure 7.4.

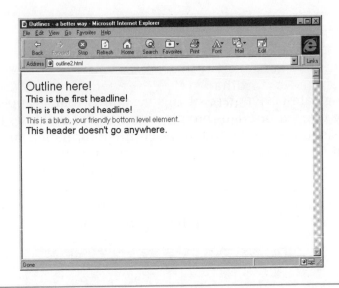

Figure 7.4 Fully expanded outline.

Viewers with Netscape 4.0 won't see the outline and won't be able to open it. Because Netscape supports cascading style sheets, the subsections will be hidden. But Netscape doesn't let you change styles dynamically, so readers won't be able to open the subsections. Be prepared with alternative routes for this situation.

When you write code such as this, perhaps the most important thing to keep in mind is that the DIV tags for most of the outline portion are nested (except the "Outline here!", which could have been nested). You have to nest these tags when one section includes other sections below it. This means that you must use window.event.cancelBubble to keep the onclick event from being processed at a higher level. Without the cancelBubble, your outline will expand and close in ways that mystify users. For example, clicking on the Blurb text would make it disappear, because the event gets processed by headline2X. That's probably not what you want to see unless you enjoy making your users scratch their heads.

Creating this example is much easier than the previous example, because the main body of the outline is generated by ordinary HTML instead of being sliced across as many functions as you have headlines. Still, if your outline is complex (three or more layers or five or more headlines), you'll want to find an easier way to make this application more compact and friendlier.

Creating Outlines with Styles and Naming Conventions

One of the most powerful ways to create simple scripts that can manage many objects is to take advantage of the ID and CLASS tags. They're handy for creating labels that make sense to humans, and they're equally handy for creating labels that make sense to your computer. Essentially, you can use these tags to explain to the computer the particular behavior your object should have. In this way, the computer can manage similar objects using the same routine instead of trying to define behaviors for every single object.

This approach can be especially useful for outlines, which have only two basic behaviors (expand and collapse) but lots and lots of parts. The way the parts fit together is strictly regulated; otherwise, an outline would be an ordinary paragraph. Hierarchical behavior is what computers are good at, after all. The code for our revised outline looks like this:

```
<HTML>
<HEAD>
<TITLE>Outline with Naming Convention</TITLE>
</HEAD>
<BODY BGCOLOR=#FFFFFF>
```

```
<SCRIPT>
function outlineHighlight(){
var source;
source=window.event.srcElement;
if (source!="Main") {source.style.color="red";}
}

function outlineDim(){
var source;
source=window.event.srcElement;
if (source!="Main") {source.style.color="black";}
}

function outlineAction(){
var source, targetID, targetObject;
source=window.event.srcElement;
if (source.className=="Manager") {
targetID=source.id + "t";
targetObject=document.all(targetID);
if (targetObject.style.display=="none") {
        targetObject.style.display="";
    }
    else {
        targetObject.style.display="none";
    }
}
}
</SCRIPT>
<DIV ID="Main" onmouseover="outlineHighlight()"
onmouseout="outlineDim()" onClick="outlineAction()">
<DIV ID="Section1" CLASS="Manager">Section 1</DIV>
<DIV ID="Section1t" CLASS="Manager"
STYLE="display:none">Section 1 Target
<DIV ID="Section1tt" STYLE="display:none">
<DIV ID="Area1" CLASS="Manager">Section 1 Target
Target - Area 1</DIV>
```

```
<DIV ID="Area1t" STYLE="display:none">Area 1
Target</DIV>
<DIV ID="Area2" CLASS="Manager">Section 1 Target
Target - Area 2</DIV>
<DIV ID="Area2t" STYLE="display:none">Area 2
Target</DIV>
</DIV>
</DIV>
<P> </P>
<DIV ID="Section2" CLASS="Manager">Section 2</DIV>
<DIV ID="Section2t" STYLE="display:none">
<DIV>Section 2 Target, line 1</DIV>
<DIV>Section 2 Target, line 2</DIV>
<DIV>Section 2 Target, line 3</DIV>
</DIV>
</DIV>
</BODY>
</HTML>
```

Note that there are only three functions and five expandable areas. One of those functions handles the expanding and collapsing of the outline; the other two functions provide added functionality (rollover highlighting) that this new structure makes possible.

In the HTML, we see the familiar nested DIV structure we used in the previous example, with a few DIVs added that contain only other DIVs without text of their own. This outline will appear fully expanded to older browsers, making compatibility a less important issue. The HTML structure is similar, but the naming structure is different. We've added a new CLASS—Manager—for outline headings that can be expanded. The IDs are also different, reflecting a targeting scheme rather than simple identifiers we can read. "Section 1" appears when the document opens (see Figure 7.5).

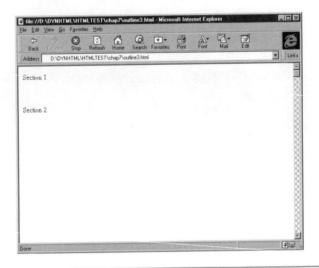

Figure 7.5 Unopened outline.

When the user clicks on **Section 1**, the DIV whose ID is Section1t will become visible (see Figure 7.6).

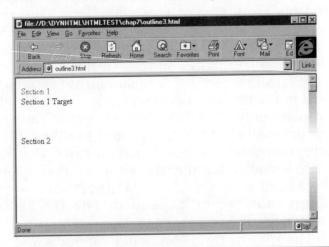

Figure 7.6 Outline opened to Section 1 Target.

The Section1t tag is also a Manager and will display the DIV whose ID is Section1tt when it gets clicked (see Figure 7.7).

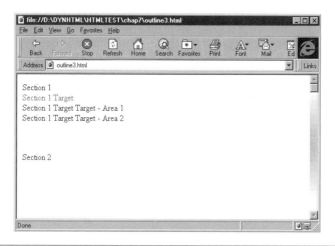

Figure 7.7 Outline opened to Section 1 Target Target.

At this point, because the Section1tt DIV includes multiple suboptions, we must change our naming convention. Section1tt includes two options, each of which has a suboption of its own. They don't need to be Section1ttt, because they're already included in the DIV targeted by Section1t. They can start over and use their own nomenclature. This will happen every time you have multiple suboptions in a layer. It doesn't matter what word you use before the number (or even what the number is) as long as it doesn't conflict with other tags. Also, note that expandable headlines are of the CLASS "Manager". If a headline won't work or if bottom-level text generates an error message when you click on it, check to make sure you've assigned the right CLASS to your objects.

Using a naming convention means that we must create a central switchboard to handle all the events for this outline and teach it how to handle those events. In this case, we'll use the outlineAction() function. Unlike the outline manipulation functions in our previous example, outlineAction() (and the other two functions in this example) gets called from the top-level DIV rather than from each headline. This technique makes for much cleaner HTML as well as much cleaner code. The user can click on any desired headline, and the onclick event will bubble all the way to our top-level DIV without encountering any event handlers.

The outlineAction() function is a bit more complicated than its predecessors:

```
function outlineAction(){
var source, targetID, targetObject;
source=window.event.srcElement;
if (source.className=="Manager") {
targetID=source.id + "t";
targetObject=document.all(targetID);
if (targetObject.style.display=="none") {
        targetObject.style.display="";
    }
    else {
        targetObject.style.display="none";
}}}
```

The outlineAction() function uses three variables to connect the source of the click to the targets of the action: source (the element that initially received the click), targetID (the name of the element to appear or disappear), and targetObject (the object representing the element that will appear or disappear). The function gets the source of the click from the srcElement property of the window.event object, and it checks to see whether the source object is a member of the Manager class. The ID of the target, following our naming convention, will be the ID of the source, with a *t* added to the end of its name. Finally, the function locates the object being targeted and makes it visible or invisible as appropriate.

The two other functions listed here are good examples of using event bubbling to make all kinds of tasks easier. The "Main" DIV specifies functions for the onmouseover and onmouseout events that will get called for rollovers by any of the elements included in the entire DIV. After checking briefly to make sure we aren't highlighting (or unhighlighting) the entire outline at once, we can make the text red for an onmouseover or black for an onmouseout. We don't need to set the cancelBubble property, because there aren't any further event handlers to worry about. The other nice thing about using the "Main" DIV to specify these event handlers is that they won't apply to text outside the outline. They'll bubble through only for the outline.

Creating Simple Pop-Up Menus

We can apply exactly the same logic to other tasks, although we may need to handle additional issues. I recently worked on a Web page for a designer who wanted to use simple pop-up menus to hide and display information selectively as the user rolled over the menu name. At the time, the only way to implement this design was to use Java, although it wasn't complicated. Dynamic HTML and some simple scripting can save the user the time spent waiting for applets to download and initialize, and the developer gains much more flexibility about what to include in a particular menu. The code is lifted from our previous outline example, with some significant additions:

```
<HTML>
<HEAD>
<TITLE>Pop-up Text Menus</TITLE>
</HEAD>
<BODY BGCOLOR=#FFFFFF>
<SCRIPT>
function popupText(){
var source, targetID, targetObject;
 source=window.event.srcElement;
if (source.className=="Menu") {
targetID=source.id + "t";
 targetObject=document.all(targetID);
 targetObject.style.display="";
//additional functionality when menu appears here
}
}
function popdownText(){
var source, targetID, targetObject;
 source=window.event.srcElement;
if (source.className=="Menu") {
targetID=source.id + "t";
targetObject=document.all(targetID);
targetObject.style.display="none";
//additional functionality when menu disappears here
}
}
function maintainText(){
//keeps menu on screen when you roll from menu title
to elements
var source;
source=window.event.srcElement;
if (source.className=="MenuArea"){
    source.style.display="";
 }
 }
function hideText(){
```

```
//puts menu away without hiding individual elements
and leaving lines
var source;
source=window.event.srcElement;
if (source.className=="MenuArea"){
     source.style.display="none";
 }
}
</SCRIPT>
<H1>Pop-up Menus demo</H1>
<DIV ID="popupArea" onmouseover="popupText()"
onmouseout="popdownText()">
<DIV ID="Menu1" CLASS="Menu">Portfolio
<SPAN ID="Menu1t" CLASS="MenuArea"
STYLE="display:none" onmouseover="maintainText()"
onmouseout="hideText()">  | <A
HREF="identity.html">Identity</A>  | 
<A HREF="print.html">Print</A>  | 
<A HREF="web.html">Web</A>
</SPAN>
</DIV>
</DIV>
</BODY>
</HTML>
```

As you can see, we broke outlineAction() into two routines, popdownText() and popupText()—because we're responding to onmouseover and onmouseout events and not a simple onclick event. The way this works is almost identical to the preceding example, although the CLASS for the activating DIV is now "Menu" instead of "Manager," and the target now has a CLASS of "MenuArea" and special methods pertaining to it. The IDs of the controlling element and the target are "Menu1" and "Menu1t", just as they would have been in the outline.

The results are slightly different from the outline (see Figure 7.8).

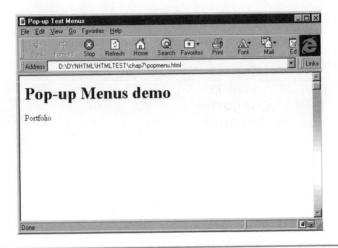

Figure 7.8 Rollover demo, unopened.

When the user rolls over **Portfolio**, or in an older browser, the screen in Figure 7.9 appears.

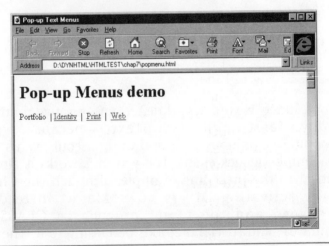

Figure 7.9 Rollover demo, menu available.

This technique is a simple way to make many choices available without cluttering the screen with options. If you wanted to, you could create a column or two of these option menus using a table, instead of creating a formal outline. Users would get easy access to a broad array of choices in categories. Because of the naming conventions, the programming would also remain simple, requiring only the preceding code.

Unfortunately, keeping the pop-up menu available is complicated by a number of event issues. When the user rolls the mouse over the word **Portfolio**, it fires an onmouseover event, which brings up the menu with popupText(). If the mouse rolls above or below the word or to the left, we want the menu to disappear, something that popdownText() handles. Unfortunately, moving the mouse to the right takes the cursor into a new object: the anchor of the first menu item (Identity). The cursor hasn't actually left the DIV, but the browser always fires an onmouseout event (setting off popdownText()) to indicate the element most recently chosen; then the browser fires the onmouseover event to pop up the element being entered. As a result, we need the maintainText() and hideText() functions, which help the menu items display and hide themselves properly.

The maintainText() function grabs the onmouseover event that takes place when the cursor moves. Even though the menu area is, technically, invisible at this point, it was visible when the event began, so it's still possible to override the disappearance of the menu without allowing a screen blink. The hideText() function makes sure that the menu appears and disappears as a unit. If you remove hideText(), the individual anchors (and not the entire menu) will disappear instead, leaving behind only the lines separating them.

Following Your Every Move

Now that we've provided practical interfaces for important tasks, it's time to lapse into frivolity. Our next example isn't especially useful, although it could (perhaps with an animated GIF) let you add flair to your site. It's a good example of how easy it can be to use the onmouseover event to create mischief, introducing some techniques we'll use in our next demonstration, which promises to be somewhat more useful.

This demonstration creates a graphic that trails the cursor. The graphic isn't always displayed (you can turn it on and off with a mouse click), but its position is updated constantly. Surprisingly, this movement drew smoothly on my underpowered 75Mhz Pentium and didn't slow my system visibly. Although you can't see the cursor in the following screen shots, it's just above and to the left of the marshmallow rabbit's left ear (see Figures 7.10 and 7.11).

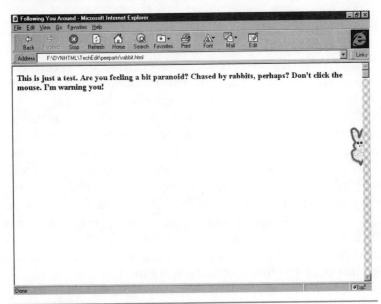

Figure 7.10 Rabbit at the edge of the screen.

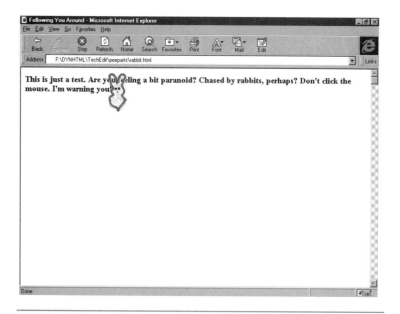

Figure 7.11 Rabbit in the middle, over text.

This effect is simple to implement. We use one function to make the rabbit follow the mouse around and a second function to make the rabbit appear and disappear with a mouse click:

```
<HTML>
<HEAD>
<TITLE>Following You Around</TITLE>
</HEAD>
<BODY BGCOLOR=#FFFFFF>
<SCRIPT>
function follower(unused,dontneed, x,y){
 if (x<0){x=-x;}
 if (y<0){y=-y;}
 rabbit.style.left=x;
 rabbit.style.top=y;
}
```

```
function showBunny(){
 if (rabbit.style.display=="none")
{rabbit.style.display="";}
 else {rabbit.style.display="none";}
}
document.onmousemove=follower;
document.onclick=showBunny;
</SCRIPT>
<H3>This is just a test.  Are you feeling a bit
paranoid?  Chased by rabbits, perhaps?  Don't click
the mouse. I'm warning you!</H3>
<IMG ID=rabbit SRC="bunnyt3.gif"
STYLE="container:positioned; position:absolute;
left:0; top:0; display:none"> </BODY>
</HTML>
```

We used the document.eventname syntax to link our functions to any onmousemove and onclick events that take place in the document, as described in Chapter 5. This means that unless you set event.cancelBubble in another element, the graphic will follow you closely.

There is one other interesting "feature" of Internet Explorer's onmousemove event: it keeps tracking the mouse even outside the browser window as long as you have a mouse button pressed. This arrangement makes sense for the kind of shell integration that Microsoft is promoting between Internet Explorer and Windows 95, but the rabbit isn't allowed to follow your cursor outside the browser. I made the follow() function check to see whether the x and y values are negative. If they are, follow() makes them positive, so dragging with the mouse outside the browser window to the top or left will make the rabbit retreat to a safe distance.

Letting the User Move Things Around

You can use the same events and properties to create simple interfaces that allow the user to move things around. My favorite Dynamic HTML demonstration from Microsoft is the Mr. Alienhead demo, which lets you decorate a supposed alien head with eyes, ears, a nose, and a mouth, all of which are made from odd pictures of fruit and vegetables. Our demonstration is simpler and more generic but uses similar tools (cascading style sheets positioning and the onmouseover event) to let the user rearrange your page.

For this demonstration, we'll let the user reposition some rectangles. You can use any graphics you want. Transparency will work just as it should, letting you see one graphic underneath the next. The example lets the user manipulate some colored blocks (which it refers to as bricks). When users first load the page, they see the screen shown in Figure 7.12.

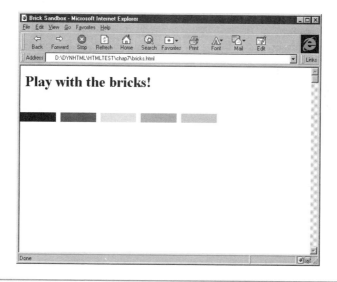

Figure 7.12 Bricks demonstration opening.

After a few minutes of clicking and dragging, the page might look like Figure 7.13.

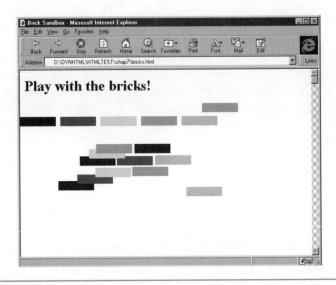

Figure 7.13 Bricks after a bit of play.

The code for this example is simple. All the images are managed by a routine called at the document level, and I haven't even had to assign them names. The routine checks to make sure we're dragging a graphic and then goes ahead and does it:

```
<HTML>
<HEAD>
<TITLE>Brick Sandbox</TITLE>
</HEAD>
<BODY BGCOLOR=#FFFFFF>
<SCRIPT>
function dragAround(button, unused, x, y){
    if (button==1) {//left button down?
        source=window.event.srcElement;
        if (source.tagName=="IMG"){
            source.style.left=x;
            source.style.top=y;
}}//end both if statements
```

```
window.event.returnValue=false;
window.event.cancelBubble=true;
}
document.onmousemove=dragAround;
</SCRIPT>
<H1 CLASS=headline>Play with the bricks!</H1>
<IMG SRC="black.gif" STYLE="container:positioned;
position:absolute; left:0; top:100"> <IMG
SRC="black.gif" STYLE="container:positioned;
position:absolute; left:0; top:100"> <IMG
SRC="black.gif" STYLE="container:positioned;
position:absolute; left:0; top:100"> <IMG
SRC="black.gif" STYLE="container:positioned;
position:absolute; left:0; top:100"> <IMG
SRC="black.gif" STYLE="container:positioned;
position:absolute; left:0; top:100"> <IMG
SRC="maroon.gif" STYLE="container:positioned;
position:absolute; left:90; top:100"> <IMG
SRC="maroon.gif" STYLE="container:positioned;
position:absolute; left:90; top:100"> <IMG
SRC="maroon.gif" STYLE="container:positioned;
position:absolute; left:90; top:100"><IMG
SRC="green.gif" STYLE="container:positioned;
position:absolute; left:180; top:100"> <IMG
SRC="green.gif" STYLE="container:positioned;
position:absolute; left:180; top:100"> <IMG
SRC="green.gif" STYLE="container:positioned;
position:absolute; left:180; top:100"> <IMG
SRC="orange.gif" STYLE="container:positioned;
position:absolute; left:270; top:100"> <IMG
SRC="orange.gif" STYLE="container:positioned;
position:absolute; left:270; top:100"> <IMG
SRC="orange.gif" STYLE="container:positioned;
position:absolute; left:270; top:100"><IMG
SRC="bluegray.gif" STYLE="container:positioned;
position:absolute; left:360; top:100"> <IMG
SRC="bluegray.gif" STYLE="container:positioned;
position:absolute; left:360; top:100"> <IMG
SRC="bluegray.gif" STYLE="container:positioned;
position:absolute; left:360; top:100">
</BODY>
</HTML>
```

The HTML is a bit messy, but it's just repeating code to give the user a few extra bricks of each color to play with. They're neatly stacked, with identical top and left properties for each color, but you could scatter them any way you like. If you wanted to, you could use a script to handle that as the page was loading.

The important part of this script is the dragAround() function, which you can use in your own code easily. First, dragAround() checks to make sure that the mouse button is depressed. If it isn't, you don't want to drag the object. Second, the function checks to make sure that an IMG tag was the source of the event, because the only parts of this page you want to move are the brick images. You could customize this to meet your needs for handling different tags, different CLASSes, or even different IDs. Once it's made certain of these conditions, dragAround() changes the graphic's top and left properties to match the position of the cursor, in the same way we made the rabbit follow the cursor earlier. Then dragAround() sets window.event.cancelBubble to true and sets window.event.returnValue to false, halting any other actions that would get in the way of dragging the object. (If you omit these events, you get jerky dragging and many accidental drops.)

Moving from Drag to Drag-and-Drop

It's fun to move bricks around, but making that capability into a useful interface means that we need to know where the brick landed. Once we can do that, we can start using dragging to do useful work. It's almost like having a GUI interface available. In our case, it'll take more script and less HTML:

```
<HTML>
<HEAD><TITLE>Brick Sandbox</TITLE></HEAD>
<BODY BGCOLOR=#FFFFFF>
<SCRIPT>
function dropOn(){
if (dragObject!=""){
  dragged=document.all[dragObject];
  x=parseInt(dragged.style.left);
  y=parseInt(dragged.style.top);
  canCheck=document.all["bluegray"];
  if (x>(parseInt(canCheck.style.left)) &&
x<(parseInt(canCheck.style.left)+parseInt(canCheck.s
tyle.width)) && y>(parseInt(canCheck.style.top)) &&
y<(parseInt(canCheck.style.top)+parseInt(canCheck.st
yle.height))) {
    alert(dragObject+" fell into the trash."); }
 }
}
function dragAround(button, unused, x, y){
  dragObject="";
  if (button==1) {//left button down?
   source=window.event.srcElement;
   if (source.tagName=="IMG"){
     source.style.left=x;
     source.style.top=y;
     dragObject=source.id;
     }
  }
window.event.returnValue=false;
window.event.cancelBubble=true;
}
document.onmousemove=dragAround;
document.onmouseup=dropOn;
dragObject="";
```

```
</SCRIPT>
<H1 CLASS=headline>Play with the bricks!</H1>
<IMG SRC="bluegray.gif" onmouseup="dropOn()"
ID="bluegray" STYLE="container:positioned;
position:absolute; left:360; top:100; height:100;
width:100;">
<IMG SRC="black.gif" ID="black"
STYLE="container:positioned; position:absolute;
left:0; top:100">
<IMG SRC="maroon.gif" ID="maroon"
STYLE="container:positioned; position:absolute;
left:90; top:100">
<IMG SRC="green.gif" ID="green"
STYLE="container:positioned; position:absolute;
left:180; top:100">
<IMG SRC="orange.gif" ID="orange"
STYLE="container:positioned; position:absolute;
left:270; top:100">
</BODY></HTML>
```

The first step is to give the bricks names; notice that I drastically reduced the number of bricks. The dragAround function now keeps track of the object it's dragging. It uses the dragObject variable, which is available to all scripts because we define it outside a function. Next, we assign the document.onmousedown event to a particular function—in this case, dropon(). It looks ugly, but all it does is to check whether the location of the object being dropped is within the bounds of the trash can object—in this case, the bluegray object. When you check this, be sure to use the parseInt() function on your property data. Internet Explorer returns the information as 365px and 100px instead of 365 and 100. Adding the values gives you "365px 100px" instead of 465, making it hard to make comparisons. The parseInt() function strips out the text and makes it numbers again. When you drop a brick in the large block, you see the screen in Figure 7.14.

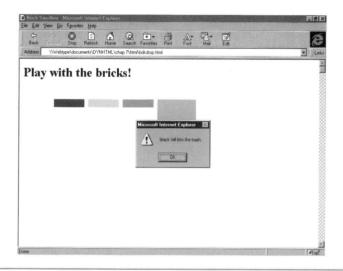

Figure 7.14 Brick dropped in the can.

This technique isn't easy to implement if you have many objects that need to receive dropped objects, but it's definitely possible. Whenever you can, you should combine your checking of drop recipients into one function that can check for all your recipients instead of checking each separately. Unfortunately, the individual objects won't receive the onmouseup notification, which goes to the object being dropped.

Making Old Interfaces New

Image maps seem to have come and gone. They still get some use, but finer HTML control has made them less necessary, and perhaps the appearance of the CSS positioning styles will drive image maps to extinction. They've gone through several phases, from server-side to client-side, and the technique I demonstrate here makes them even more client-side than they were before. This program treats the client-side image map more as a data container than as a link. It produces a simple, unified interface by shifting graphics and links around according to naming conventions.

Client-side image maps can be manipulated easily in Microsoft Internet Explorer 4.0. Both the IMG tag and the AREA tags that make up the map are exposed directly, and you can even shift the coordinates covered by a portion of the image map if you like. This program doesn't go that far, but it makes it easy to create an image map that works for multiple applications without calling back to the server for new instructions.

There are three pages to this image map, although you could create as many as you like. I've created some simple graphics to demonstrate the changes you can make based on a simple city information center. It provides weather, arts, events, and hotel information on New York, San Francisco, and Chicago. Instead of putting it all on one page, the application shows you New York first, allowing you to click the bottom row of city abbreviations to move from city to city. A local skyscraper silhouette lets you know which city you're in (see Figure 7.15).

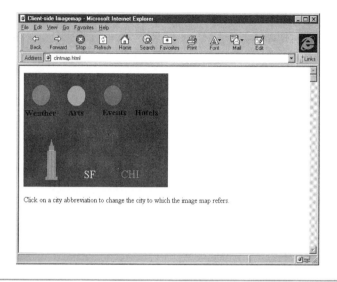

Figure 7.15 New York client-side image map.

If you click on the CHI, you'll see the same map for Chicago (see Figure 7.16).

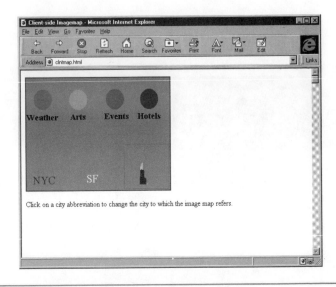

Figure 7.16 Chicago client-side image map.

Unfortunately, the most important thing about this change is invisible in the picture. IN addition to the picture, the links on the circles change—from weather1.html to weather3.html, from arts1.html to arts3.html, and so on. For speed, we also loaded the additional images as the page loaded, so the map should move quickly as you click. The code looks like this:

```
<HTML>
<HEAD>
<TITLE>Client-side Image Map</TITLE>
</HEAD>
<BODY BGCOLOR=#FFFFFF>
<SCRIPT>
function changeCity(){
source=event.srcElement.id
City.src=(source+".gif");
```

```
cityNumber=source.substring(4,5);
weather.href="weather"+cityNumber+".gif";
arts.href="arts"+cityNumber+".gif";
events.href="events"+cityNumber+".gif";
hotels.href="hotels"+cityNumber+".gif";
}
var imageInit = new Array(3);
numberCities=3;
for (x=0;(x<numberCities);x++){
imageInit[x]=new Image();
imageInit[x].src="city"+x+".gif";
}
</SCRIPT>
<MAP ID=cityMap>
<AREA ID=weather SHAPE="RECT" COORDS="0,13,78,104"
HREF="weather1.html"> <AREA ID=arts SHAPE="RECT"
COORDS="82,13,155,104" HREF="arts1.html"> <AREA
ID=events SHAPE="RECT" COORDS="163,13,237,104"
HREF="events1.html"> <AREA ID=hotels SHAPE="RECT"
COORDS="240,13,320,104" HREF="hotels1.html">
<AREA ID=City1 SHAPE="RECT" COORDS="0,144,96,240"
onclick="changeCity();"> <AREA ID=City2 SHAPE="RECT"
COORDS="113,144,186,240" onclick="changeCity();">
<AREA ID=City3 SHAPE="RECT" COORDS="219,144,320,240"
onclick="changeCity();">
</MAP>
<IMG SRC="City1.gif" ID=City STYLE="height:240;
width:320" USEMAP="#cityMap">
<P>Click on a city abbreviation to change the city
to which the image map refers.</P> </BODY>
</HTML>
```

The changeCity() function does all the work. Within the MAP are three areas, one for each city. Their names are City1, City2, and City3, something that makes it easy to extract the requested city using the JavaScript substring() method. These areas don't take you anywhere with an HREF when you click; instead, they call changeCity(). It determines which button called it and uses the number to change the graphic image and all the HREFs in the image map at the same time. This approach isn't complicated; it's just a matter of changing some properties of the image map.

The initialization routine isn't part of a function. It gets called when the page is loaded. The array of images it creates isn't used for anything, but loading the image into the array puts the image file into the browser's cache for instant access later.

The Document as Dataset

We took a big leap in the previous example, although you probably didn't notice it. We began by using naming conventions to push objects around, and we moved to using them to store data in the document. Because the names of the city AREAs end in numbers, we can determine the requested city. Our next example will use the same technique in a more sophisticated way, making the document itself store most of the program data.

One of the first examples I planned for this book was the classic sliding puzzle, in which an image is chopped up into squares and scrambled. It seemed to be a good way to demonstrate how to use graphics and tables and might even provide people with a few minutes of enjoyment. I figured I'd need a program with an array to keep track of the location of each piece, as well as a complex connection among that array, the user's actions, and the display on the screen. As soon as I started programming, it became clear that the array and the complexity it introduced weren't necessary. A table is a natural array that's composed of columns and rows. Because I was using a naming convention to manipulate the pieces and their positions in the table, I could look up the name of any piece in the table and find out which one it was at any time. The example takes a little more work than that—the src property of an image returns an absolute URL—but one function later I was ready to go.

When you first start the puzzle, it's already solved. I could have scrambled it, but that would have meant more programming and the slight possibility of creating an unsolvable puzzle. This example uses a three-by-three grid, but you could expand it considerably without having to change any of the code. It begins as a simple table holding a chopped-up image (see Figure 7.17).

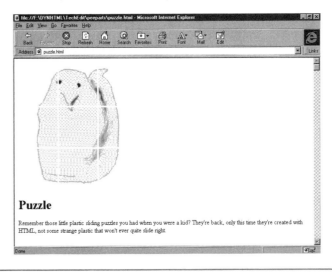

Figure 7.17 Puzzle at opening.

To move a piece, you click on it. If the empty space (blank gray in this set of images) is adjacent to the piece you clicked on, the piece moves. If all spaces around it are full, nothing happens. Just as in the plastic version, no diagonal moves are allowed. A few moves later, your puzzle may look like Figure 7.18.

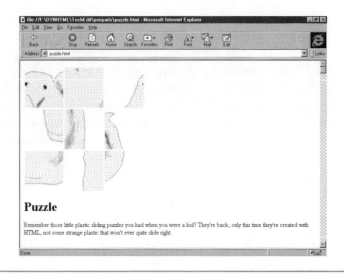

Figure 7.18 Puzzle slightly scrambled.

If you aren't careful, you can get tangled in the code to create this. It's easy to forget that the ID name of an object isn't quite the object itself, producing odd errors and undefined results. Also keep in mind that this code is designed to be expandable. You can create a puzzle with as many as nine rows or columns simply by building a larger table (with the same naming convention) and changing the numberColumns and numberRows variables.

```
<HTML>
<HEAD>
<TITLE>Puzzle Madness</TITLE>
</HEAD>
<BODY BGCOLOR=#FFFFFF>
<SCRIPT>
function extractPiece(fullURL){
return fullURL.substring((fullURL.length-
6),(fullURL.length-4));
```

```
}
function space(location){
empty=0;
x=location/10;
x=Math.round(x);
y=location-(x*10);
if (x!=1) {
     //check left
     check="space"+(x-1)+y;
     pieceFull=document.all(check);
     piece=extractPiece(pieceFull.src);
     if (piece==emptySquare) {empty=((x-1)*10+y)};
}
if (x!=numberColumns) {
     //check right
     check="space"+(x+1)+y;
     pieceFull=document.all(check);
     piece=extractPiece(pieceFull.src);
     if (piece==emptySquare) {empty=((x+1)*10+y)};
}
if (y!=1) {
     //check above
     check="space"+x+(y-1);
     pieceFull=document.all(check);
     piece=extractPiece(pieceFull.src);
     if (piece==emptySquare) {empty=(x*10+(y-1))};
}
if (y!=numberRows) {
     //check below
     check="space"+x+(y+1);
     pieceFull=document.all(check);
     piece=extractPiece(pieceFull.src);
     if (piece==emptySquare) {empty=(x*10+(y+1))};
}
 return empty;
}
```

```
function slide(){
 if (window.event.srcElement.tagName=="IMG"){
     source=window.event.srcElement.id;
     puzzleFull=window.event.srcElement.src;
     puzzlePiece=extractPiece(puzzleFull);
     puzzleLoc=source.substring(5,7);
     if (puzzlePiece!=emptySquare) {
         emptySpace=space(puzzleLoc);
         if (emptySpace!=0) {
             //swap pieces
             newSpace=document.all("space" +
emptySpace);
             oldSpace=document.all(source);
             blankPiece=newSpace.src;
             newSpace.src=oldSpace.src;
             oldSpace.src=blankPiece;
         }
     }
 }
}
var numberRows, numberColumns, emptySquare;
numberRows=3;
numberColumns=3;
emptySquare=11;
</SCRIPT>
<TABLE onClick="slide()">
<TR>
<TD><IMG SRC="peep11.gif" ID="space11"></TD>
<TD><IMG SRC="peep21.gif" ID="space21"></TD>
<TD><IMG SRC="peep31.gif" ID="space31"></TD> </TR>
<TR>
<TD><IMG SRC="peep12.gif" ID="space12"></TD>
<TD><IMG SRC="peep22.gif" ID="space22"></TD>
<TD><IMG SRC="peep32.gif" ID="space32"></TD> </TR>
<TR>
```

```
<TD><IMG SRC="peep13.gif" ID="space13"></TD>
<TD><IMG SRC="peep23.gif" ID="space23"></TD>
<TD><IMG SRC="peep33.gif" ID="space33"></TD> </TR>
</TABLE>
<H1>Puzzle</H1>
Remember those little plastic sliding puzzles you
had when you were a kid?  They're back, only this
time they're created with HTML, not some strange
plastic that won't ever quite slide right.
</BODY>
</HTML>
```

The table is simple. All image containers and graphics files are identified with two numbers. The first number represents the column, and the second number represents the row. Numbers for graphics files identify their places in the solved puzzle, and numbers for image containers stay put. Graphics file numbers are part of the URL: in this case, the picture that goes in row 2, column 3 is identified as peep23.gif. Image container numbers are part of the ID: the IMG tag in row 2, column 2 is identified as space23. (If I had used an array, I'd be counting the first row as zero, but we're spared that problem so we might as well make this example vaguely friendly to humans as well as computers.)

Most of the script revolves around figuring out which piece was clicked on and whether it has any empty spaces next to it. The actual movement is very simple. The onclick event is picked up at the table level; the table includes all the graphics but none of the text, so this approach makes sense and avoids most unnecessary clicks. The slide() function is the main logic routine. First, it checks to make sure that the click came from an element that uses the IMG tag. If the user had clicked on a table border, the program would process it and get a runtime error (a nasty warning box) when it couldn't find an src property for a table. The next task is to figure out which image element reported the click and to extract the number from its ID property using the same substring() string method we used in the client-side image map example. Once slide() knows what we've clicked, it sends that location to the space() function to see whether there's an adjacent empty space. If an adjacent space is empty, space() returns zero and the slide() function exits without moving anything. If there is, space() returns the location of the empty space and the slide() function ends by switching the graphic of the chosen piece with the empty space graphic.

The space() function provides most of the intelligence for the program. By checking, as appropriate, the spaces above and below and to the left and the right of the piece that was clicked, the space() function can determine which graphics occupy those squares. If any one of them is the empty space graphic (whose value is set by emptySquare when the page loads), space() returns the number of the square containing that graphic. If emptySquare is 11 and the graphic peep11.gif is in row 3, column 3, space will return 33 *if* the initial value it was sent is next to that space (32 and 23 would return 33; anything else would return zero).

The space() function uses the extractPiece() function to figure out which graphic is which. The extractPiece() function takes the src property of an image element and extracts the number of the graphic from the full URL. Because we know what we expect the file names to be, it's easy to teach the computer that the significant part of that URL ranges from six characters before the end of the string to four characters before the end of the string. In that way, we don't get the useless information at the front of the URL or the ".gif" at the end. All we get is a simple two-digit code that tells us where that piece started in the puzzle.

You can use similar tools to manipulate other kinds of content, especially structured information such as tables with their easily defined rows and columns. Naming conventions aren't always a substitute for heavy-duty programming logic, but they make it easy to script many tasks with Dynamic HTML that might otherwise require a much more powerful language environment. Throughout the rest of the book you'll see other applications for naming conventions, and I hope you'll find plenty of practical use for them in your own pages.

CHAPTER 8

Interactive Documents II: Changing Document Content

Both Netscape and Microsoft are counting on the browser becoming an important part of the everyday user interface. Netscape has discussed ending Microsoft's dominance of the operating systems market by replacing the operating system with the browser. For its part, Microsoft has made good on its promise to integrate the browser and the Windows interface with shell extensions to Internet Explorer 4.0. Making the browser the interface, however, will require much more than using the browser to handle slow, simple transactions managed mostly by the server. For the browser to become remotely as useful as the current GUI interfaces, it must be nearly as flexible. Dynamic HTML gives developers the flexibility they need to create powerful applications that share work smoothly across client and server.

Just as the ability to manipulate properties has made many new things possible, the ability to change HTML code after the document has loaded makes Dynamic HTML powerful enough to become an interface in its own right. Developers can use the textRange object to modify their code and rebuild their pages many times from a common base. This approach may not always be the best way to do it—there are still many reasons to use multiple pages instead of a single 1000K file—but this new flexibility means that a single page is now capable of doing what it once took many pages to do. Internet Explorer 4.0 has not reached the point where you can write a word processor or a spreadsheet with HTML, but it's the closest any browser has come yet.

Remember, examples in this chapter are guaranteed to work only in Internet Explorer 4.0. If you want to use some of these techniques in mixed-browser environments, you should implement the kind of browser detection code explained in Appendix A.

N O T E

textRanges and the Object Model

We first visited the textRange object in Chapter 4, and we saw an example of how not to use it in Chapter 7. Although it gives developers tremendous power with a fairly manageable learning curve, it's not always the best solution. If your task involves displaying data selectively, you'll be much happier with the style properties we discussed in Chapter 7. On the other hand, if your task involves changing the structure of your document or if you need to present information created by an object (especially an ActiveX object), textRange manipulation is what you're looking for. This chapter will provide a complete explanation of the capacities of the textRange object, and then we'll use it in Chapter 9 to build interactive HTML interfaces.

The textRange object is not yet a standard in anyone's eyes except Microsoft's. Be warned: information on textRanges is subject to the same kind of changes as the information on event models presented in Chapter 5.

N O T E

Different Worlds: textRanges vs. Properties

So far, most of the work we've done has been with property manipulation. Internet Explorer makes it simple to access element properties, rarely requiring you to create extra variables that mirror the contents of the document's own object and property values. When we've done so, it's been mostly as a convenience, and, as we saw with the puzzle example in Chapter 7, using properties can spare us the need for additional variables. The easy scriptability of properties, combined with an event model that lets you easily pinpoint the source and nature of an event, makes it possible to create lightweight, powerful code.

Working with textRanges is more demanding. You must create a variable to hold a textRange object; textRange objects are not "natural" objects of a document. You won't find them in the all collection. Every time you want to create a textRange, you must determine which element you'll use as the base for your textRange and decide how to access that data. Because the methods for creating textRanges are exposed on the document object, you must always refer to document methods when you create them. Changing the content of your textRange, except in very simple situations, requires that you make a method call (to pasteHTML) instead of just setting a value.

This extra work means, however, that you can change anything in your document at any time. If you want to remove a section of your page and replace it, you can. If you want to excise an object that hasn't been responding the way you wanted, you can. If you want to make changes to the document based on the content of the document, you can.

NOTE The textRange object is new and not yet stable. Although it's safe to use, be sure you test it first. Results will be repeatable but aren't always predictable, especially when you overwrite tags.

The way the textRange handles elements strongly resembles the way that event bubbling passes objects.

Elements are contained within other elements, making it possible to collect many elements with the same request. For example, let's take a simple HTML document:

```
<HTML><BODY ID=bodydoc>
<H1 ID=headline>This is the headline</H1>
<P ID=main>This document contains some <B
ID=bolded>bold</B>, <I ID=italicized>italic</I>, and
<SPAN ID=ordinary>plain</SPAN> text.  All of it is
contained within the "main" paragraph element, which
itself is contained by the "bodydoc" body
element.</P>
<P ID=minor>This minor paragraph is contained only
by the "bodydoc" body element</P>
</BODY></HTML>
```

Figuring out the structure here is reasonably simple. If you want to create a textRange based on the BODY tag, it will include the headline and both paragraphs, including all the subsections of the "main" paragraph. If you create textRanges based on the headline or the "minor" paragraph, they'll contain only the text within their tagsets. The main paragraph would include its own text, even including all the small sections created by the formatting tags and the SPAN. The formatting tags and the SPAN would create textRanges that included only the text within them. Table 8.1 goes into more detail.

Table 8.1 Ways to create textRanges

Declaration	**Resulting Value of r**
r=document.body.createTextRange();	<H1 ID=headline>This is the headline</H1> <P ID=main>This document contains some <B ID=bolded>bold</B>, <I ID=italicized>italic</I>, and <SPAN ID=ordinary>plain</SPAN> text. All of it is contained within the "main" paragraph element, which itself is contained by the "bodydoc" body element.</P> <P ID=minor>This minor paragraph is only contained by the "bodydoc" body element</P>
r=document.rangeFromElement(main);	This document contains some <B ID=bolded>bold</B>, <I ID=italicized>italic</I>, and <SPAN ID=ordinary>plain</SPAN> text. All of it is contained within the "main" paragraph element, which itself is contained by the "bodydoc" body element.
r=document.rangeFromElement(bolded);	bold

This approach is simple but powerful. The textRange object also has several properties you should keep in mind as we continue through the chapter (see Table 8.2).

Table 8.2 textRange Properties

Property	Contents
end	Contains the end value for the textRange relative to the entire document, in characters. You can read and write this property.
start	Contains the start value for the textRange relative to the entire document, in characters. You can read and write this property.
htmlSelText	Contains the HTML for the selected text (see notes on selections). Read-only.
htmlText	Contains the HTML contained in the space marked off by the text range object. Read-only. (Use pasteHTML.)
text	Contains the text contained in the range without any HTML. You can read and write this value.

Remember that a textRange object doesn't actually contain the text that you use to access it. The text, htmlText, and htmlSelText properties are a little misleading. They aren't properties in the same sense that a color is a property of a style. The textRange is a window onto the document you're working with, and start and end provide the window frame's boundary. What you see through that window is material on the other side of the glass and not a painting directly on the glass. This means that you can't use the duplicate method (as in rangeBackup=rangeOriginal.duplicate) to preserve the original content of your range. When the contents of rangeOriginal change, the contents of rangeBackup also change. After all, they're similar window frames looking out at the same scenery. To create a backup variable successfully, you must create a different variable—a string rather than a textRange—to store the htmlText of your range.

Also keep in mind that the start and end properties count characters starting at zero. Technically, character position 0 is right in front of the first character in the range. If you have trouble dealing with this, try to think of these values as cursor positions, always one in front of the character you're about to type in.

Creating textRange Objects From Elements

There are two ways to use the document structure to create a textRange, both of them methods of the document object. The first one, document.createTextRange(), creates a text range that includes the entire content of the body section of the document, unless you specify start and end parameters. The second method, which you'll probably use more frequently, is document.rangeFromElement(), which takes an element as its argument.

At least initially, you'll probably want to use the textRange object to manipulate the contents of your document. It's easy to do so, but there are a few things you should keep in mind. First, unless you use the pasteHTML method, you'll be changing only the content of the textRange and not its formatting—and you can get unpredictable results when you paste over objects or scripts. Second, replacing initial text with textRange objects isn't a great way to "hide" data. You can do it, but anyone who looks at your source code can tell what you're trying to hide. Finally, adding HTML to your document with pasteHTML forces the browser to parse the entire contents of the string you hand it. If you make a mistake and include elements that have duplicate IDs or remove important parts of your page by accident, the browser won't stop you. Everything will look as if it's working—until your script finds it can't reach the objects it was expecting and starts producing strange error messages that are hard to trace. Overall, textRange objects are a blunt tool for working with HTML, and you'll frequently find better solutions in other styles of scripting.

Our initial examples will be simple: a page with some text and a few controls to let you modify it. If you need to experiment with what will happen when you paste HTML into a document, you'll be much better off checking it out with a simple testbed application such as this one than your fully developed Web application. After you've made the parts work in isolation, you can put them together with the confidence that each part works well on its own.

```
<HTML>
<HEAD><TITLE>textRange object testing
zone</TITLE></HEAD>
<BODY BGCOLOR=#FFFFFF>
<H1 ID=headline>Testing Zone...</H1>
<P ID=para1>Please put on your helmet.  HTML may
shift <SPAN ID=span1
STYLE="color:red">violently</SPAN> in this
location.</P>
<P ID=para2>Management is not responsible for
developers who choose not to wear protective <SPAN
ID=span2>headgear</SPAN>.</P>
<INPUT TYPE="button" VALUE="Action 1"
onclick="action1()">
<INPUT TYPE="button" VALUE="Action 2"
onclick="action2()">
<INPUT TYPE="TEXT" ID=entryBox>
<SCRIPT LANGUAGE="JavaScript">
function action1(){
}
function action2(){
}
</SCRIPT>
</BODY>
</HTML>
```

Within this simple framework, we'll explore the possibilities of the textRange object and prepare ourselves for real work. You need only enter the function code in the examples that follow, and our prefab laboratory will do the rest. Clicking on **Action 1** will launch the action1() function, and clicking on **Action 2** will launch action2() (see Figure 8.1).

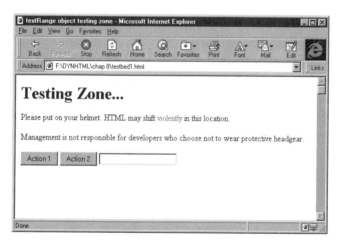

Figure 8.1 The prefab textRange laboratory.

First, let's use the action1() function to create a textRange object from the span1 ("violently") element and replace that text with whatever you've entered in the text box.

```
function action1(){
var replaceRange;
replaceRange=document.rangeFromElement(span1);
replaceRange.text=entryBox.value;
}
```

If you try this, you'll see that you can type anything you like into the text box, and Internet Explorer will obligingly place it where the word *violently* used to be. Unfortunately, it doesn't do anything with embedded HTML tags. They appear in the text with the rest of the document, as shown in Figure 8.2.

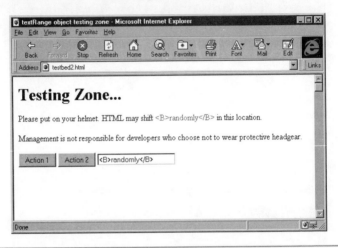

Figure 8.2 HTML tags flown boldly.

If we want to eliminate the tags, we'll need to use a different means of changing the text. Rather than change its text property, we'll use the pasteHTML method:

```
function action2(){
var replaceRange;
replaceRange=document.rangeFromElement(span1);
replaceRange.pasteHTML(entryBox.value);
}
```

You can type in any HTML code you like, and the document will reflect what you've typed (see Figure 8.3).

You can even enter tags for images and other multimedia elements if you like. It's quite a change from the usual edit-and-load cycle, a strange improvement on the current generation of HTML editors.

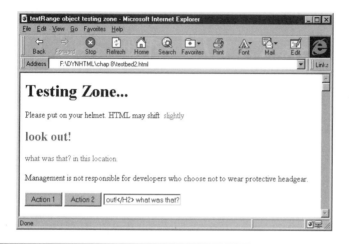

Figure 8.3 Document with simple HTML added.

The pasteHTML method makes it possible to change any part of your document any time. When the structure you've built isn't enough and you want to knock it all down, you can use pasteHTML to start afresh. (You could also load a new page, but you can't easily load only part of a page.) Try it with a few tags to see what happens. One problem you'll encounter quickly is that any tags you put at the beginning of your entry will hang over your page forever, or at least until you refresh the view. If you put a space in front of your entry, though, you can prevent this, but at the cost of strange spacing between words. The space is enough of a placeholder that you can bounce out the code the next time around. On the bright side, tags you forget to close aren't allowed to interfere with the rest of your page. Try entering **<I>italic** and see what happens (very little). (There are a few glitches, though, especially with cascading style sheet tags.)

Creating your textRange objects based on elements or even the entire document doesn't limit you to working with the entire content of the textRange you initially created. The textRange object includes several methods to let you be more selective. You can use the move method to change your range, choosing a start point within the current range:

```
function action2(){
var replaceRange;
replaceRange=document.rangeFromElement(span1);
replaceRange.move("Character",2);
replaceRange.pasteHTML(entryBox.value);
}
```

If you try this odd action, type test and click the **Action 2** button. You'll see the screen shown in Figure 8.4.

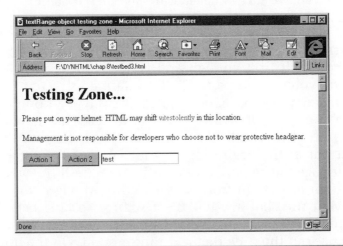

Figure 8.4 Text landing after position 2.

The move method and its siblings moveEnd and moveStart allow you to specify targets with a new syntax. If you use only move, the whole range collapses, becoming more of a cursor than a range. The moveEnd and moveStart methods let you build a larger range, moving only one of the endpoints of the range instead of the whole thing. You can use the move method with the kinds of units shown in Table 8.3.

Table 8.3 textRange units

Unit	Meaning
character	Counts in characters
Word	Counts in words separated by spaces
Sentence	Takes you to the beginning of the nth sentence. It seems to use periods, question marks, and exclamation points as the breaking characters.
Story	Appears in practice to take you to the next paragraph.

The syntax for all three of these methods is the same: move(unit, count). You don't have to specify how many units to move. The default is 1.

Three other methods can help you manage ranges. The collapse method collapses your range to its start or its end. If you specify true, you get the start; if you specify false, you get the end. The expand method takes a unit for its argument and helps you gather the stray half a word or quarter of a sentence you missed when you moved mathematically. It expands the range's beginning and end so that they include whole units. The setRange function takes a beginning and an end argument (in characters) to set your textRange object to the position you specify.

Now that we've covered the basics of textRange objects, we'll explore some of their more powerful features. By the end, you may think you're getting a programmer's view of Microsoft Word. I suspect that's what Microsoft has in mind for these controls.

Creating and Manipulating Content-Based textRange Objects

Creating textRange objects from elements can be useful when you're building an interface, but there may be times when you need to create your ranges more flexibly. The method document.rangeFromText() allows you to search for a specific piece of text and make the next occurrence of it in the document into a textRange you can manipulate. This method is most useful for a find function or a search-and-replace, which we'll implement in this section. We'll use the same interface we created earlier, adding to it as necessary until we've implemented a full search-and-replace function like that in a simple word processor.

First, we need a search engine. Microsoft has obligingly given us the document.rangeFromText() method, which takes a string to search for, a parameter named count that indicates whether to search backward or forward, some simple flags, and the range to search in. All the parameters except the text to search for are optional. The misleadingly named count parameter works very simply. If you give it a positive number, it searches forward from the current insertion point; if you give it a negative number, it searches backward. Giving it zero limits your search to the range supplied in the final parameter, which is the entire document if you don't supply a range. There are two flags you can use: htmlMatchWord (equal to 2) and htmlMatchCase (equal to 4). If you need to match both word and case, you can enter (htmlMatchWord AND htmlMatchCase), which equals 6, as the parameter. The final parameter, range, is optional. If you supply it a range (and set count to zero), the method will search only within that range, ignoring the rest of the document.

Let's try this and see how it works. Instead of making the **Action 1** button replace text, we'll make it find and highlight it.

```
function action1(){
var seekRange;
seekRange=document.rangeFromText(entryBox.value);
seekRange.select();
}
```

It's simple, but it should give you an idea of what's coming (see Figure 8.5).

We used a new method of the textRange object to highlight the text: select(). It doesn't take any parameters or return any values; it makes your textRange into the current selection. As we'll see, select() is the first arrival of a new set of tools.

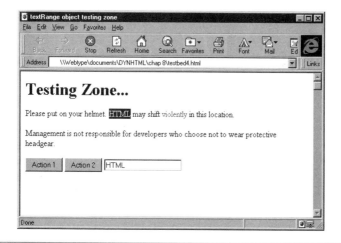

Figure 8.5 Searching for HTML.

You can refine this search in several ways. We'll start by adding a few check boxes to the form to make it easy to use more of this function's power:

```
<HTML>
<HEAD><TITLE>textRange object testing
zone</TITLE></HEAD>
<BODY BGCOLOR=#FFFFFF>
<H1 ID=headline>Testing Zone...</H1>
<P ID=para1>Please put on your helmet.  HTML may
shift <SPAN ID=span1
STYLE="color:red">violently</SPAN> in this
location.</P>
<P ID=para2>Management is not responsible for
developers who choose not to wear protective <SPAN
ID=span2>headgear</SPAN>.</P>
<INPUT TYPE="button" VALUE="Action 1"
onclick="action1()">
<INPUT TYPE="button" VALUE="Action 2"
onclick="action2()">
<INPUT TYPE="TEXT" ID=entryBox><BR>
<INPUT TYPE="CHECKBOX" ID=Word>Match Whole Word<BR>
<INPUT TYPE="CHECKBOX" ID=Case>Match Case<BR>
<SCRIPT LANGUAGE="JavaScript">
function action1(){
var seekRange, matchFlags;
matchFlags=0;
if (Word.checked==true)  {matchFlags=2;}
if (Case.checked==true)  {matchFlags+=4;}
seekRange=document.rangeFromText(entryBox.value,0,ma
tchFlags);
if (seekRange != null )
  {seekRange.select();}
}
function action2(){
}
</SCRIPT>
</BODY>
</HTML>
```

If you try it, your results should look something like
Figure 8.6.

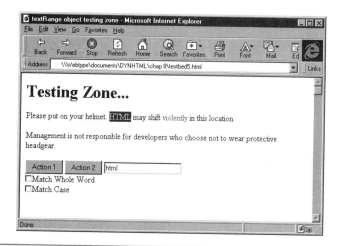

Figure 8.6 Qualified search results.

Now that we've built our little search engine, it's time to
tie it to additional tools that will let it do some work. So
far, we've used the entire document as our range, without
worrying about insertion points or selections. By creating
an additional variable to make our textRange object
persistent, we'll be able to create a search-and-replace
function worthy of a simple word processor.

```
<HTML>
<HEAD><TITLE>textRange object testing
zone</TITLE></HEAD>
<BODY BGCOLOR=#FFFFFF>
<H1 ID=headline>Testing Zone...</H1>
<P ID=para1>Please put on your helmet.  HTML may
shift <SPAN ID=span1
STYLE="color:red">violently</SPAN> in this
location.</P>
```

```
<P ID=para2>Management is not responsible for
developers who choose not to wear protective <SPAN
ID=span2>headgear</SPAN>.</P>
<INPUT TYPE="button" VALUE="Search"
onclick="action1()">
<INPUT TYPE="button" VALUE="Replace"
onclick="action2()"> <BR>
<INPUT TYPE="CHECKBOX" ID=Word>Match Whole Word<BR>
<INPUT TYPE="CHECKBOX" ID=Case>Match Case<BR>
Search Text:<INPUT TYPE="TEXT" ID=entryBox
onblur="action1"><BR>
Replace Text:<INPUT TYPE="TEXT" ID=replaceBox><BR>
<SCRIPT LANGUAGE="JavaScript">
function action1(){ //search function
     var matchFlags;
     matchFlags=0;
     if (Word.checked==true)  {matchFlags=2;}
     if (Case.checked==true)  {matchFlags+=4;}

seekRange=document.rangeFromText(entryBox.value,0,ma
tchFlags);
     if (seekRange != null ){
            seekRange.select();
     }
}
function action2(){//replace function
     action1();//find it, if they forgot to do that.
     if (seekRange != null ){
          seekRange.pasteHTML(replaceBox.value);
     }
}
var seekRange;
</SCRIPT>
</BODY>
</HTML>
```

It's not the most elegant interface yet, but it's getting there (see Figure 8.7).

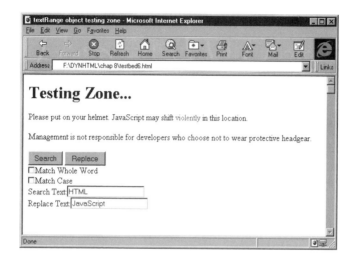

Figure 8.7 Search and replace with HTML and JavaScript.

Now that we have a simple search-and-replace function, we need to start thinking about what it is we're replacing with this blunt instrument. We're adding and deleting objects, and the computer is doing its best to keep up, but you'll frequently find that you need to take control of the object management. Creating pages that make extensive use of textRange objects is difficult. It's easy to inadvertently refer to objects that you either just deleted or haven't yet created.

Managing Objects and Elements That Get Trapped in Your textRange

The first part of managing elements involves determining where you are in the document. Fortunately, two textRange methods can give you some basic orientation. The parentElement() method takes as its argument an integer that represent the character position of the

location you're checking. We'll use our search framework
to try this:

```
<HTML>
<HEAD><TITLE>textRange object testing
zone</TITLE></HEAD>
<BODY BGCOLOR=#FFFFFF>
<H1 ID=headline>Testing Zone...</H1>
<P ID=para1>Please put on your helmet.  HTML may
shift <SPAN ID=span1
STYLE="color:red">violently</SPAN> in this
location.</P>
<P ID=para2>Management is not responsible for
developers who choose not to wear protective <SPAN
ID=span2>headgear</SPAN>.</P>
<INPUT TYPE="button" VALUE="Search"
onclick="action1()">
<INPUT TYPE="button" VALUE="Look up"
onclick="action2()"> <BR>
<INPUT TYPE="CHECKBOX" ID=Word>Match Whole Word<BR>
<INPUT TYPE="CHECKBOX" ID=Case>Match Case<BR>
Search Text:<INPUT TYPE="TEXT" ID=entryBox
onblur="action1"><BR>
<SCRIPT LANGUAGE="JavaScript">
function action1(){ //this is the same search
routine as before
     var matchFlags;
     matchFlags=0;
     if (Word.checked==true)  {matchFlags=2;}
     if (Case.checked==true)  {matchFlags+=4;}

seekRange=document.rangeFromText(entryBox.value,0,ma
tchFlags);
     if (seekRange != null ){
          seekRange.select();
     }
```

```
    }
function action2(){
    action1();
    checkNumber=seekRange.start;//we want to check
the first character

checkElement=seekRange.parentElement(checkNumber)
//get element
    checkID=checkElement.id //get just ID of
element
    alert(checkID); //announce ID
    }
var seekRange;
</SCRIPT>
</BODY>
</HTML>
```

The action1() function here is the same one we just used in our search; the new developments take place in the action2() function. First, we get the start value for the seekRange object we just found. Then we use the parentElement method to find out which element contains that first character. The parentElement method returns a full object reference, which is useful if we want to make changes to the object. In our case, we want to announce its name to the world (see Figure 8.8).

The textRange object also offers a lightweight method for using similar code to determine whether the character you're looking at with parentElement is an embedded object (an applet, image, ActiveX object, multimedia, and so on). The isEmbed method, like the parentElement method, takes a character count as its parameter and returns a true or false value:

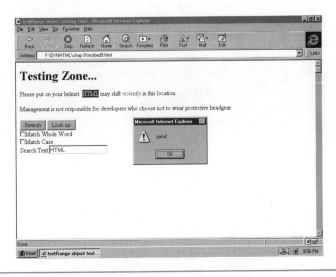

Figure 8.8 Revealing the parent.

```
function action2(){
    action1();
    checkNumber=seekRange.start;//we want to check
the first character
    checkElement=seekRange.isEmbed(checkNumber)
//get element
    alert(checkElement); //announce yes(true) or
no(false)
}
```

If you try this in our simple testbed, you'll always get a false response, because there aren't any embedded objects here. Add some elements if you want to experiment. The isEmbed method is a quick way to check that you're not incinerating objects, but you'll need to use the parentElement() method to find out which element you've encountered.

Whether or not a textRange crosses element boundaries, you can find the element that completely contains it by using the commonParentElement method. We need only change the action2() method slightly:

```
function action2(){
    action1();
    checkElement=seekRange.commonParentElement()
//get common element
    checkID=checkElement.id //get just ID of
element
    alert(checkID); //announce ID
}
```

It's hard to find words when they're broken across paragraph boundaries, but you can try crossing the SPANs easily. For instance, "shift violently" returns the result shown in Figure 8.9.

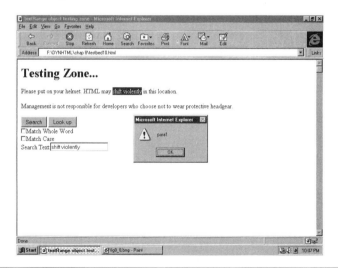

Figure 8.9 Returning the element that contains both words.

TextRange objects have one other oddly intriguing method—scrollIntoView()—which takes true or false for a parameter. If you supply true, the window scrolls to the beginning of your textRange object; if false, it scrolls to the end.

Internet Explorer 4.0 also includes a few intriguing but undocumented (and, so far, unfunctional) methods for the document and textRange objects. It appears that Microsoft wants to make it possible to add commands to Internet Explorer using a similar technology to one used for adding VBScript macros to the Visual Studio line of products. The textRange object has an executeCommand() method that accepts a command ID number and a variant value as parameters. The Internet SDK documentation suggests that this method executes "a command on the range. For example, changing the formatting of the text." It doesn't work yet, at least with the documents I've been able to create, but it looks as if this method will be the hook for adding text manipulation functions to the browser. The methods you can use to change for commands—queryCommandEnabled(cmdID), query-CommandIndeterm(cmdID), queryCommandState-(cmdID), queryCommandSupported(cmdID), and query-CommandText(cmdID)—all seem to be connected to the load cycle of ActiveX and other objects that we saw in Chapter 5. When these methods appear, expect the functions to provide the text processing power your scripts will need to actively manage text, incoming as well as outgoing.

Microsoft is starting to make it possible to create full-fledged applications in its browser, but it needs to provide a more comprehensive set of tools that can respond to user selections as well as user actions such as clicking and dragging and dropping. The tools we have now are a bit crude, but they have enough power to make a start of it. Microsoft hasn't yet implemented but has described the document.createRange() method (which turns the current selection into a textRange object) and the selection object, both of which will make it possible to create something more akin to a word processor. When those objects are complete, Internet Explorer will have the beginnings of a system that will let users manage the content of Web pages directly.

Keep an eye on the MIS:Press Web site (http://www.mispress.com/ dynamichtml) for updates to the information in this chapter.

N O T E

CHAPTER 9

Interactive Documents III: Communicating with the User

Now that we can make the browser jump through hoops, it's time to apply this technology to create interfaces for getting work (and play) accomplished. By combining Dynamic HTML with existing tools, such as frames, forms, and windows, we'll start creating a fully featured environment that can even include its own virtual psychiatrist.

NOTE Examples in this chapter are guaranteed to work only in Internet Explorer 4.0. If you want to use some of these techniques in mixed-browser environments, you should implement the kind of browser detection code explained in Appendix A.

Multiframe and Multiwindow Examples

All the examples we've worked with have been single-document applications. Everything takes place in one window, without any frames. It's easier to work that way for simple projects, but sometimes you may need to work with information in multiple locations. It's possible to concentrate much of your code in a single frame or window, making it accessible to other frames as they need it. This strategy has hazards (especially if someone closes the window or loads a frame individually), but there will be times when you need to refer to information in multiple-document objects.

Targeting Frames

The syntax for managing Dynamic HTML in multiple document applications is the same as when you are working with ordinary scripting and HTML. Windows and frames are identified by their NAME attributes and can be addressed using that name. For example, we'll create a set of two frames:

```
<HTML>
<HEAD><TITLE>Frames workspace</TITLE></HEAD>
<FRAMESET COLS="150,*">
<FRAME FRAMEBORDER=0 SRC="controls.html"
NAME="controls">
<FRAME FRAMEBORDER=0 SRC="targeted.html"
NAME="targeted">
</FRAMESET>
</HTML>
```

The left side ("controls") will contain scripts to let us change things on the right ("targeted"). Our target side contains just enough HTML elements to let us make changes:

```
<HTML>
<BODY>
<H3 ID=juniper STYLE="color:red">Target side.</H3>
<P ID=hideaway STYLE="display:none">This paragraph
is the target side's secret weapon.</P>
<P ID=blues STYLE="color:blue; font-size:24">It's
rough being on the target side.  You don't have any
```

```
<SPAN id=rePlace>control</SPAN> over what
happens.</P>
</BODY>
</HTML>
```

The controls.html file has all the scripts for the example:

```
<HTML>
<SCRIPT LANGUAGE="JavaScript">
function hilite(){
  parent.targeted.juniper.style.color="green";
}
function showHide(){
  current=parent.targeted.hideaway.style.display;
  if (current=="none"){
  parent.targeted.hideaway.style.display="";
  shower.value="Hide It";
  }
  else{
  parent.targeted.hideaway.style.display="none";
  shower.value="Show It";
  }
}
function changeIt(){
    newText=replaceValue.value;

r=parent.targeted.document.rangeFromElement(parent.t
argeted.rePlace);
    r.pasteHTML(newText);
}
</SCRIPT>
<BODY>
<H3 onclick="hilite()">Control side</H3>
<P><INPUT TYPE=BUTTON ID=shower onclick="showHide()"
VALUE="Show It"></P>
<P><INPUT TYPE=TEXTBOX ID=replaceValue SIZE=15><BR>
```

```
<INPUT TYPE=BUTTON ID=replaceIt onClick="changeIt()"
VALUE="Change Text"></P>
</BODY>
</HTML>
```

There are several key things to notice. The first is the parent.framename notation you use to refer to elements in other frames. This notation isn't hard to deal with, but you must use it every time except in one case. It isn't documented, but textRange objects appear to understand which document they came from originally and will let you make changes to them (as we do in the changeIt() function) without the extra work of listing out the frame notation.

Our initial page looks like the one shown in Figure 9.1.

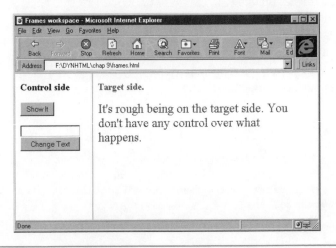

Figure 9.1 Frameset with fresh target.

After making some changes on the control side, it can look like Figure 9.2.

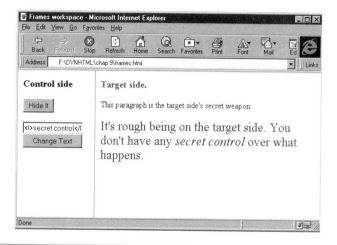

Figure 9.2 Frameset with modified target.

Targeting Windows

You can do the same thing with windows, with one difference: you don't use the keyword parent. Windows have their own identities, and you can pass references to window variables. We'll make a similar target2.html. When it opens, this codes create the control panel as a floating remote control window:

```
<HTML><HEAD><TITLE>Targeted</TITLE></HEAD>
<SCRIPT LANGUAGE="JavaScript">
newWin=window.open("control2.html","Control","width=
150 height=200");
newWin.creator=self;
</SCRIPT>
<BODY>
<H3 ID=juniper STYLE="color:red">Target window.</H3>
```

```
<P ID=hideaway STYLE="display:none">This paragraph
is the target side's secret weapon.</P>
<P ID=blues STYLE="color:blue; font-size:24">It's
rough being on the target side.  You don't have any
<SPAN id=rePlace>control</SPAN> over what
happens.</P>
</BODY>
</HTML>
```

The main change is the addition of code that creates a
new window for the control panel and passes the identity
of this window (self) to the new window as an object
named creator. The main window has no name, and you
cannot assign it a name, so passing the window reference
is the only way to make this work. The control2.html file
is similar to its predecessor; the only change is that
parent.targeted has been replaced in all instances by
creator. (If the target window had a name, we could have
used that instead of the creator object.)

```
<HTML>
<SCRIPT LANGUAGE="JavaScript">
function hilite(){
   creator.juniper.style.color="green";
}
function showHide(){
   current=creator.hideaway.style.display;
   if (current=="none"){
   creator.hideaway.style.display="";
   shower.value="Hide It";
   }
   else{
   creator.hideaway.style.display="none";
   shower.value="Show It";
   }
}
function changeIt(){
```

```
    newText=replaceValue.value;

r=creator.document.rangeFromElement(creator.rePlace)
;
    r.pasteHTML(newText);
}
</SCRIPT>
<BODY>
<H3 onclick="hilite()">Control window</H3>
<P><INPUT TYPE=BUTTON ID=shower onclick="showHide()"
VALUE="Show It"></P>
<P><INPUT TYPE=TEXTBOX ID=replaceValue SIZE=15><BR>
<INPUT TYPE=BUTTON ID=replaceIt onClick="changeIt()"
VALUE="Change Text"></P>
</BODY>
</HTML>
```

When you open the target2.html file in Internet Explorer, it creates another browser window that contains the control panel (see Figure 9.3).

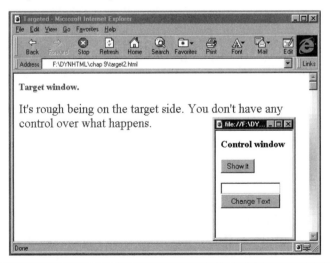

Figure 9.3 Control and target windows before making changes.

The control window has just as much power to change the contents of the target window as the control frame had over the target frame (see Figure 9.4).

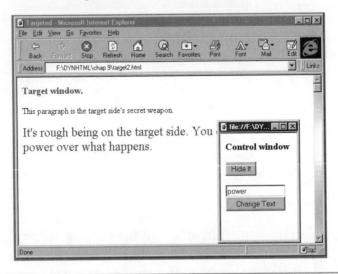

Figure 9.4 Control and target windows after changes.

Frames and windows have always been useful for loading in new content without disturbing the old. Those techniques now give us the power to make changes in the old from a central command center, making it easier to coordinate and centralize code.

Hiding Information: The Comic Strip

One the loudest complaints about the Web has come from content creators, who feel that anything they post instantly becomes a part of the public domain. Text and graphics can be pilfered with ease and printed, edited, or redistributed without the creator's knowledge. Dynamic HTML gives developers a few more tools in the war between the content owners and the content thieves, although these tools are hardly foolproof. They also create a wide variety of new interface possibilities that promise to make pages more responsive to users.

Our example is a simple comic strip with three panels. Instead of presenting the strip as one large GIF or JPEG that users can save to their hard drives, we'll break it into various pieces, first by panel and then by layer. Every panel of the comic strip has three successive layers: a background graphic, a foreground graphic, and a text graphic. The foreground and text graphics are transparent, and the background is opaque. (Splitting the foreground and background makes it easy to create comics that share background elements. It also creates an additional graphic that potential thieves must download and merge.) When the strip first loads, the background and foreground graphics are visible, but the text is hidden (see Figure 9.5).

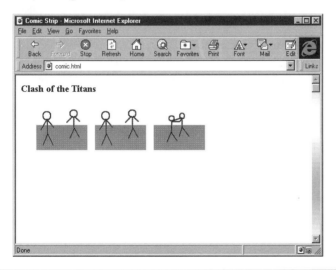

Figure 9.5 Comic strip as loaded.

To make the text appear, the user must roll the mouse over one of the panels. The text appears but only in the current panel; only one panel has text at any given time (see Figure 9.6).

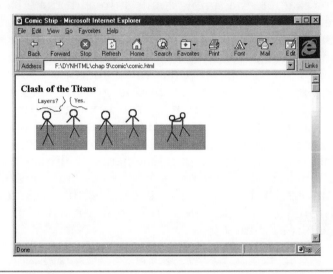

Figure 9.6 Comic strip, first panel text visible.

Anyone who wants to copy the strip must take a lot of screen shots and cut and paste them. It's possible, but it's much more work. The code to implement the comic strip needs only one function along with numerous positioned and named graphics:

```
<HTML>
<HEAD><TITLE>Comic Strip - Internet
Explorer</TITLE></HEAD>
<BODY BGCOLOR=#FFFFFF>
<SCRIPT LANGUAGE="JavaScript">
function showIt() {
     origin=event.srcElement.id;
     whichOne=origin.substring(origin.length-1,
origin.length);
```

```
      for (i=1;i<4; i++){
            if (i==whichOne){

document.all["txt"+whichOne].style.display="";
            }
          else{

document.all["txt"+i].style.display="none";
            }
      }
}
</SCRIPT>
<H3>Clash of the Titans</H3>
<!-Comics here ->
<IMG SRC="bg1.gif" ID="bg1"
STYLE="container:positioned; position:absolute;
top:40; left:40; height:100; width:100">
<IMG SRC="bg1.gif" ID="bg2"
STYLE="container:positioned; position:absolute;
top:40; left:155; height:100; width:100">
<IMG SRC="bg1.gif" ID="bg2"
STYLE="container:positioned; position:absolute;
top:40; left:270; height:100; width:100">
<IMG SRC="fg1.gif" onmouseover="showIt()" ID="fg1"
STYLE="container:positioned; position:absolute;
top:40; left:40; height:100; width:100">
<IMG SRC="fg2.gif" onmouseover="showIt()" ID="fg2"
STYLE="container:positioned; position:absolute;
top:40; left:155; height:100; width:100">
<IMG SRC="fg3.gif" onmouseover="showIt()" ID="fg3"
STYLE="container:positioned; position:absolute;
top:40; left:270; height:100; width:100">
<IMG SRC="txt1.gif" ID="txt1"
STYLE="container:positioned; position:absolute;
top:40; left:40; height:100; width:100;
display:none">
<IMG SRC="txt2.gif" ID="txt2"
STYLE="container:positioned; position:absolute;
```

```
top:40; left:155; height:100; width:100;
display:none">
<IMG SRC="txt3.gif" ID="txt3"
STYLE="container:positioned; position:absolute;
top:40; left:270; height:100; width:100;
display:none">
</BODY>
</HTML>
```

The foreground graphics call the showIt() routine when they receive an onmouseover event. The showIt() function determines which graphic called the routine and makes the appropriate text graphic visible while hiding all the others. We don't need to worry about the onmouseout event, because showIt() takes care of hiding graphics as well as displaying them. This arrangement also helps keep blinking to a minimum. For the closing panels of this fine strip, check out Chapter 12, where we create the same page in Netscape.

Extending this principle to a variety of other situations is fairly simple. You could add panels by changing the for loop to accommodate them. You could also use this style of display to create comics that changed depending on the sequence in which the user read them; you would add code to showIt() that kept track of which graphics had been displayed and respond accordingly. I hope that Dynamic HTML doesn't reduce Web pages to a strange kind of hide-and-seek, but it opens new possibilities for interfaces that depend on hiding information as well as displaying it.

Eliza: Creating an Interface with textRange Objects

When I first started experimenting with Dynamic HTML, I was struck by how it returned me to my earliest days of programming in Applesoft: old-style BASIC, with all its ugly print statements and inputs. After years of thinking in terms of events and pages, I was suddenly able to revert to the old text interfaces, and I wanted to create a sample program that harked back to those earlier days. Eliza, the classic relic from that period, simulated a psychotherapist by responding to keywords in text entered by the user. Eliza generated simple questions that often echoed large portions of the text the user entered. Although it was a poor excuse for a psychologist, Eliza was one of the early artificial intelligence programs that could fool users into believing that the computer was capable of sustaining a conversation. It wasn't, of course, but it demonstrated the power of using a keyword database and some simple rules to create readable sentences.

Our example will present an extremely simple version of Eliza. My point isn't to make the computer seem human but rather to demonstrate a simple, text-based interface that works smoothly on the client. It uses textRange objects for data storage and to present responses to the user, taking advantage of its relatively powerful tools for managing text and breaking it into workable chunks. Our Eliza program is easy to extend; you can add to the keyword and response lists quite easily, although you'll notice a slowdown as the list grows.

NOTE

After all the JavaScript, why is this example in VBScript? There are a few reasons. First, most of the implementations I've seen of Eliza were from the late 1970's, and written in BASIC. VBScript continues a long tradition of including string matching as a standard, easy-to-use function within the language. Second, even though I believe that JavaScript will be the way to go in the long term, it's still worthwhile to know how to use VBScript. This example applies several of the techniques used elsewhere in this book, albeit with a slightly different accent. I hope JavaScript developers will take a look at this example to get a sense of the differences among scripting languages and styles.

First, we need to create an interface. I had originally hoped to keep the entire conversation on the screen, scrolling along to keep up with the user entries and computer responses, but that was prevented by a severe limitation in the way the pasteHTML method works. I wanted to append the text to the end of a <DIV></DIV> section, but pasteHTML puts the text outside the end tag. When you try to append a new piece of conversation, it appears in front of the older comments and not after them. As a result, I had to use a simpler interface that displays only one response at a time (see Figure 9.7).

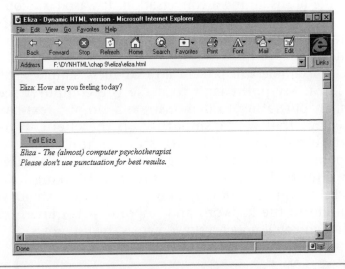

Figure 9.7 Eliza opening.

We can create this much with just a skeleton of the Eliza interface, using a placeholder for the elizaThink function that will eventually produce the interactive "conversation" our users expect:

```
<HTML><HEAD><TITLE>Eliza - Dynamic HTML
version</TITLE></HEAD>
<BODY>
```

```
<SCRIPT LANGUAGE="VBScript">
function elizaThink(userSpeak)
elizaThought="I don't have a brain yet."
  elizaThink= elizaThought
end function

sub respond
'This part just prints what you typed.
userResponse=response.value
set wholeRange=document.rangeFromElement(Response1)
wholeRange.pasteHTML("<P ID=Response1>You: " +
userResponse+"</P>")

'This part will call the Eliza routines and report
the response
elizaResponse=elizaThink(userResponse)
set wholeRange=document.rangeFromElement(Eliza1)
wholeRange.pasteHTML("<P ID=Eliza1>Eliza: " +
elizaResponse + "</P>")

'clears the input box
response.value=""
end sub

</SCRIPT>
<P ID=Response1>Eliza: How are you feeling
today?</P>
<P ID=Eliza1> </P>

<DIV ID=Input1><INPUT TYPE=TEXT SIZE=100
ID=response>
<INPUT TYPE=BUTTON onclick="respond" VALUE="Tell
Eliza"></DIV>
<CITE>
Eliza - The (almost) computer psychotherapist<BR>
For best results, please don't use punctuation.<BR>
</CITE>
```

```
</BODY>
</HTML>
```

The Response1 and Eliza1 paragraphs will be the targets for the text of our conversation. I've put Eliza's opening statement in the top space (it looks more natural), but all subsequent user comments will appear in the top (Response1) paragraph. Note that we include the full <P ID=xxxxx1></P> code in our call to pasteHTML. If you don't include it, the code works the first time and then crashes the browser the second time. One of the hardest things about directly manipulating the HTML is that it's hard to see what the browser thinks you've done. **View Source** brings up the original code and not your modified version. Apparently, pasteHTML overwrites the tags we use to identify the paragraphs, obliterating the ID information we need to write to them a second or third time. Including the extra code skirts that problem.

Another potential bug is the need to use a set statement when you're assigning a textRange in VBScript. I couldn't make this code work. I ported it to JavaScript, where it performed happily. In desperation, I added a set statement and it worked. This statement isn't supposed to be necessary, but in this case omitting it produces objects that don't quite hold their values. Trying to call methods or attempting to access properties of a textRange that was created without the set statement produces runtime errors every time.

You can reuse this simple interface by replacing the elizaThink function with your own code to process user input. Our placeholder function doesn't do much (see Figure 9.8).

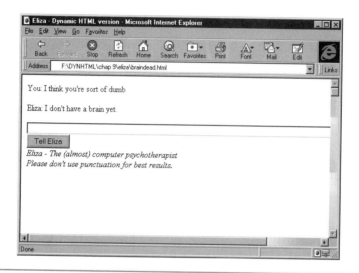

Figure 9.8 Eliza on a stupid day.

It's time to give Eliza a brain. We'll take advantage of another feature of Dynamic HTML to store the data to interpret user responses. We can read from a textRange as well as write to it, and we can create invisible data storage structures that will hold our keywords and responses. VBScript doesn't have any kind of READ...DATA structure (nor does it have the GOTO that most of the early Eliza programs used extensively), so we'll use the HTML document itself. We'll put the data in a DIV structure with the ID dataPlace. We won't provide multiple responses to keywords, but we will allow multiple keywords to trigger the same response. To do this, we'll alternate keywords and responses. Each section will conclude with an ENDKWD or ENDRESP to let the program know that one section is ending and another one is beginning:

```
anger angry mad mean grumpy ENDKWD
Have you been under a lot of stress lately? ENDRESP
sad tired depressed bored listless cry weep ENDKWD
What makes you so sad? ENDRESP
```

You can't see it, but you need to include a space after ENDRESP and ENDKWD. Internet Explorer sometimes adds white space at the end of these lines when we search them—but not always. You'll find that Eliza behaves much more consistently if you include the spaces, even if you have line breaks between your sections. (If it frustrates you, you can modify the code with some Trim() functions.) At the end of the list is an ENDALL, which tells the computer it's reached the end of the list without finding a match.

NOTE You could also use the Tabular Data Control (covered in Chapter 11) to provide much of the same functionality as our hidden data. In this way, you could build a more powerful Eliza that draws its responses from a separate text file.

The logic we use in the elizaThink function to match keywords to the user's text is a series of loops that navigate the data, advancing forward one word at a time and skipping unnecessary responses:

```
function elizaThink(userSpeak)
if userSpeak="" then
    'empty space response
    elizaThought="Come on, say something!"
else
    'search initialization
    set
searchRange=document.rangeFromElement(dataPlace)
    searchRange.collapse(true) 'start at beginning
of data
        searchRange.moveEnd("Word")      'enclose the
first word
```

```
        wordNow=""
    Do While matchFound=""
                'data search loop
                'this loop checks keywords
                Do While wordNow<>"ENDKWD "
                    wordNow=searchRange.text
                    if wordNow="" or wordNow="ENDALL
" then
                        'ran out of words to match
                        matchFound="NONE"
                        wordNow="ENDKWD "
                        'need to break out of loop
                    else
                    'is word in user string?

wordPos=InStr(1,userSpeak,wordNow,1)
                        if wordPos<>0 then
                            matchFound=wordNow
                            set
matchRange=searchRange
                        end if
                    'move on to the next word
                    searchRange.moveStart("Word")
                    searchRange.moveEnd("Word")
                    end if
            Loop
            if matchFound="" then
                'cycle through to end of line if no
match
                Do While wordNow<>"ENDRESP "
                    wordNow=searchRange.text
                    searchRange.moveStart("Word")
                    searchRange.moveEnd("Word")
                Loop
            else
                if matchFound<>"NONE" then
                    'pull out reply
```

```
                searchRange.moveEnd("Sentence")
                matchFound=searchRange.text
          end if
        end if
   Loop
   if matchFound="NONE" then matchFound="Could you
be more specific?"
     elizaThought=matchFound
end if
elizaThink= elizaThought 'sets return value
end function
```

Because there can be any number of keywords in a list, we use do...while loops instead of the for...next loops we've used elsewhere in the book. This function has three loops. The outermost loop keeps the program looking through all the lines of keywords until it finds a match or runs out of responses. The first inner loop cycles through all the keywords in a section and uses the InStr() function to check whether any keyword is included in the user's input. InStr() takes four arguments. First is the starting position to search from, which in our case will be 1 (the beginning of the string in VBScript). The second argument is the string in which to search, followed by the string we're searching for. The fourth argument is the most important one; if it is set to zero, the strings must match exactly, including case. We set it to 1, letting us ignore case. InStr() will return zero if the string doesn't appear, or a number indicating its starting position. A more sophisticated version of Eliza could use that number for parsing, but for this example it will suffice to know that we have a match.

The second part of the function gets called when we've finished searching a set of keywords. If we don't yet have a match, the second inner loop cycles past the words in the response to avoid producing false matches. If we have

a match, the code pulls out the response and we're ready
to exit the loops and return a response (see Figure 9.9).

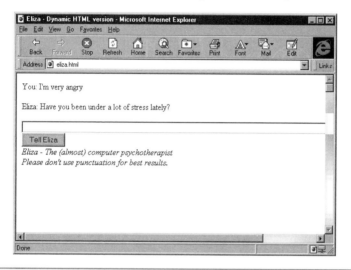

Figure 9.9 Eliza with an angry patient.

With all its data, the program is moderately long but still
a fairly quick download. To give Eliza new conversation,
just add to the list at the bottom of the document or
write your own extensions for parsing text and
responding.

```
<HTML><HEAD><TITLE>Eliza - Dynamic HTML
version</TITLE> </HEAD>
<BODY>
<SCRIPT LANGUAGE="VBScript">
function elizaThink(userSpeak)
if userSpeak="" then
    'empty space response
    elizaThought="Come on, say something!"
else
    'search initialization
```

```
    set
searchRange=document.rangeFromElement(dataPlace)
    searchRange.collapse(true) 'start at beginning
of data
        searchRange.moveEnd("Word")        'enclose the
first word
        wordNow=""
    Do While matchFound=""
                'data search loop
                'this loop checks keywords
                Do While wordNow<>"ENDKWD "
                    wordNow=searchRange.text
                    if wordNow="" or wordNow="ENDALL
" then
                        'ran out of words to match
                        matchFound="NONE"
                        wordNow="ENDKWD "
                        'need to break out of loop
                    else
                    'is word in user string?

wordPos=InStr(1,userSpeak,wordNow,1)
                        if wordPos<>0 then
                            matchFound=wordNow
                            set
matchRange=searchRange
                        end if
                    'move on to the next word
                    searchRange.moveStart("Word")
                    searchRange.moveEnd("Word")
                    end if
            Loop
            if matchFound="" then
                'cycle through to end of line if no
    match
                Do While wordNow<>"ENDRESP "
                    wordNow=searchRange.text
```

```
                        searchRange.moveStart("Word")
                        searchRange.moveEnd("Word")
                Loop
            else
                if matchFound<>"NONE" then
                    'pull out reply
                    searchRange.moveEnd("Sentence")
                    matchFound=searchRange.text
                end if
            end if
    Loop
    if matchFound="NONE" then matchFound="Could you
be more specific?"
        elizaThought=matchFound
end if
elizaThink= elizaThought 'sets return value
end function
sub respond
'This part just prints what you typed.
userResponse=response.value
set wholeRange=document.rangeFromElement(Response1)
wholeRange.pasteHTML("<P ID=Response1>You: " +
userResponse+"</P>")
'This part calls the Eliza routines and reports the
response
elizaResponse=elizaThink(userResponse+" ")
set wholeRange=document.rangeFromElement(Eliza1)
wholeRange.pasteHTML("<P ID=Eliza1>Eliza: " +
elizaResponse + "</P>")
'clears the input box
response.value=""
end sub
</SCRIPT>
<P ID=Response1>Eliza: How are you feeling
today?</P>
<P ID=Eliza1> </P>
```

```
<DIV ID=Input1><INPUT TYPE=TEXT SIZE=100
ID=response>
<INPUT TYPE=BUTTON onclick="respond" VALUE="Tell
Eliza"></DIV>
<CITE>
Eliza - The (almost) computer psychotherapist<BR>
For best results, please don't use punctuation.<BR>
</CITE>
<DIV ID=dataPlace STYLE="display:none">
anger angry mad mean grumpy ENDKWD
Have you been under a lot of stress lately? ENDRESP
sad tired depressed bored listless cry weep ENDKWD
What makes you so sad? ENDRESP
sleep rest relax ENDKWD
Have you been getting enough rest? ENDRESP
dynamic layers Microsoft Netscape ENDKWD
I think you need to relax more and think less about
computers. ENDRESP
shoot punch beat break smash injure kick hurt kill
ENDKWD
Violence isn't the answer, you know. ENDRESP
kiss love adore hug hold ENDKWD
Love is a wonderful thing. ENDRESP
crash storm shatter accident ENDKWD
It's a pity our world is so violent. ENDRESP
you your ENDKWD
This isn't about me, you know. ENDRESP
mother mom mamma momma ENDKWD
Do you often think of your mother? ENDRESP
father dad daddy ENDKWD
Do you have a good relationship with your father?.
ENDRESP
ENDALL
</DIV>
</BODY>
</HTML>
```

We've taken advantage of Internet Explorer's new flexibility in a number of ways. The new style information lets us keep data hidden without requiring us to create complex code. The textRange object lets us read and write our document, making it possible to create code that responds to the context of the document and present replies to the user without requiring a trip back to the server. These examples are only a small start, but you can combine and extend them to build new interfaces in an entirely new kind of Web page.

CHAPTER 10

Multimedia Effects

In a bid to make ActiveX controls more widely used, Microsoft has included a set of fairly sophisticated multimedia effects with Internet Explorer 4.0. These controls can make ordinary HTML text much more interesting, and their scriptability means that low-bandwidth animated effects are built into the browser. I suspect that these controls will get a lot of use in kiosk applications and other stand-alone multimedia systems where HTML's flexibility and ease of modification will be a refreshing change from the all-in-one approach of most other authoring tools. The hardest part of working with ActiveX controls is dealing with the ActiveX CLASSIDs, especially because some of these controls nest controls inside of controls. Although this arrangement makes these controls easy for the computer to interpret, they're difficult for average human beings.

All the examples in this chapter are for Internet Explorer 4.0 only. It is possible that Netscape will adopt some of Microsoft's ActiveX technology or that a plug-in such as NCompass will make it possible to use these tools with Netscape, but it's probably not a good bet to expect anyone except users of Internet Explorer 4.0 for Windows 95 and NT to be enjoying these controls anytime soon. Most of the examples in this chapter are written in VBScript. It's easier to control ActiveX objects from VBScript, because you can create subroutines to handle object events. This approach also helps keep Netscape from getting confused and producing JavaScript errors for objects it can't find, because it won't even attempt to run VBScript.

Transitions

Transitions are probably the easiest of the multimedia effects to use. They require little hassle except that they're connected to meaningless numbers. The available effects are listed in Table 10.1.

Table 10.1 Available Transition Effects

Name	Number
Box in	0
Box out	1
Circle in	2
Circle out	3
Wipe up	4
Wipe down	5
Wipe right	6
Wipe left	7
Vertical blinds	8
Horizontal blinds	9
Checkerboard across	10
Checkerboard down	11
Random dissolve	12
Split vertical in	13
Split vertical out	14
Split horizontal in	15
Split horizontal out	16
Strips left down	17
Strips left up	18
Strips right down	19
Strips right up	20
Random bars horizontal	21
Random bars vertical	22
Random	23

As you can see, you have many options. Unfortunately, you must always use the number to identify the effect you want, a practice that isn't exactly user-friendly. I suspect that most people will pick one or two favorite effects, rather than spray transitions across the screen.

You insert the ActiveX control as you do any other control, but you don't have to worry about specifying CODEBASE, which comes preinstalled with Internet Explorer 4.0. There's only one long hex number to deal with for this control:

```
<OBJECT ID=yourTransition CLASSID="CLSID:F0F70103-
6A8F-11d0-BD28-00A0C908DB96">
     <PARAM NAME="Transition" VALUE="10"></OBJECT>
```

There's only one parameter: Transition. You can set the value here or change it with scripting—it's simply yourTransition.Transition. The way you call it is a bit more complicated and needs an example:

```
<HTML>
<HEAD>
<TITLE>Transitions</TITLE>
</HEAD>
<BODY BGCOLOR=#FFFFFF>
<SCRIPT LANGUAGE="VBScript">
Dim Speed
Speed=750
sub Window_OnLoad
     breakNews.style.visibility="hidden"
     call Announce()
end sub
Sub breakNews_onclick
     breakNews.style.visibility="hidden"
     call Announce()
end Sub
```

```
Sub Announce()
    breakNews.stopPainting(yourTransition)
    breakNews.style.visibility="visible"
    breakNews.startPainting(Speed)
end sub
</SCRIPT>
<OBJECT ID=yourTransition CLASSID="CLSID:F0F70103-
6A8F-11d0-BD28-00A0C908DB96">
    <PARAM NAME="Transition" VALUE="10"></OBJECT>
<DIV id="breakNews" STYLE="color:red; font-
face:sans-serif; font-size:24; position:Absolute;
width:150; height:100%; left:10; top:10"> This just
in...</FONT></DIV>
<P> </P>
The battle for Dynamic HTML supremacy is heating up.
The contenders have entered the arena.  One strikes,
the other parries.  One feints, the other
overreacts. It's a heavy duty-battle here, folks!
</BODY></HTML>
```

This code will produce a bit of checkerboarding, a fairly nice effect.

The important parts of the script are the two functions breakNews_onclick and Announce. The first one sets the visibility of our headline to hidden, giving us something to transition from. The second function calls the stopPainting method with the name of the transition, makes the headline visible, and tells the transition to go ahead (startPainting) at a certain speed, given in milliseconds. You'll have to experiment to figure out which speed is best for a given transition in your particular situation. You don't have to break this effect into two sections, but it seems to help Internet Explorer keep up with the action.

Visual Filters

Visual filters are fun, and they make available some sophisticated effects for developers who don't want to go anywhere near Adobe Photoshop, Corel PhotoPaint, or other photo-retouching or painting tools. Visual filters can't do everything, but they make many different things possible. Because they're scriptable, you can make them happen or not happen, and you can change the way they happen. The only thing complicated about visual filters is that you must use (at least) two extraordinarily long and tedious CLASSIDs. Fortunately, cut and paste can spare you a lot of trouble once you've built a library of effects.

Our example is simple, operating on plain HTML text and transforming it into something bizarre (see Figures 10.1 and 10.2).

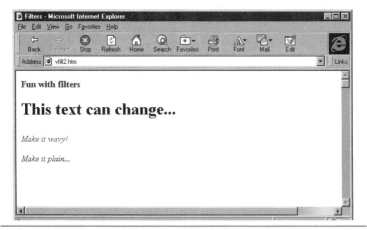

Figure 10.1 Happy normal HTML text.

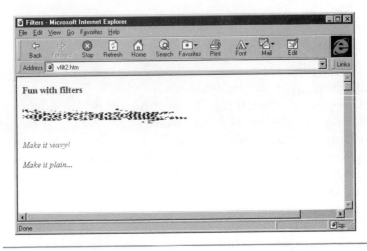

Figure 10.2 Thoroughly distorted, unreadable text.

You probably don't want to put all your text through the highly distorting wave effect, but it's a nice one to examine first. The code is simple except for the OBJECT tag:

```
<HTML>
<HEAD>
<TITLE>Filters</TITLE>
</HEAD>
<BODY BGCOLOR=#FFFFFF>
<H3 style="color:blue">Fun with filters</H3>
<DIV ID=target STYLE="LAYOUT: Fill; HEIGHT:50; LEFT:
100; TOP: 0; WIDTH: 700;ZINDEX:0"> <H1>This text can
change...</H1>
</DIV>
<P>
<P STYLE="color:red; font-style=italic"
ONCLICK="Wavy()"> Make it wavy!</P>
<P STYLE="color:blue; font-style=italic"
ONCLICK="Plain()"> Make it plain...</P>
<OBJECT ID="wavyWave"
```

```
     CLASSID="CLSID:DA9E9D23-3661-11D0-BDC2-
00A0C908DB96">
     <PARAM NAME="Effect0.CLSID" VALUE="{13B3D462-
43AD-11d0-BDC2-00A0C908DB96}">
</OBJECT>
<SCRIPT LANGUAGE="VBScript">
Sub window_onLoad()
     visual.bufferDepth = 8
End Sub
Sub Wavy
     wavyWave(0).Freq = 3
     wavyWave(0).LightStrength =40
     wavyWave(0).Strength = 20
     wavyWave(0).Add = 0
     target.Filter = Nothing
     target.Filter = wavyWave
End Sub
Sub Plain
     target.Filter = Nothing
End Sub
</SCRIPT>
</BODY>
</HTML>
```

The OBJECT tag contains two CLASSIDs. The first ID sets up the object as a filter, and the PARAM class ID makes it into a wave filter. You can combine multiple PARAM elements to create multipart effects; the effects take place in sequence. Effects must be named "Effect0", "Effect1", "Effect2", and so forth in sequence. You can define the effect's parameters here, or you can wait and assign them as properties in the script. Our example uses the scripting approach. Unfortunately, at this point in Internet Explorer's development you must assign the effect with a Window_onLoad routine rather than a filter attribute. Varying the parameters can have a dramatic effect on your results, and I highly recommend experimentation.

Table 10.2 lists the effects and their associated class ID values.

Table 10.2 Multimedia effects and associated class ID values

Name	Class ID	Description	Properties and Methods
Visual filters	DA9E9D23-3661-11D0-BDC2-00A0C908DB96	The main filter control. You call this in the OBJECT tag, and the rest are PARAMs.	All the other filters, as Effect*n*
Chromakey	7D0CD243-5910-11d0-823A-00A0C908DB96	Makes a particular color transparent (such as blue screening).	color (to make transparent)
Drop Shadow	D68FC8F4-6B17-11d0-80E6-00AA006EC537	Creates an offset shadow.	color (of shadow), OffX (x-offset), OffY(y-offset), Positive (0 shadows transparent pixels only)
Flip Horizontal	F6167903-5479-11d0-8236-00A0C908DB96	Makes a horizontal mirror image.	None
Flip Vertical	67741683-547D-11d0-8236-00A0C908DB96	Makes a vertical mirror image.	None
Grayscale	73F2B3A3-5474-11d0-8236-00A0C908DB96	Drops all color information	None
Invert	254E8EA4-4924-11d0-A787-00A0C91BBEE1	Reverses hue, saturation, and brightness.	None
Lights	F1631E43-47F8-11d0-80D4-00AA006EC537	Plays lights across target to your specs.	Methods: AddAmbient, AddCone, AddPoint, ChangeColor, ChangeStrength, Clear, MoveLight

Mask	4709E4E3-6B05-11d0-80E6-00AA006EC537	Turns an object into a transparent mask.	Color (to paint transparency)
Motion Blur	A380D684-4A3B-11d0-A787-00A0C91BBEE1	Gives the illusion an object is moving.	Add (true adds original image to blurred image), Direction (in degrees clockwise), Strength (pixel length of blur)
Opacity	3EE8A933-4D3F-11d0-97D0-00AA00BBB6E2	Allows you to set how transparent or opaque an object is.	Opacity (0=transparent, 100=totally opaque)
Shadow	6165A063-5F6A-11D0-B8F1-000000000000	Casts a shadow along an edge of the object.	Color (of shadow), Direction (in degrees clockwise)
Wave	13B3D462-43AD-11d0-BDC2-00A0C908DB96	Applies a sine wave to the object along the x axis.	Add (true adds original image to blurred), Freq (number of waves to apply), light (in percent), offset (0=0, 25=90°), strength (intensity)
XRay	45588FF3-51FA-11d0-8236-00A0C908DB96	Reduces an object to edges.	None

Paths

The Paths control provides some of the easiest animation I've seen. In the past, developers who needed to move objects along a simple path had to resort to Java or Java-based tools. The Paths control makes it all much easier, letting you move ordinary HTML objects around the page. I've brought back one of the bricks from Chapter 7 to dance around the page for our viewing pleasure (see Figure 10.3).

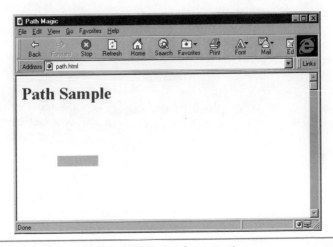

Figure 10.3 Brick in motion.

The code is simple:

```
<HTML>
<HEAD>
<TITLE>Path Magic</TITLE>
</HEAD>
<BODY BGCOLOR=#FFFFFF>
<H1 STYLE="color:blue">Path Sample</H1>
<IMG ID=brick SRC="bluegray.gif"
STYLE="position:absolute;LEFT: 15; TOP: 70">
<OBJECT ID="path"  CLASSID="CLSID:E0E3CC60-6A80-
11D0-9B40-00A0C903AA7F">
<PARAM NAME=AutoStart VALUE=-1>
<PARAM NAME=TickInterval VALUE=50>
<PARAM NAME=EdgeAction VALUE="2">
<PARAM NAME=XSeries
VALUE="0,20;20,100;30,100;50,40;80,10">
<PARAM NAME=YSeries
VALUE="20,80;35,100;40,240;55,240;80,60">
</OBJECT>
<SCRIPT LANGUAGE="VBScript">
Sub Window_onLoad
```

```
path.Target = brick.Style
End Sub
</SCRIPT>
</BODY>
</HTML>
```

All the action takes place in the object except for the small intervention in the window_onLoad routine that connects the brick to the path object. The AutoStart parameter tells the Path to start moving the object immediately. If this parameter were set to zero, the Path object would wait until its Play() method was explicitly called. The TickInterval parameter sets an interval (in milliseconds) after which an internal timer will make our brick jump to the next step in the path. You can also send ticks manually using the Tick() method. The EdgeAction parameter tells the path to wrap to the beginning and continue along the same path. If EdgeAction had been set to 1, the brick would have reversed itself and followed the path backward, bouncing again when it reached the beginning. If the parameter is set to zero, the brick stops at the end of the path.

The XSeries and YSeries parameters specify the actual path. Our brick lurches about, because the X and Y values don't make any particular sense. The values are grouped in pairs, with the pairs separated by semicolons and the members of each pair separated by commas. The first number specifies at which tick the object should be at a certain location; the second number is the location. The computer interpolates intermediate paths to make the action fairly smooth.

Structured Graphics

The Structured Graphics control brings a different kind of graphic to the Web: vector graphics, which are defined by shapes and fills. Internet Explorer isn't the only tool offering these kinds of effects on the Web; Macromedia's Shockwave includes a similar, equally small vector graphics tool (formerly FutureSplash) as one part of its many offerings. Microsoft's is interesting, however, in its programmability. Each of these graphics is a program in its own right, and you can use scripting to add to the graphic after it's finished setting itself up. (This feature didn't work at press time, so I'm afraid you'll have to settle for canned graphics.)

The big advantage of vector graphics is that it allows you to put a lot of information into a very small space. Bitmaps offer precision and photorealism, but they take up lots and lots of space and precious bandwidth. With vector graphics, you need only send a brief set of instructions telling the computer what kind of shape to draw where. Because Microsoft has built the engine into Internet Explorer (as an ActiveX object), it doesn't take much effort to make this work. The following example uses the Structured Graphics tool to put a few shapes on the screen, including some text.

```
<HTML>
<HEAD>
<TITLE>Structured Graphics</TITLE>
</HEAD>
<BODY BGCOLOR=#FFFFFF>
<H3 STYLE="color:blue">Structured Graphics
Sample</H3>
<TABLE><TR><TD>
<P id=Polygonal>Polygon </P>
<OBJECT ID=Polygon1
STYLE="HEIGHT:80;WIDTH:110" CLASSID="CLSID:5FD6A143-
372A-11D0-A521-0080C78FEE85">
<PARAM NAME="Line0001" VALUE="SetLineColor(0,0,0)">
<PARAM NAME="Line0002"
VALUE="SetFillColor(255,0,0,0,0,255)">
```

```
<PARAM NAME="Line0003" VALUE="SetFillStyle(1)">
<PARAM NAME="Line0004" VALUE="SetLineStyle(1)">
<PARAM NAME="Line0005"
VALUE="Polygon(8,10,20,10,30,20,30,45,30,40,10,40,10
,30,0,20,0,0)"> </OBJECT>
<P>Rectangle (Rect)</P>
<OBJECT ID=sgRect1
STYLE="HEIGHT:70; WIDTH:110"
CLASSID="CLSID:5FD6A143-372A-11D0-A521-
0080C78FEE85">
<PARAM NAME="Line0001"
VALUE="SetLineColor(255,255,255)">
<PARAM NAME="Line0002"
VALUE="SetFillColor(255,0,0,0,0,255)">
<PARAM NAME="Line0003" VALUE="SetFillSTYLE(1)">
<PARAM NAME="Line0004" VALUE="SetLineSTYLE(1)">
<PARAM NAME="Line0005" VALUE="Rect(0,0,60,30,0)">
</OBJECT>
</TD><TD><HR WIDTH=150><TD>
<P>Text</p>
<OBJECT ID=Text1
STYLE="HEIGHT:80;WIDTH:150;"
CLASSID="CLSID:5FD6A143-372A-11D0-A521-
0080C78FEE85">
<PARAM NAME="Line0001" VALUE="SetFont('Arial',
36,700,1,0,0)">
<PARAM NAME="Line0002"
VALUE="SetLineColor(255,0,255)">
<PARAM NAME="Line0003"
VALUE="SetFillColor(255,0,0,0,0,255)">
<PARAM NAME="Line0004" VALUE="SetFillSTYLE(1)">
<PARAM NAME="Line0005" VALUE="SetLineSTYLE(1)">
<PARAM NAME="Line0006" VALUE="Text('HTML',-25,0,0)">
</OBJECT>
<P>Oval</P>
<OBJECT ID=Oval1
STYLE="HEIGHT:70;WIDTH:110;"
```

```
CLASSID = "CLSID:5FD6A143-372A-11D0-A521-
0080C78FEE85">
<PARAM NAME="Line0001"
VALUE="SetLineColor(255,255,255)">
<PARAM NAME="Line0002"
VALUE="SetFillColor(255,0,0,0,0,255)">
<PARAM NAME="Line0003" VALUE="SetFillSTYLE(1)">
<PARAM NAME="Line0004" VALUE="SetLineSTYLE(1)">
<PARAM NAME="Line0005" VALUE="Oval(0,-25,20,50,0)">
</OBJECT>
</TD></TR>
<SCRIPT LANGUAGE=VBScript>
</SCRIPT>
</BODY>
</HTML>
```

The results aren't beautiful (see Figure 10.4).

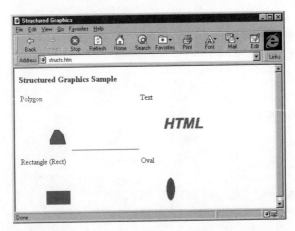

Figure 10.4 Assorted structured graphics.

There are several important things to note about the way this control works. First, it doesn't matter what you want to draw; the CLASSID is always the same. The kind of drawing gets set as one of the lines in the program. Second, the parameters are issued like lines in a program, and you must use the LINEnnn formula for NAME attributes for your commands if you want to hard-code them into the HTML. They will be executed in sequence. (Be sure to specify fill and line color before drawing your object, or your results may be strange.)

You should check the Microsoft documentation for the full details on all 22 of this control's methods (from Arc to Translate) and their required parameters. You'll also find out whether they've become programmable, and, if so, how programmable.

Sequencer

The Sequencer control is the last control we'll cover in depth, and I must admit that it's my favorite. The Sequencer makes it easy to set up complex routines that previously required a lot of work with the setTimeout method, as we did in Chapter 4. The Sequencer makes it possible to fire a wide array of exciting routines using scripts and ActiveX objects. Our example is simple, but the potential for this control (especially in a kiosk) is endless.

Our example uses a single routine to handle the Sequencer's output, but it should give you a picture of how to program the Sequencer and put it to use in more exciting situations.

```
<HTML>
<HEAD>
<TITLE>Sequencing Magic</TITLE>
</HEAD>
<BODY BGCOLOR=#FFFFFF>
<H3 id=headliner>Sequencing Magic</H3>
<SCRIPT LANGUAGE="VBScript">
```

```
Sub window_OnLoad
    call seqMain.Play()
End Sub
Sub VBPlay(A)
    if A mod 2=1 then
headliner.style.visibility="Hidden"
    if A mod 2=0 then
headliner.style.visibility="Visible"
    if A=2 then headliner.style.color="#FF00FF"
    if A=3 then headliner.style.color="#00FF00"
End Sub
Sub Window_OnUnload
    seqMain.Stop()
End Sub
</SCRIPT>
<OBJECT ID="seqMain" CLASSID="CLSID:37992B41-F5E3-
11CF-97DF-00A0C90FEE54" STYLE="position: absolute;
TOP:0; LEFT:0; WIDTH:20; HEIGHT:20">
<PARAM NAME="Action1" VALUE="AT 0:0.0,1,0:0.0
VBPlay(0),1">
<PARAM NAME="Action2" VALUE="AT 0:0.200,1,0:0.0
VBPlay(1),1">
<PARAM NAME="Action3" VALUE="AT 0:0.400,1,0:0.0
VBPlay(2),1">
<PARAM NAME="Action4" VALUE="AT 0:0.800,4,0:1.0
VBPlay(3),1">
<PARAM NAME="Action5" VALUE="AT 0:1.500,4,0:1.0
VBPlay(4),1">
</OBJECT>
</BODY>
</HTML>
```

The window_onLoad and window_onUnload start and stop the Sequencer, respectively. It's always a good idea to shut down an object this way, although it didn't produce any errors on my machine when I went from page to page without turning it off. The Play() routine responds to input from the Sequencer, which calls it and sends it a number. As we'll see, the Sequencer sends Play() 3 and 4 a few times. If you watch this example run, you'll see the different intervals between actions and catch the repeats at the end.

Again, the control itself is the center of the action. After the obligatory CLASSID, the parameters bring us to the real story: which actions should take place and when. As with the Structured Graphics control, the parameters write a sort of program, and all the name values must be in the format Action*n*, where *n* is a sequential integer. The VALUE attribute must start with AT, followed by the start time, the number of times this action will repeat, how often it should repeat, the action to take, and a tiebreak number that assigns priority if two actions collide on the same millisecond.

The time at which the action should take place is relative to the time the Sequencer Play() method was first called, specified as follows:

```
minutes: seconds.milliseconds
```

The repeat value can be zero or 1 (no repeats), -1 (infinite repeats), or a positive number of times the action should take place. The next value is in the same format as the starting time and represents the amount of time the Sequencer should wait after the first time the action takes place to repeat it. If you use zero, it's interpreted as soon as possible," which can tie up the user's machine. The next parameter is the action, either a script function call (with parameters included) or an ActiveX control call in this form:

```
object.method(parameter-list)
```

This means that you can sequence almost anything you can program into a Dynamic HTML page. That should give you enough possibilities to work with for a long time.

Other Controls

Microsoft has released a few other controls and may add more as Internet Explorer matures. Two released controls don't appear to work (their demos won't work on my machines at all) but sound promising. The Sprite control gives you easy access to powerful graphics routines for creating flipbook animation on your page. The Mixer control extends the media to music, making it easy to load and play WAV files simultaneously on multiple channels. This makes it possible to create a page that combines background music, for example, with interviews in a documentary or sound effects in a Web game. Combined with the Sequencer, this control will let you create interesting soundscapes, although as usual you'll have to wait for the files to download.

ActiveX controls can make possible many exciting effects, and Microsoft has made them easier to use by including this starter set with the Internet Explorer. If you're developing with Windows generally, you can also write programs that expose the same methods and properties and thereby access these same controls on any machine that has Internet Explorer 4.

For updates to this information, keep an eye on MIS:Press' Web site (http://www.mispress.com/dynamichtml).

N O T E

CHAPTER 11

Binding Data
to Your Documents

Multimedia controls are fun and a great way to spice up your pages, but data binding makes it easy to get real work done over the Web. Microsoft's latest additions to its set of tools for connecting databases to Web pages give developers and network administrators new flexibility and new power to build stable, user-friendly applications. Suddenly, you don't have to connect the database to the Web server directly, and you don't need to burden your Web server with the overhead of managing and manipulating database requests. That task can be distributed to the client machines, taking advantage of the processing power of the user's own machine rather than slowing down the server for everyone.

As it did with the multimedia controls, Microsoft has implemented the data connection controls as ActiveX objects that are included with Internet Explorer 4. Microsoft is also making it possible for developers to use JavaBeans, a new Java component specification from Sun, to connect to databases with these tools. In addition, Microsoft has proposed extensions to HTML that make it possible to include data objects from multiple sources on a page. In the long term, some of these new tools may also be available in Netscape and other browsers. Like

Dynamic HTML and the document object model itself, these standards are currently before the W3 committee and are subject to change. They may eventually be supported by other browsers, but, as usual, syntax may be inconsistent. As a result, most of this chapter will be devoted to Internet Explorer and other Microsoft products. Although some sections may be applicable to more general Internet practice, most of this chapter aims to help you develop intranet business applications with Internet Explorer 4.0.

NOTE   Because this is a single chapter in an introductory book, the examples are fairly simple, and references are given for advanced documentation. This chapter could easily become an entire book, and I'm sure one will appear soon. The Java Beans information is not yet available. Check the Microsoft Sitebuilder site (http://www.microsoft.com/sitebuilder/) for further information.

A Quick Introduction to Databases and the Web

If you've never worked with a database more complex than a simple list, the world of relational and object databases may seem alien to you. Fortunately, one of the tools we'll cover, the Tabular Data Control, gives you new options without requiring you to learn the ins and outs of relational database development. If you're working with complex data, though, you'll quickly find that you need powerful tools to help manage it.

NOTE   If you are already familiar with relational databases, SQL, ODBC, and client-server development, you may want to skip to the next section, which details Microsoft's approach to solving the problems outlined here. If you don't have any interest in dealing with data more complex than a list, you may also want to skip ahead to the "HTML Data Binding" and "Tabular Data Control" sections of this chapter.

Relational databases were developed from tools created in the 1970s and matured in the 1980s, becoming the predominant way for businesses to store easily structured critical business data. At first, relational databases existed primarily on mainframes and large servers, but over the past ten years they've arrived on the desktop and have become much more approachable. Microsoft Access helped thousands of small databases sprout on users' desks, letting people keep track of and share megabytes of data easily (and often to the frustration of MIS managers who couldn't control their growth). If you've never used a relational database, you'll probably find Access the best place to start, because it will walk you through the difficult parts of creating a database application with reasonably simple and powerful graphical tools. (Our examples for the rest of this section and most of the rest of this chapter will be created in Access. In addition to being easy to use, it connects most easily to the Microsoft products we'll be using here.)

Tables

A relational database is built of tables made up of rows and columns that contain data. The data is linked by *keys*—pieces of information unique to each row of a column—that can be used to identify rows and combine information across tables. For example, here are three simple tables in Access:

- Students: StudentID, FirstName, LastName
- Classes: ClassID, ClassTitle
- Rosters: RosterID, StudentID, ClassID

As you can see, each of these tables has an ID number, which we'll let the database create. This ID number makes it easy for us to refer to specific students, classes, and rosters without having to go through a complicated search by name. Such a search takes the computer much more time and is also less reliable; typos can keep you from finding what you want. The students table and the classes table don't link to each other directly; there aren't any entries in the students table for the classes a student is taking, nor are there entries in the classes table to indicate which students are in the class. Instead, the roster table holds that information, linking students to classes (see Figure 11.1).

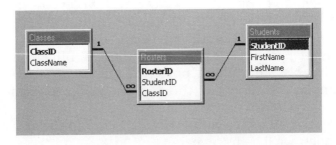

Figure 11.1 Tables with relationships.

Queries

To find out which students are taking which classes, we run a query. Queries constitute most of the action in a relational database, letting you read, filter, update, and add data. For most of our work with our database connectivity tools we'll use queries. Learning to use queries (and Structured Query Language, or SQL, the language they're usually written in) is most of the battle of learning to work with relational databases. You don't necessarily need to learn SQL. You can use Access or another tool to create queries and then copy the SQL that your tool has created.

NOTE

If you need a quick but thorough introduction to SQL for Web development, you may want to read Edward Sfreddo's chapter (Chapter 17) of Reaz Hoque's *Practical JavaScript Programming* (MIS:Press, 1997). It's aimed at Netscape LiveWire developers, but pages 415–431 are the best quick reference to SQL that I've found yet, providing much more information than I give here.

We'll use the tables we created earlier to find out which courses students are taking. The SQL statement is (at least at first) pretty simple:

```
SELECT Students.FirstName, Students.LastName,
Classes.ClassName
FROM Students
INNER JOIN (Classes INNER JOIN Rosters ON
Classes.ClassID = Rosters.ClassID) ON
Students.StudentID = Rosters.StudentID;
```

The INNER JOIN part of it, unfortunately, is messy, and that's why I suggest you use the tools at first. We'll apply the preceding statement to tables with the data shown in Tables 11.1, 11.2, and 11.3.

Table 11.1 The Students Table

StudentsID	FirstName	LastName
1	Jim	Marks
2	Rachel	Abernathy
3	Karen	Miller
4	Thomas	Hart

Table 11.2 The Classes Table

ClassID	ClassName
1	Introductory Spanish
2	Introductory Calculus
3	Advanced Calculus

Table 11.3 The Rosters Table

RosterID	StudentID	ClassID
1	1	1
2	1	2
3	2	3
4	3	1
5	3	3
6	4	2

Our results are shown in Table 11.4.

Table 11.4 Query Results

FirstName	LastName	ClassName
Jim	Marks	Introductory Spanish
Jim	Marks	Introductory Calculus
Rachel	Abernathy	Advanced Calculus
Karen	Miller	Introductory Spanish
Karen	Miller	Advanced Calculus
Thomas	Hart	Introductory Calculus

This is just the beginning. You can change this query to ask for the courses Thomas Hart is taking or to find out who's taking Advanced Calculus. Any time you want to read the information from a database, you'll use the SELECT statement in one form or another. The syntax is simple, although I recommend that you start with Access or another tool to create your queries. Data is added to the database with INSERT statements, changed with UPDATE statements, and removed with DELETE statements. For most of this chapter, we'll use SELECT statements, but you can use the others as appropriate.

Applications

The most important part of a database, at least to a programmer, is the underlying data structure. If there isn't a solid structure, the data won't make sense to either the computer or the user. To the user, though, the interface is the important part, making it possible to work with the information. This division has worked itself out in the technology world to produce client-server computing, in which each side of a database application can do what it's good at. On the client side, developers create friendly programs that make it easy to find, manage, and manipulate data. On the server side, other developers create complex database systems that can store all that data and relay it to the client whenever the client needs it. In this way, the front end (client) of the database can look like the GUI tools users are familiar with, and the back end (server) can include industrial-strength data management without wasting processor cycles on niceties such as windows, toolbars, and forms.

The Web has taken all this to a new level, because HTML provides much of the graphical interface users are accustomed to without demanding much effort from the machine. Dynamic HTML has taken this another step further, making it possible to create interfaces with a level of functionality comparable to Windows or the Macintosh for certain applications. HTML promises to be the medium of choice for client-server applications, but it still lacks the ability to connect to and work with data at the server. Another set of tools included in Internet Explorer promises to move us past that bottleneck, letting us move much of the work needed to manipulate data from the server to the client, allowing us much more flexibility than before.

Old Technology, New Technology

We're going to back up technologically a little so that we can consider Microsoft's newest tools—the Tabular Data Control (TDC) and Advanced Data Control (ADC)—in the light of their server-side predecessors Internet Database Connectivity (IDC/HTX) and Active Server Pages (ASP). Using TDC and ADC requires that you use Microsoft's Internet Explorer; IDC/HTX and ASP require that you use Microsoft's Internet Information Server (IIS) 3.0 or its cousins, Peer Web Services for NT Workstation and the Personal Web Server for Windows 95. If you can't count on your users running Internet Explorer, you may want to examine the Microsoft server-side solutions closely. If you happen to be using an IIS, they offer a relatively easy path to database connectivity and publishing.

On the Server Side

Although IIS supports all the technologies we listed in Chapter 1, Microsoft decided to offer a few additional techniques for creating dynamic pages based on databases. The two that have lasted are IDC (and HTX, an associated standard for HTML templates), which is fairly simple, and ASP, which requires more tools and more horsepower on the server machine. An IDC solution consists of two files: one (with the extension .idc) that includes the query information, and one (with the .htx extension) that provides a template for posting the data. An ASP solution includes one file, which acts as a program that creates pages on demand. Neither IDC or ASP is compatible with CGI or other non-Microsoft gateway standards.

ASP is more flexible and more complex, providing a much more comprehensive solution that allows you to build complete applications for the Web in a structured programming environment. It offers much of the "live" power of ADC, as we'll see later in this chapter. Unfortunately, ASP also requires a good deal more knowledge of database and BASIC programming environments than IDC or any of the other technologies in this chapter, and it functions quite differently. Developers interested in building Active Server Pages should be prepared to use heavier-duty development environments, such as Microsoft Visual Studio and Microsoft Visual InterDev. Because of these requirements, we'll focus on IDC.

NOTE Finding documentation for these two solutions is difficult. *Building Applications with Microsoft Access 97*, the manual that ships with Access, includes about 10 pages of information that can get you started. Other sources on IDC are Chapter 8 of the IIS documentation (which doesn't come with the Windows 95 Personal Web Server) and a Microsoft "Job Forum" white paper at http://www.microsoft.com/accessdev/AccWhite/ jobforpa.htm. ASP documentation is available at http://www.microsoft.com/IIS/.

One of the nicest things about ASP and IDC is that it's easy to create certain kinds of pages with Microsoft Access. Access includes wizards for exporting forms and datasheets to both IDC/HTX and ASP, making it simple to create basic applications without having to do much work. Unfortunately, Microsoft hasn't done nearly so well in the reports department, allowing you to export reports only to static pages. What's more, reports are broken into individual pages, forcing you to click from page 1 to page 2. Although this approach preserves page headers and footers, it makes navigating and printing long documents tedious or nearly impossible. IDC/HTX doesn't offer as many frills as the standard Access report writer, but IDC/HTX makes it possible for developers to publish live data to the Web. We'll use it here to create a simple reporting solution for our class tracking database.

The step is to make the database available to ODBC, the Open Database Connectivity standard. The control panel on your Windows 95 or NT machine has an icon marked **32-bit ODBC**. Open it and you'll see a list of drivers. If your database (probably Access) isn't listed, check your documentation and find out how to install it. If you can't connect through ODBC, you can't use IDC. If it is there, click the **Add** button. You choose which database driver you want to use, and then the somewhat daunting dialog box shown in Figure 11.2 appears.

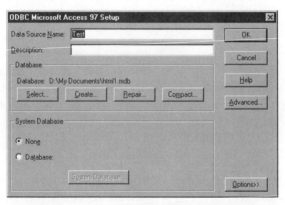

Figure 11.2 Adding a database to ODBC.

Enter a simple data source name (DSN) for your database. A single word is probably easiest, because we'll use this name to refer to the database from now on. In my case, I called it **test**. You can also enter a description if you like. Choose your database by clicking **Select** and browsing on your hard drive to find it. When you've finished, press **OK** button. (If the database is open in another application, you'll get an error. Close it and try again.)

Next, we create our .idc and .htx files. For this example, I've used the Access Save as HTML command on the query we created in the previous section. I specified which query to export, told Access the DSN, and let it do the rest of the work. (You must put these files into a directory with execute permissions, such as the scripts directory.) The IDC file looks like this:

```
Datasource:Test
Template:RosterList_1.htx
SQLStatement:SELECT Students.FirstName,
Students.LastName, Classes.ClassName
+FROM Students INNER JOIN (Classes INNER JOIN
Rosters ON Classes.ClassID = Rosters.ClassID) ON
Students.StudentID = Rosters.StudentID;
Password:
Username:
```

It specifies the ODBC data source, the HTML template, the SQL statement (note the + used on the FROM statement, because it's on a separate line), and a password and username if they're needed to get into a secured database. The password and username are optional but are included in plain text if they're needed. This arrangement can create many problems for you if you're working with secured databases; make sure that the .idc file is in a directory where users can execute it but not read it. If you're developing an intranet using Microsoft technology (NT networking and SQL Server), the Web server can also get the user's Microsoft authentication (from when the user logged into the machine) and use that to attempt to collect the database information.

You can modify the SQL in this file any way you like. You can even make it add, modify, or delete data by coding the appropriate query. (Access won't help you do this. It exports only SELECT queries.) To use these other features you must create the query, copy the SQL, and create the IDC file by hand with a text editor. Remember to include the + sign on every line after a return, or you'll get strange generic errors from the server about failed queries and missing parameters. You can easily make IDC files search or modify based on information returned by a form: just have the FORM method POST the data to the IDC file, and all of its fields will be accessible to your IDC file as parameters. For example, if the user submitted a form with a lastName field to this IDC, you could search based on that entry by adding the following line between the SELECT and the +FROM lines of the query:

```
+WHERE LastName=%lastName%
```

It's extremely simple, and it works.

The HTX file Access creates is also simple, although it piles in font and color information that takes up a lot of real estate:

```
<HTML>
<HEAD>
<META HTTP-EQUIV="Content-Type"
CONTENT="text/html;charset=windows-1252">
<TITLE>RosterList</TITLE>
</HEAD>
<BODY>
<TABLE BORDER=1 BGCOLOR=#ffffff CELLSPACING=0><FONT
FACE="Arial" COLOR=#000000>
<CAPTION><B>RosterList</B></CAPTION>
<THEAD>
<TR>
<TH BGCOLOR=#c0c0c0 BORDERCOLOR=#000000 ><FONT
SIZE=2 FACE="Arial"
COLOR=#000000>FirstName</FONT></TH>
<TH BGCOLOR=#c0c0c0 BORDERCOLOR=#000000 ><FONT
SIZE=2 FACE="Arial"
COLOR=#000000>LastName</FONT></TH> <TH
BGCOLOR=#c0c0c0 BORDERCOLOR=#000000 ><FONT SIZE=2
FACE="Arial" COLOR=#000000>ClassName</FONT></TH>
</TR>
</THEAD>
```

```
<TBODY>
<%BeginDetail%>
<TR VALIGN=TOP>
<TD BORDERCOLOR=#c0c0c0 ><FONT SIZE=2 FACE="Arial"
COLOR=#000000><%FirstName%><BR></FONT></TD>
<TD BORDERCOLOR=#c0c0c0 ><FONT SIZE=2 FACE="Arial"
COLOR=#000000><%LastName%><BR></FONT></TD> <TD
BORDERCOLOR=#c0c0c0 ><FONT SIZE=2 FACE="Arial"
COLOR=#000000><%ClassName%><BR></FONT></TD>
</TR>
<%EndDetail%>
</TBODY>
<TFOOT></TFOOT>
</TABLE>
</BODY>
</HTML>
```

Most of this page is ordinary, and you can customize it any way you like. Access has already created table headers that contain the names of the columns. (You can't do that part dynamically with any of the tools in this chapter.) The part that's most interesting is the *detail section* between the <%BeginDetail%> and <%EndDetail%> tags. Whatever you put between these tags will repeat as many times as there are records in the dataset returned by the IDC file. This feature makes it easy to create tables that include a complete listing of the query contents, although you can use a simple down-the-page list if you'd rather present the information that way. If there are no records in the list, the detail section will be skipped. Individual fields are referenced by placing their names in <%xxxx%> tags.

When you open these files (you request the IDC file and put a question mark at the end of the URL), you'll see the display shown in Figure 11.3.

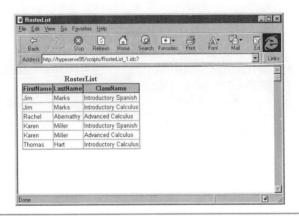

Figure 11.3 Table created with IDC/HTX technology.

This isn't much yet, but it's only a small beginning. You can include if...then statements in your tags. For example, if a first name was missing, you could make the server notify you of that problem with the following:

```
<%if FirstName EQ
""%>UNKNOWN<%else%><%FirstName%><%endif%>
```

You can also check (in your <%if%> statement only) which record is being listed by using the <%CurrentRecord%> variable and find out how many records are available by using the <%MaxRecords%> variable. If you passed query information to the .idc file in the first place, you can retrieve that as <%idc.nameOfVariable%>. Those variables will remain constant whatever part of the document you're in, detail or not. For more information, explore the IIS documentation, Chapter 8.

One last word on IDC and HTX. You can use Microsoft FrontPage 2.0 to edit these files, although it's much more useful for HTX than for IDC. All it does with IDC is to verify the syntax; it won't help you build queries or connect to databases. For HTX, though, FrontPage provides a number of tools that make it easier to manage if...then statements and data fields.

T I P If you ever need to dump database information to static HTML files, IDC can provide a simple solution. Because the server parses all these strange <%xxx%> tags, by the time your browser receives the document it's become a clean file, containing only the formatted data. You can save these pages from your browser to regular HTML files and put them on whatever kind of server you need. This approach isn't convenient for files you update every day, but for occasional updates I find it to be workable. After all, nearly anything is better than the standard HTML report output that's built into Access.

On the Client Side: HTML Data Binding

Microsoft's client side tools are similar to the IDC standards in many ways. They allow you to do similar kinds of things but make them easier to adjust to user needs. The Microsoft tools also let you distribute processing between the server and the client, and they give you more options for setting up your network infrastructure. They aren't the answer in every situation, especially if you don't control which browser is being used, but they open up many new vistas.

Before we get to the ActiveX controls you use to connect to your data source, we'll take a look at Microsoft's proposed data-binding extensions to HTML. We'll cover the event handlers that accompany them when we reach the ADC control to which they apply. For the most part, the HTML extensions provide similar functionality to the <%xxx%> tags described in the IDC section, although with a few different quirks and a different kind of scriptability.

Microsoft has divided the world of HTML data binding into data sources and data consumers. The data consumers are all tags we've seen before—TABLE, DIV, SPAN, SELECT, INPUT, TEXTAREA, MARQUEE, IMG, OBJECT, and APPLET—but Microsoft adds three new attributes to the mix. DATASRC applies to all these consumers, DATAFLD applies to all these consumers except TABLE, and DATAFORMATAS applies only to SPAN, DIV, and MARQUEE.

The DATASRC attribute specifies where an object should get its data. This attribute will always be a reference to another object: the Tabular Data control, the Advanced Data control explored later, or something else, possibly a JavaBean. DATASRC takes the pound sign and the NAME attribute of the object source as its value. For example, if a document contained an object in which NAME="ClassList" as a datasource object, a table that was to list the entire set of data included in that object could be set up as follows:

```
<TABLE DATASRC="#ClassList"><!--Table info here-
></TABLE>
```

The table would contain as many rows as necessary to list the contents of the data object, and all the DATAFLD attributes contained in the table tags would inherit their DATASRC from the TABLE tag. Generally, objects enclosed by a tag with a DATASRC attribute will inherit that DATASRC.

DATAFLD is even simpler. It fills the default text of an object with the contents of the field it specifies. To continue the preceding example, if SalesTable contained the columns FirstName, LastName, and ClassName, you could list the entire table with the following code:

```
<TABLE DATASRC="#ClassList">
<TR>
<TD><SPAN DATAFLD="FirstName"></SPAN></TD>
<TD><SPAN DATAFLD="LastName"></SPAN></TD>
<TD><SPAN DATAFLD="ClassName"></SPAN></TD>
</TABLE>
```

The DATASRC binding on the table would make it repeat as many rows as necessary, and the DATAFLD attribute would fill the SPANs with data. DATAFLD can be especially interesting when used with form elements such as radio buttons and select boxes; the value of DATAFLD will become the default choice in the box or the button set. This makes it easy to create forms with values you can modify later.

DATAFORMATAS is useful in several situations. It takes three values: "text", "html", and "none". The default is "text". If you're including HTML codes in your data and you need them to be parsed by the browser, specify DATAFORMATAS="html". If you've included nontextual information, such as numbers, specifying DATA-FORMATAS="none" should ensure predictable display in the data's original format.

Tabular Data Control

Now that we have the means to display data, it's time to look at the ways to acquire that data. For Internet Explorer 4, Microsoft supplied an easy way to collect data and a more complicated but more powerful way to collect, manage, and modify data. The Tabular Data Control, the simpler way, provides a useful solution to small problems. It allows the user to connect to delimited text files and view them using the HTML extensions we've just covered. In addition, the TDC provides simple sorting and filtering controls to help users navigate large quantities of data. Although it doesn't provide any server-side functions (no changes can be made to the server database), the TDC makes it easy to present catalog and other information for user browsing and selection.

Delimited files are much simpler than the databases we've been discussing. They don't have any linked tables; they're made up of one table, which is listed in a text file. All entries are separated by a delimiter character, usually a comma. (You can specify any character, a useful feature if your data is riddled with commas.) The first line of the table usually lists the column headings, and all the other lines are rows of data under those column headings. Our class roster query results, for example, would look like this:

```
FirstName, LastName, ClassName
Jim, Marks, Introductory Spanish
Jim, Marks, Introductory Calculus
Rachel, Abernathy, Advanced Calculus
Karen, Miller, Introductory Spanish
Karen, Miller, Advanced Calculus
Thomas, Hart, Introductory Calculus
```

It's easy to create delimited files from databases or spreadsheets, which usually have an option to export the data as text. Although this isn't cutting-edge technology, it's much simpler to work with. If you have data that needs to be refreshed only occasionally (or, better yet, never), it's easy to post information this way. Even if people can't get to it with your sharply designed Internet Explorer 4.0 Web site, you can still post the URL for the data, which users can download and analyze with their own tools.

Connecting this table to your Web page is also simple. You create a TDC object whose DataURL value is the URL of this text file:

```
<OBJECT id=ClassList CLASSID="clsid:333C7BC4-460F-
11D0-BC04-0080C7055A83">
<PARAM NAME="DataURL" VALUE="ClassList.txt">
<PARAM NAME="UseHeader" VALUE="True">
</OBJECT>
```

This object will link smoothly to the examples we used earlier for the DATASRC and DATAFLD attributes. This object has 13 properties and one method. The two most important properties are used here. DataURL specifies the URL from which the object should draw the delimited data. In this case, ClassList.txt is in the same directory as the file referencing it. The UseHeader property indicates that this file's first row is column names, and that lets us refer to the columns in DATAFLD attributes as "FirstName", "LastName", and "ClassName" instead of

"Column1", "Column2", and "Column3". (The Column*x*-style names will still work, though.) The other available properties are listed in Table 11.6.

Table 11.6 TDC Properties

Property	Description
CharSet	Defaults to Latin1. Specifies the character set of the data.
EscapeChar	Allows you to specify a character to "escape" the delimiter character. If you specified "/", then "eggs/, beaten" would enter as "eggs, beaten".
FieldDelim	Allows you to specify the delimiter character. A comma is the default.
Language	An ISO 369 language specifier for the file. The default is "eng-us."
RowDelim	Specifies the character at the end of the row. Default is a newline.
FilterColumn	Specifies column to use for filtering.
FilterCriterion	Specifies relationship between column data and FilterValue. Default is "=".
FilterValue	Gives the value that FilterColumn is compared with when filtering.
SortAscending	If true, the column in SortColumn will be sorted A–Z. If false, Z–A.
SortColumn	Specifies which column to sort. By default, "", which does no sorting.
Reset (Method)	Method to call after setting sort or filter criteria. Refreshes all data fields.

As a demonstration, we'll create a page that uses the TDC and our class data, allowing the user to view, filter, and sort data. Our HTML looks like this:

```
<HTML>
<HEAD><TITLE>TDC Demonstration</TITLE></HEAD>
<BODY BGCOLOR=#FFFFFF>
<H1>Class Roster Information</H1>
```

```
<OBJECT id=ClassList CLASSID="clsid:333C7BC4-460F-
11D0-BC04-0080C7055A83">
<PARAM NAME="DataURL" VALUE="ClassList.txt">
<PARAM NAME="UseHeader" VALUE="True">
</OBJECT>
<TABLE DATASRC=#ClassList BORDER=1>
<TR>
<TD><SPAN DATAFLD="FirstName"></SPAN></TD>
<TD><SPAN DATAFLD="LastName"></SPAN></TD>
<TD><SPAN DATAFLD="ClassName"></SPAN></TD>
</TR>
</TABLE>
</BODY></HTML>
```

The results aren't a multimedia spectacular, but it works
(see Figure 11.4).

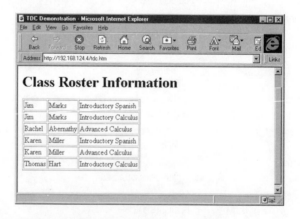

Figure 11.4 The TDC-generated table.

So far this is a handy way to present the class list.
Unfortunately, it will become unwieldy when we have more
than four students. We'll take advantage of the sorting
capabilities of the TDC first and then try the filtering. Both
functions are easy to use. You set the appropriate properties
and then call the data object's Reset() method.

```
<P STYLE="color:red"
onclick="SortIt('FirstName')">Sort by first name</P>
<P STYLE="color:blue"
onclick="SortIt('LastName')">Sort by last name</P>
<P STYLE="color:green"
onclick="SortIt('ClassName')">Sort by class name</P>
<SCRIPT LANGUAGE="JavaScript">
function SortIt(ColName){
ClassList.SortColumn=ColName;
ClassList.Reset();
}
</SCRIPT>
```

This simple sort method takes the column name and tells the TDC to sort the table (in ascending order, the default) by that column. You can try all three columns for entertainment. "Sort by class" produces the table shown in Figure 11.5.

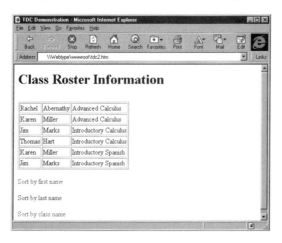

Figure 11.5 Table sorted by the class column.

Now we're getting worried, because we expect a deluge of students to come through any minute. We need to be able to enter only a student's last name and find out which courses the student is taking. We need to add a simple filter routine to let us do that:

```
Last Name:<INPUT TYPE="TEXT" ID="FilterName"
onchange="FilterIt()">
<INPUT TYPE="RESET" ID="FilterClr"
onclick="FilterClear()">
<SCRIPT LANGUAGE="JavaScript">
function FilterIt(){
  ClassList.FilterColumn="LastName";
  ClassList.FilterValue=FilterName.value;
  ClassList.Reset();
}
function FilterClear(){
  ClassList.FilterColumn="";
  ClassList.FilterValue="";
  ClassList.Reset();
}
</SCRIPT>
```

Our TDC page now lets us sort and filter the list at will (see Figure 11.6).

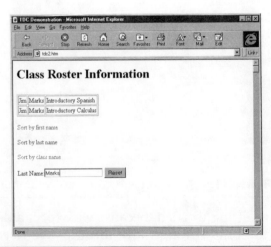

Figure 11.6 Class list with sorting and filtering.

All this sorting and filtering is interesting, but it seems that there should be a way to access the elements of the tabular data in the same way that we access the rest of our HTML document. Fortunately, the TDC lets you get to the data (read-only as usual) through its recordset object. It has two methods for moving through rows and two properties to let you know at which row the recordset is currently positioned. MovePrevious() moves you to the previous record; (for example, ClassList.recordset.MovePrevious()). MoveNext() takes you to the next record. The AbsolutePosition property returns the index number of the current row as an integer, and the RecordCount property returns the total number of rows.

In our example, we let the TABLE tag's DATASRC field manage the proper display of rows and fields. If, for example, we wanted to show only one row at a time, we'd use a different approach. Every data element would have both a DATASRC and a DATAFLD attribute, binding them directly to the TDC. We'd then use the TDC's recordset to manipulate which row was being displayed:

```
<HTML>
<HEAD><TITLE>TDC Demonstration</TITLE></HEAD>
<BODY BGCOLOR=#FFFFFF>
<H1>Class Roster Information</H1>
<OBJECT id=ClassList
     CLASSID="clsid:333C7BC4-460F-11D0-BC04-
0080C7055A83">
<PARAM NAME="DataURL" VALUE="ClassList.txt">
<PARAM NAME="UseHeader" VALUE="True">
</OBJECT>
First Name:<SPAN DATASRC=#ClassList
DATAFLD="FirstName"></SPAN><BR>
Last Name:<SPAN DATASRC=#ClassList
DATAFLD="LastName"></SPAN><BR>
```

```
Course: <SPAN DATASRC=#ClassList
DATAFLD="ClassName"></SPAN><BR>
<P><INPUT TYPE="Button" ID=previous VALUE="Previous"
onclick="goBack()"><INPUT TYPE="Button" ID=previous
VALUE="Next" onclick="goForward()"></P>
<SCRIPT LANGUAGE="JavaScript">
function goBack(){
if (ClassList.recordset.AbsolutePosition > 1)
{ClassList.recordset.MovePrevious();}
else {alert("This is the first record already!");}
}
function goForward(){
if (ClassList.recordset.AbsolutePosition <
ClassList.recordset.RecordCount)
{ClassList.recordset.MoveNext();}
else {alert("This is the last record already!");}
}
</SCRIPT>
</BODY></HTML>
```

Our results appear in Figure 11.7.

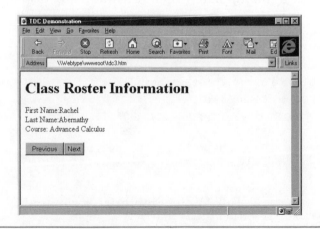

Figure 11.7 One row at a time.

It may not be the easiest way to view the data, but it's one possibility among many. Unfortunately, you can't yet reach the data directly with these methods. Asking the script for ClassList.recordset.FirstName, ClassList.FirstName, or even ClassList.recordset.Column1 returns an undefined value. I'm sure this oversight won't last very long. (You can get around it by binding your data to INPUT fields and checking their value property, but this technique isn't always convenient.)

There's one other way you may want to use the TDC. Before Dynamic HTML, Microsoft created a set of ActiveX objects that displayed and stored recordsets. The Grid and Chart controls are just two of the many possibilities. They aren't included with the Internet Explorer 4.0 browser but are available at http://www.microsoft.com/ActiveX. Instead of assigning them long lists of data with PARAM tags, you can include the DATASRC attribute within the OBJECT tag.

For all its limitations, the TDC is a powerful tool for creating data-based applications. Microsoft has created two demonstrations, both available at http://www.micro-soft.com/ie/ie40/, that use the TDC quite powerfully. The Arcadia Bay Company uses tabular data to present a full catalog of goods, and Microsoft's Best of the Web demonstration uses the TDC to present a deluge of information about all kinds of available resources. The simple step of separating the data from the HTML pages makes many development tasks much simpler.

An Introduction to Advanced Data Control

The Advanced Data control starts where the TDC ends and extends to enormous enterprise-scale applications, the kinds you can use to run Fortune 500 companies. Or so Microsoft hopes. Because of its growing complexity, there's no way to cover everything you can do with this control (actually, set of controls) in what's left of this chapter. Instead, we'll focus on the architecture of the ADC and explain how to integrate it with your Web development applications.

The most important changes from TDC to ADC involve the kind of data you're working with and what you can do with it. TDC pages aren't exactly static, but they deal with a static set of textual data. You can't make changes to the data and don't have to worry about reflecting changes in another part of the document. ADC data is "live," at least if you have read/write permission. As with a database, changes made to INPUT fields take effect (with some programming) when you leave the record. Changes made in one place are reflected throughout your document dynamically, a great feature for databases that rely on calculated fields.

Unfortunately, working with live database data isn't very much like working with tabular text files. The server side is much more complicated, requiring serious attention to the architecture of your servers and your network. Using ADC requires you to use an IIS 3.0 Server with ASP support installed and an ODBC-compliant database. For most of these applications, you'll find Access insufficient. You will need SQL Server or a database from Oracle, Informix, Sybase, or a similar manufacturer. You'll also need to install several components from Microsoft on your Web server to create the server-side AdvancedDataFactory object that manages communication between your Web server and the ODBC database.

The client side is simpler, because Microsoft has packaged the two controls you'll need with Internet Explorer 4.0. The AdvancedDataControl object works very much like the TDC and has similar properties. Most Web developers will focus on this piece of the puzzle. The AdvancedDataSpace object is also supported on the client and acts as a proxy for the server-side AdvancedDataFactory object. All these controls can be modified by developers to support custom needs; our discussion will cover them only in the form that Microsoft ships them.

Using these objects creates a complex chain of interactions between the client and the server. Data requests arise in bound elements and from event handlers. The AdvancedDataControl routes most of these requests (except sorting and filtering, which it can manage itself) to either the AdvancedDataSpace control, which provides proxy and caching services, or the AdvancedDataFactory. The AdvancedDataSpace uses the HTTP, HTTPS, or DCOM protocol as appropriate to communicate with the AdvancedDataFactory object on a server (possibly but not necessarily the same Web server that holds the pages). The AdvancedDataFactory then makes a request of the actual database server through OLE DE (a Microsoft protocol layered on top of ODBC) and sends the database response back up through all the layers. The process looks roughly like Figure 11.8.

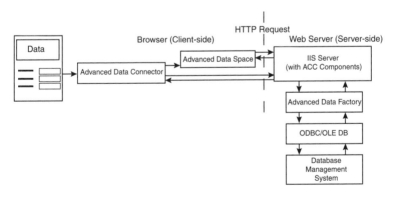

Figure 11.8 ADC communications.

Setting up the ADC isn't much harder than dealing with the TDC. The main differences are a new CLASSID and different values for your data source:

```
<OBJECT classid="clsid:BD96C556-65A3-11D0-983A-
00C04FC29E33" ID=ADCStudentList HEIGHT=10 WIDTH =
10>
        <PARAM NAME="SQL" VALUE="Select * from
Students">
        <PARAM NAME="SERVER"
VALUE="http://data.school.edu">
        <PARAM NAME="CONNECT"
VALUE="dsn=Rosters;UID=General;PWD=public;">
</OBJECT>
```

It looks a little different, but the results are similar to what the TDC might produce. Here, for simplicity, we've called in all the records from the students table with the SQL parameter. (The asterisk, *, is a wildcard for all records.) The AdvancedDataFactory from which we'll collect the records is on the server data.school.edu, and we'll use the HTTP protocol to send information back and forth. The CONNECT parameter gives the AdvancedDataFactory the information it needs to find our database. The parameters are a lot like the ones we used in the IDC example: the ODBC data source name of the database and the UserID and password needed to access it. In this case, the administrator created an open account, General, for anyone to use. It should be an account with few privileges; as we mentioned, including usernames and passwords in plain text is dangerous. If you're on an all-Microsoft solution (Internet Explorer, NT 4 IIS, and SQL Server), you can use the more secure (and automatic) network authentication instead.

The recordset contained in the ADC can be accessed and manipulated with the same tools you used for the TDC, with one major difference: ADC data is live and still connected to the database. You can make changes in your browser, and they'll be reflected at the database even before you press a submit button. This arrangement applies only to data bound to INPUT tags. This makes it possible to create fully functional client-server applications. It also means that the Web developer has a few new responsibilities to shoulder.

Events and ADC

Now we're getting to the data-binding events we first mentioned in Chapter 5. Most Web developers won't get very excited about these events, but database developers will find them critical. Data-binding events allow you to manage data validation and entry when the user is working live on a database that manages transactions with commits and rollback. Without these events, your users could enter random data that might damage the integrity of your database, and you'd have a harder time knowing when users have made changes.

Microsoft has proposed four new events to help developers manage database issues. The onbeforeupdate event is unquestionably the most important, because it lets you validate your data before it gets transmitted to the database. The other three events are onafterupdate, onrowenter, and onrowexit. The sequence in which they occur (with other INPUT element events is as follows:

```
onbeforeupdate
onafterupdate
onchange
onrowexit
onblur
onfocus
onrowenter
```

The sequence in which these events takes place plays a critical role in how you use them.

onbeforeupdate

The onbeforeupdate event occurs immediately when a data-bound element loses focus. The data will transfer back to the database before onchange, and this means that you must do your field-level validation in onbeforeupdate. (It's possible, although unlikely, that you would still want to use onchange for additional validation.) Otherwise, this event behaves exactly like onchange. To prevent the data update from passing back to the server, make the function that handles this event return false.

onafterupdate

The onafterupdate event takes place after a data-bound element has updated the back-end database. This event lets you know that the onbeforeupdate event was not canceled. You could use it to reformat the data that was just entered if necessary.

onrowexit

The onrowexit event happens right before the user changes the current record, whether by moving from row to row in a data-bound table or by using the MoveNext() recordset method. The onrowexit event exists to allow you to perform validation on the entire set of records to ensure that there aren't conflicting values. As with onbeforeupdate, returning false to this event cancels it, preventing the user from leaving the row (or even the page). You can either change the data to reflect a more appropriate value or stall the user's progress until the information is fixed. It isn't foolproof, though—a user could change records and then exit a program suddenly (**Ctrl-Alt-Delete** comes to mind).

onrowenter

The onrowenter event exists to let you do preprocessing of a new recordset, adjusting formats, changing help text, or even skipping to the next record if you like. Unlike onrowexit, the onrowenter event isn't coercive. It can't be canceled and doesn't accept a return value.

Implications of ADC and Data Objects

Microsoft's ADC technology promises programmers a reasonably simple means for transferring complex client-server applications to a Web interface. At the same time, it almost provides Web developers with a way to connect to back-end databases from the client without having to put extra loads on the server. Unfortunately, programmers and Web developers will need a lot of assistance from their system administrators to make the various parts of this system—the browser, the Web server, the database server, and all the objects in between—talk with each other the way they need to. This middle tier of installed software isn't difficult to work with, but neither Web developers nor database programmers will be the ones to handle installation and maintenance. This situation isn't very different from the current situation with Web servers—only a few developers maintain their own servers themselves—but it is vastly more complicated than the average Web server, even with server-side scripting.

ADC over the Web offers client-server developers a lot of promise for creating database-enabled solutions, but it still has a few limitations. Until data-binding extensions become available on other platforms, possibly through Java Beans, the Web offers little intrinsic advantage over developing client-server applications directly in Windows applications. It's easier to distribute upgraded Web pages than upgraded programs, and if you have thousands of users, this benefit might be enough to make it worthwhile. Politically, a Web-based database might sound better, and it might provide a friendlier, more familiar interface, but it isn't sufficiently different or better (in fact, it's more restrictive) than the other options to compel its use. If, on the other hand, Microsoft and its opponents can find a graceful end to the object wars (COM/ActiveX vs. Corba and IIOP, ActiveX controls vs. Java applets) and make this technology available across multiple browsers and platforms, it could make many Web developers very happy.

CHAPTER 12

Layers Upon Layers: Netscape Tools for Dynamic HTML

Although this book has spent a lot of time covering Microsoft-only technologies, I remain one of those idealists who hope that each of the useful tools presented by the vendors will find its niche and prosper. Layers have been portrayed as a promised land and a designer's nightmare, and both myths need dispelling. As we'll see, layers offer much of the same functionality as Microsoft's Dynamic HTML. For certain situations, layers may be more convenient. In many cases, users can't differentiate which tool was used except for the brand name on the browser window.

Netscape's approach makes different assumptions about your style of programming. Microsoft's system relies almost entirely on the structure of the document to determine which objects you can program and which events you can manage. Netscape has developed structures that require you to specify which objects you'll be manipulating and which elements will be handling events. This approach has advantages and disadvantages. The most obvious advantage is that it's somewhat easier to debug layers, because they aren't as prone to mysterious errors created by miscoded HTML and unclosed tags. If a layer object doesn't appear, it's easy to track down the problem, and it is usually separate from any problems you may be having with the contents of the layer. The other advantage of layers is that they make it easy to put objects into groups for simpler management, even to the extent of putting the groups in separate files. This option gives you a lot of flexibility that Microsoft's simpler approach lacks. On the other hand, having to declare every layer explicitly can make for garbled HTML, especially when layers get nested inside layers inside layers. The Netscape event model is somewhat more difficult to work with, although you can create pages that respond neatly to user input.

Layers: An Introduction

The Microsoft document object model lets you break your HTML document into elements. The Netscape layers model lets you break it into sheets. Layers are areas of HTML that can be positioned on the screen with x, y, and z-layer properties much as we manipulated objects earlier in this book. You can hide and display layers, clip their viewing areas, and load them from separate files. They're capable of most of the same things Dynamic HTML provides, with their own set of limitations and extensions.

Layers come packaged in two new HTML tags. <LAYER> tags need to be positioned absolutely on the screen, whereas <ILAYER> tags are part of the flow of the document. By default, the contents of a layer tag have a transparent background, and graphics with transparency will remain transparent. Unless you've declared a background color, you can see the layer "underneath" the top layer through the top layer and through the transparent areas of any graphics. (Background colors make the layer opaque.) The <LAYER> and <ILAYER> tags can accept the attributes listed in Table 12.1.

Table 12.1 Attributes of the <LAYER> and <ILAYER> Tags

Attribute/ Property	Description
NAME (or ID)	The identification for the layer. All references to the layer must be by name or through the layers collection.
LEFT	The position of the left edge of the layer, expressed in pixels or as a percentage of the window's width. For LAYER tags, this positions the layer in absolute terms; for ILAYER tags, it positions the layer relative to its parent element.
TOP	The position of the top edge of the layer, expressed in pixels or as a percentage of the window's height. For LAYER tags, this positions the layer in absolute terms; for ILAYER tags, it positions the layer relative to its parent element.
WIDTH	The width of the layer, expressed in pixels or as a percentage of the window's height. Used for text wrapping and default clipping.
HEIGHT	The height of the layer, expressed in pixels or as a percentage of the window's height. Used to handle child layers that specify their positioning with percentages.
CLIP	Specifies a rectangle (as "x1,y1,x2,y2" or "x2,y2" where zeros are assumed for x1 and y1) that contains the section of the layer that should be drawn. A "window" on the layer.
Z-INDEX	Specifies the stacking order of the layer, as an integer. Higher numbered Z-Indexes will appear stacked on top of those with lower numbers.
ABOVE	Specifies the name of the layer on top of which the current layer should appear. An alternative way to set the Z-INDEX.
BELOW	Specifies the name of the layer below which the current layer should appear. An alternative way to set the Z-INDEX.
VISIBILITY	Whether or not to display the layer. Accepts "SHOW," "HIDE," and "INHERIT." "INHERIT" is the default.
BGCOLOR	Accepts an RGB color or a named HTML color. If used, makes the layer opaque.

continued on next page

Attribute/ Property	Description
BACKGROUND	Sets the background to a tiled image. Transparent areas of the image will still be transparent, allowing users to see through to the lower layers.
SRC	Specifies a URL that contains the content of the layer.

Netscape also provides a <NOLAYER> tag, which contains text that Communicator 4 will not display. Unfortunately, unless you're creating all your layers from well-hidden JavaScript code or strictly using layers stored in outside files, other browsers (including Internet Explorer 4.0) will likely trip over the contents of your layer tags and spray them across the page.

The way that Netscape has implemented layers makes them almost subdocuments. Each layer can have its own source file and its own collections of images, applets, anchors, and even other layers. The document object contains a collection of layers, and every layer object includes a document object, which can itself hold more layers. Layers are scriptable, exposing as properties some of their attributes as well as their position in the document structure and also providing simple methods for manipulating them. You can address layer properties as *layerName.propertyName* and *layerName.methodName*, which is compatible JavaScript syntax.

N O T E

If you need to address collections of a layer, such as the images collection, it'll be strange if you're referencing them from the main document or from a different layer. Remember that every layer includes its own document object with all the properties and methods of the main document object. The syntax looks like this:

```
document.layers["layerName"].document.image
s.["imageName"].
```

The properties of a layer object include those in Table 12.2.

Table 12.2 Some Properties of a Layer Object

Property Name	Modifiable?	Description
name	no	The name of the layer, specified in the NAME or ID attribute.
left	yes	The position of the left edge of the layer relative to the enclosing layer, in pixels.
top	yes	The position of the top edge of the layer relative to the enclosing layer, in pixels.
visibility	yes	Can be set to "hide" or "inherit."
clip.left clip.top clip.right clip.bottom clip.height clip.width	yes	Define the clipping rectangle. Try to use clip.bottom *or* clip.height and not both. Conflicting values may produce strange results. The same applies to clip.height and clip.width.
siblingAbove	no	Returns the layer above this layer (by z-order), or null if this is already the top layer.
siblingBelow	no	Returns the layer below this layer (by z-order), or null if this is already the bottom layer.
parentLayer	no	The layer in which this layer is nested. Returns null if there is no layer enclosing this layer.
layers	no, but...	The associative array containing all the layers nested in this layer. This array cannot be scripted, but the properties of the layer objects included in it can be scripted if they are normally modifiable.

In addition to these properties, layers have methods that let you manipulate them more thoroughly (see Table 12.3).

Table 12.3 Methods Used with Layers

Method Name	Description
moveBy(*deltaX,deltaY*)	Changes the layer's x and y positions by adding the deltaX and deltaY parameters to the object's current location.
moveTo(*x,y*)	Changes the layer's x and y positions to the values specified in the x and y parameters.
resizeBy(*deltaWidth, deltaHeight*)	Changes the layer's clipping rectangle by adding the deltaX and deltaY parameters to the object's current clipping rectangle.
resizeTo(*width,height*)	Changes the layer's clipping rectangle to cover the values specified in the width and height parameters.
moveAbove(*layer*)	Changes the layer's Z-index to place it above the layer specified.
moveBelow(*layer*)	Changes the layer's Z-index to place it below the layer specified.

Now that we have these components, let's put them together in a simple example. We'll create some basic text layers to demonstrate how easy it is to load, move, and stack layers in a document.

Client-Side includes Made Real

The inclusion of an SRC attribute makes the ILAYER tag a prime candidate for handling a simple task that HTML couldn't deal with previously: nesting HTML files within HTML files. This tag breaks down the one-file-to-a-document structure, giving developers an alternative to complex framesets. It gives layers functionality that

Microsoft's Dynamic HTML lacks, and it can make many projects far easier to implement. Best of all, creating these documents is just like creating any other HTML document.

Our parent document includes two child layers, one of which has a different background color. The parent code looks like this:

```
<HTML>
<HEAD><TITLE>Parent Document with
ILAYERS</TITLE></HEAD>
<BODY BGCOLOR=#FFFFFF>
<P>This text is in the original parent document.</P>
<P><ILAYER SRC="child1.html"></ILAYER></P>
<P><ILAYER SRC="child2.html"></ILAYER></P>
</BODY>
</HTML>
```

The code for the first child layer is as follows:

```
<HTML><BODY>
This text is in the first child document.
</BODY></HTML>
```

Here's the code for the second child layer:

```
<HTML><BODY BGCOLOR=#00FF00>
This text is in the second child document.
</BODY></HTML>
```

Layer document traits such as background color are respected by the browser (see Figure 12.1).

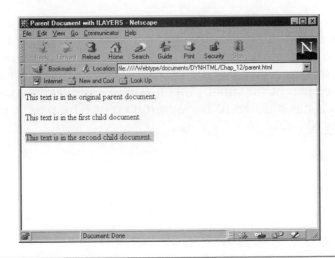

Figure 12.1 Using layers as client-side includes.

This technique is simple and powerful. In the early days of the Web, there were good reasons not to permit such client includes. For one thing, HTTP is not a very efficient protocol for retrieving multiple files, and the overhead of calls for hundreds of small text files could well have overwhelmed early browsers and servers. HTTP 1.1 addressed many of those deficiencies and opened the floodgates. No doubt there will be purists who decry the breakdown of document structure that this approach represents, but I suspect that developers will clamor for the feature until it becomes a standard part of all browsers. I'd also like to see an SRC attribute implemented for the DIV tag.

Unfortunately for developers who want to create outlines, the current ILAYER tag lacks collapsibility. Netscape Communicator will not resize the layer to reflect a change of content, nor will it collapse the space occupied by a hidden ILAYER. Figure 12.2 shows a sample based on the outline code from Chapter 7.

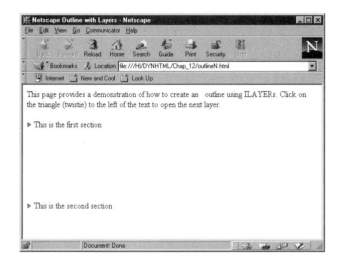

Figure 12.2 Unexpanded outline attempt.

This program produces the screen in Figure 12.3.

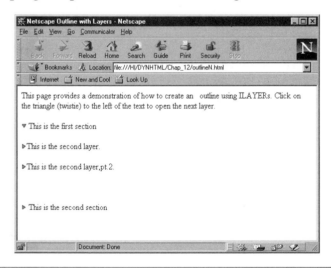

Figure 12.3 Expanded outline attempt.

As you can see, the hidden ILAYER takes up all the space it would have if it were shown. When you click on the twistie graphic, you get the screen shown in Figure 12.3. This makes it difficult to use ILAYER for information-hiding applications, except perhaps to hide the answers on a test temporarily. LAYER elements don't have these restrictions, but you'll need to know much more about where on the screen you want your information to appear.

Hiding Information with Layers

Although they may not work well with outlines, layers can still be useful for hiding large amounts of information and displaying it instantly when desired. We'll build a small page that holds information on a variety of topics and displays it on the right-hand side of the screen at the user's request. We'll use a naming convention to make certain that our layers are displayed and hidden in the proper sequence. We'll also use positioning information and a background layer.

The task we'll manage is usually done with frames, but layers can make it look much more appealing. The list of five items will be on the left side of the page, with the descriptions on the right. We'll create our layers in several different ways. In the first version of the example, the source code for the layers will simply be a part of the HTML code. The second time around, we'll load the layers from separate files, an approach that makes it much easier to manage the item data. Then we'll look at an alternative that is more useful if you want to show multiple layers simultaneously.

Our first version includes one JavaScript function that responds to user clicks, some HTML that the user sees at all times, and a set of layers we'll manipulate to display additional information:

```
<HTML>
<HEAD><TITLE>Layers Hiding Info Demo</TITLE></HEAD>
<BODY BGCOLOR=#FFFFFF>
<SCRIPT LANGUAGE="JavaScript">
function showIt(selectItem) {
//this function makes all the layers except the
selected one invisible.
//then it sets the twistie graphic
for (i=1; i<6; i++){
  if (i==selectItem) {
  document.layers["Odd"+i].visibility="inherit";
  document.images["OddT"+i].src="twist2.gif";
  }
  else {
  document.layers["Odd"+i].visibility="hide";
  document.images["OddT"+i].src="twist1.gif";
  }
}}
</SCRIPT>
<H2>Museum of Odd Things</H2>
<P>Here at the Museum of Odd Things, we've collected
an ensemble of strange objects and mysterious
devices.  If you can't come in to browse our
collection, please explore the following links to a
few of our finest oddities.</P>
<!-Note:The following links use a number and naming
convention that we can use to select the appropriate
layer and change the twistie gif to reflect an
'opened' subject.  ->
<P><A HREF="javascript:showIt(1)"><IMG
SRC="twist1.gif" NAME="OddT1" BORDER=0>Tesla
Coils</A></P>
<P><A HREF="javascript:showIt(2)"><IMG
SRC="twist1.gif" NAME="OddT2"
BORDER=0>Theremin</A></P>
<P><A HREF="javascript:showIt(3)"><IMG
SRC="twist1.gif" NAME="OddT3"
BORDER=0>Carburetors</A></P>
```

```
<P><A HREF="javascript:showIt(4)"><IMG
SRC="twist1.gif" NAME="OddT4" BORDER=0>Static
Ball</A></P>
<P><A HREF="javascript:showIt(5)"><IMG
SRC="twist1.gif" NAME="OddT5" BORDER=0>Web
browsers</A></P>
<!-Note:The following layers use a naming convention
(OddX) the script will use to make them visible and
invisible as appropriate.  ->
<LAYER BGCOLOR=#000000 LEFT="300" TOP="110"
HEIGHT="250" WIDTH="300" VISIBILITY="inherit"
NAME="Background"></LAYER>
<LAYER BGCOLOR=#FF0000 LEFT="300" TOP="110"
HEIGHT="250" WIDTH="300" VISIBILITY="hide"
NAME="Odd1"><H3>Tesla Coils Info</H3></LAYER>
<LAYER BGCOLOR=#00FF00 LEFT="300" TOP="110"
HEIGHT="250" WIDTH="300" VISIBILITY="hide"
NAME="Odd2"><H3>Theremin Info</H3></LAYER>
<LAYER BGCOLOR=#0000FF LEFT="300" TOP="110"
HEIGHT="250" WIDTH="300" VISIBILITY="hide"
NAME="Odd3"><H3>Carburetor Info</H3></LAYER>
<LAYER BGCOLOR=#FF00FF LEFT="300" TOP="110"
HEIGHT="250" WIDTH="300" VISIBILITY="hide"
NAME="Odd4"><H3>Static Ball Info</H3></LAYER>
<LAYER BGCOLOR=#00FFFF LEFT="300" TOP="110"
HEIGHT="250" WIDTH="300" VISIBILITY="hide"
NAME="Odd5"><H3>Web Browser Info</H3>
The Web browser arrived on this planet in 1991, in
Geneva, Switzerland. Since then, it has spread
around the world.  For more information, try these
links:
<UL>
<LI><A HREF="http://www.netscape.com">Netscape -
Communicator</A>
<LI><A HREF="http://www.microsoft.com">Microsoft -
Internet Explorer</A>
```

```
<LI><A HREF="http://www.w3.org">W3 Consortium -
Arena</A>
</UL></LAYER>
</BODY></HTML>
```

When users first load the page, they'll see the screen in Figure 12.4.

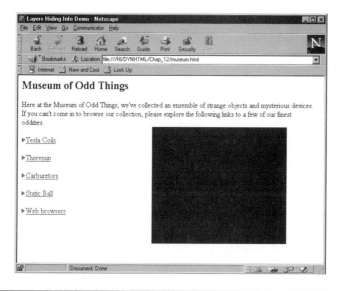

Figure 12.4 Museum of oddities at opening.

The black box on the right is a little ominous. You'll probably want to use a BACKGROUND attribute instead of the BGCOLOR attribute to make the opening screen display your logo or other filler material. When users click on the final item, they'll see the screen shown in Figure 12.5.

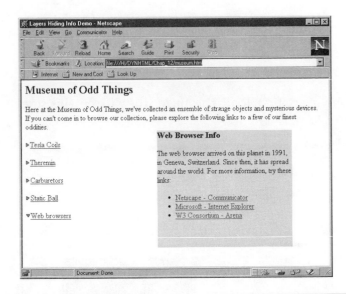

Figure 12.5 Museum of oddities, Web browsers selected.

If you keep clicking the various items, they'll appear and disappear at will. The demo works smoothly, without much overhead. If you want to, you could make the layers different sizes or even make them move. All that's happening here is one property change for the layer and one change for the graphic. The visibility and the twistie are both turned on (made visible, or rotated) for the selected item and turned off for the other items.

If you add many more items to the demonstration or want to create multiple layers, you'll need to take a more complex approach. The first step is to break the layers out into separate files. In this way, you can manage and manipulate the data in subdocuments without having to worry about breaking the main document. We'll break the layers into the files Odd1.html, Odd2.html, and the like so that we can use the same naming convention.

This small change creates some different-looking code in the layers area:

```
<LAYER BGCOLOR=#FF0000 LEFT="300" TOP="110"
HEIGHT="250" WIDTH="300" VISIBILITY="hide"
SRC="Odd1.html" NAME="Odd1"></LAYER>
<LAYER BGCOLOR=#00FF00 LEFT="300" TOP="110"
HEIGHT="250" WIDTH="300" VISIBILITY="hide"
SRC="Odd2.html" NAME="Odd2"></LAYER>
```

I've shown only two of the five layers here. You need to change the code for each layer to add an SRC attribute that consists of the layer name and ".html" and then put the former contents of the layer into a file by that name. The Odd1.html file contains what used to be in the main document's Odd1 layer:

```
<HTML><BODY>
<H3>Tesla Coils Info</H3>
</BODY></HTML>
```

The results are identical to the first version. Functionally, nothing much has changed—all the layers are loaded as the page comes in, and the showIt() function hides and displays them as before. Our last version changes the showIt() function slightly. If you wanted to be able to show multiple pieces of information at once, it might be useful to move a layer to the top rather than show it and hide it. Our layers initially load with the background on the bottom, Odd1 next up, Odd2 next up, and so on, with Odd5 on the top. We'll move the user-activated layer to the top. To do this, we'll make background the last layer, which gives it the highest position in the z-order. Then we use the moveAbove() layer method to send our layers to the top:

```
<HTML>
<HEAD><TITLE>Layers Hiding Info Demo</TITLE></HEAD>
<BODY BGCOLOR=#FFFFFF>
<SCRIPT LANGUAGE="JavaScript">
function showIt(selectItem) {
//this NEW line moves the selected item to the top
document.layers["Odd"+selectItem].moveAbove(document
.layers["Background"]);
//the next line isn't actually necessary in Netscape
PR4.
document.layers["Odd"+selectItem].visibility="inheri
t";
//then it sets the twistie graphic
for (i=1; i<6; i++){ //still need to set twistie
  if (i==selectItem)
{document.images["OddT"+i].src="twist2.gif";}
  else {
document.images["OddT"+i].src="twist1.gif";}
}}
</SCRIPT>
<H2>Museum of Odd Things</H2>
<P>Here at the Museum of Odd Things, we've collected
an ensemble of strange objects and mysterious
devices.  If you can't come in to browse our
collection, please explore the following links to a
few of our finest oddities.</P>
<!—Note:The following links use a number and naming
convention that we can use to select the appropriate
layer and change the twistie gif to reflect an
'opened' subject.  —>
<P><A HREF="javascript:showIt(1)"><IMG
SRC="twist1.gif" NAME="OddT1" BORDER=0>Tesla
Coils</A></P>
<P><A HREF="javascript:showIt(2)"><IMG
SRC="twist1.gif" NAME="OddT2"
BORDER=0>Theremin</A></P>
```

```
<P><A HREF="javascript:showIt(3)"><IMG
SRC="twist1.gif" NAME="OddT3"
BORDER=0>Carburetors</A></P>
<P><A HREF="javascript:showIt(4)"><IMG
SRC="twist1.gif" NAME="OddT4" BORDER=0>Static
Ball</A></P>
<P><A HREF="javascript:showIt(5)"><IMG
SRC="twist1.gif" NAME="OddT5" BORDER=0>Web
browsers</A></P>
<!-Note:The following layers use a naming convention
(OddX) the script will use to move them. Note that
Background is now the last layer rather than the
first, which pushes it to the top of the screen. ->
<LAYER BGCOLOR=#FF0000 LEFT="300" TOP="110"
HEIGHT="250" WIDTH="300"  SRC="Odd1.html"
NAME="Odd1" VISIBILITY="hide"></LAYER>
<LAYER BGCOLOR=#00FF00 LEFT="300" TOP="110"
HEIGHT="250" WIDTH="300"  SRC="Odd2.html"
NAME="Odd2" VISIBILITY="hide"></LAYER>
<LAYER BGCOLOR=#0000FF LEFT="300" TOP="110"
HEIGHT="250" WIDTH="300"  SRC="Odd3.html"
NAME="Odd3" VISIBILITY="hide"></LAYER>
<LAYER BGCOLOR=#FF00FF LEFT="300" TOP="110"
HEIGHT="250" WIDTH="300"  SRC="Odd4.html"
NAME="Odd4" VISIBILITY="hide"></LAYER>
<LAYER BGCOLOR=#00FFFF LEFT="300" TOP="110"
HEIGHT="250" WIDTH="300"  SRC="Odd5.html"
NAME="Odd5" VISIBILITY="hide"></LAYER>
<LAYER BGCOLOR=#000000 LEFT="300" TOP="110"
HEIGHT="250" WIDTH="300"  NAME="Background"></LAYER>
</BODY></HTML>
```

Keep in mind that all the layers must be the same size and in the same place for this version to work in the same way as the previous versions. If your document is more of a collage—with layers all over the place—the preceding code could add some visual interest, letting users pull pieces from the pile.

Hidden Information: The Comic Strip

Whereas the previous example let us avoid using frames in a simple interface, our next example puts the layer information to a real purpose: breaking down and presenting information in a way that may give artists a bit more legal control over their work. This basic comic strip demonstrates a technique you can use to make your Web documents a bit more ephemeral—interesting to read but hard to steal and harder to print. You may also find it a handy way to mark up documents, displaying comment information in an overlay only when the reader is ready to move from the original material to the comments.

Our comic strip has three blocks, much like a simple newspaper strip. Each block has three layers: a background layer, a foreground layer, and a text layer that contains our characters' thoughts or words. It's an easy way to organize a strip, and it lets you reuse material easily without having to redraw everything every time. The text layer appears only when the mouse is over that particular block, letting the user read the conversation but making it difficult to print. It's possible to download all three images, piece them together, and print the complete strip, but the difficulty of it should discourage casual readers from distributing our mysteriously valuable strip.

The HTML and the code for this example are simple. All we're doing is showing and hiding a few layers in response to onmouseover and onmouseout events. It's much like a rollover except that we're displaying a layer instead of changing a graphic.

When the user loads the page, it looks like Figure 12.6.

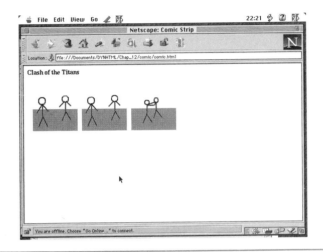

Figure 12.6 Initial screen, no text.

After the mouse rolls over the first block, users see the screen in Figure 12.7.

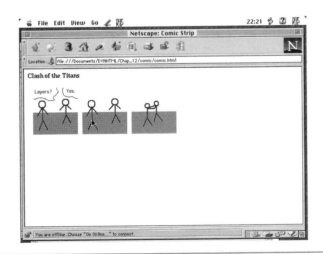

Figure 12.7 First block of text.

The second block puts away the text in the first block and displays its own text (see Figure 12.8).

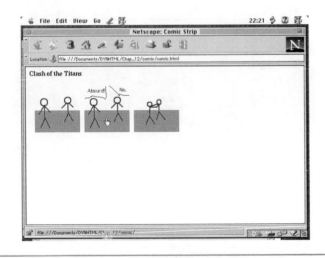

Figure 12.8 Second block only.

The final block displays the dramatic conclusion to our saga (see Figure 12.9).

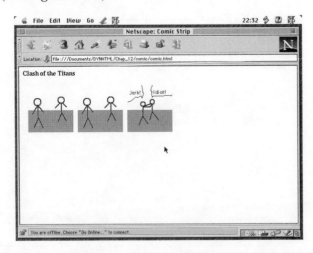

Figure 12.9 Final block only.

Following is the code for this example:

```
<HTML>
<HEAD><TITLE>Comic Strip</TITLE></HEAD>
<BODY BGCOLOR=#FFFFFF>
<SCRIPT LANGUAGE="JavaScript">
function showIt(whichOne) {
     for (i=1;i<4; i++){ //runs through layers
          if (i==whichOne){//turns on the right one

document.layers["txt"+whichOne].visibility="inherit"
;}
          else{//turns off the others

document.layers["txt"+i].visibility="hide";}
     }
}
</SCRIPT>
<H3>Clash of the Titans</H3>
<LAYER NAME="bg1" TOP=40 LEFT=20 HEIGHT=100
WIDTH=100><IMG SRC="bg1.gif"></LAYER>
<LAYER NAME="bg2" TOP=40 LEFT=130 HEIGHT=100
WIDTH=100><IMG SRC="bg1.gif"></LAYER>
<LAYER NAME="bg3" TOP=40 LEFT=240 HEIGHT=100
WIDTH=100><IMG SRC="bg1.gif"></LAYER>
<LAYER NAME="fg1" TOP=40 LEFT=20 HEIGHT=100
WIDTH=100><A HREF=""  ONMOUSEOVER="showIt(1)"><IMG
SRC="fg1.gif" BORDER=0></A></LAYER>
<LAYER NAME="fg2" TOP=40 LEFT=130 HEIGHT=100
WIDTH=100><A HREF="" ONMOUSEOVER="showIt(2)"><IMG
SRC="fg2.gif" BORDER=0></A></LAYER>
<LAYER NAME="fg3" TOP=40 LEFT=240 HEIGHT=100
WIDTH=100><A HREF="" ONMOUSEOVER="showIt(3)"><IMG
SRC="fg3.gif" BORDER=0></A></LAYER>
<LAYER NAME="txt1" TOP=40 LEFT=20 HEIGHT=100
WIDTH=100 VISIBILITY="hide"><IMG
SRC="txt1.gif"></LAYER>
<LAYER NAME="txt2" TOP=40 LEFT=130 HEIGHT=100
WIDTH=100 VISIBILITY="hide"><IMG
SRC="txt2.gif"></LAYER>
```

```
<LAYER NAME="txt3" TOP=40 LEFT=240 HEIGHT=100
WIDTH=100 VISIBILITY="hide"><IMG
SRC="txt3.gif"></LAYER>
</BODY></HTML>
```

Our strategy for making the information appear and disappear is simple. When the cursor rolls over one of the foreground (stick figure) images, it calls the showIt() function. This function shows the one layer we want to see—the one with the text for this block—and hides the rest of the blocks. You could achieve something similar by using the onmouseout event to determine when the cursor has left the block, but unfortunately both it and the onmouseover event happen when the cursor is in motion, making the text blink wildly. The user can also sneak out of the block, leave the text on-screen, then proceed to the next block and do the same. A screenshot would give would-be art thieves an instant printable copy of your document.

You can use this technique with many kinds of rollovers. It would be great to build a funhouse using layers that appear in response to user clicks and mouseovers and could also be handy for creating menus that appear only as necessary. As usual, simple techniques can produce a wide variety of interfaces.

Animation with Layers

You can use the CSS-style positioning with layers to create animations as long as you remember to give the browser a break to refresh the screen. For our example, we'll create a black layer and move it across the screen in a sine curve—a classic up-and-down motion. We'll use the setTimeout() function instead of a simple for loop, because the browser won't redraw the screen while we remain in the script.

```
<HTML>
<HEAD><TITLE>Sine curve layers
demonstration</TITLE></HEAD>
<BODY BGCOLOR=#FFFFFF>
<LAYER NAME="active" TOP=100 LEFT=0 HEIGHT=10
WIDTH=10 BGCOLOR=#000000></LAYER>
<SCRIPT LANGUAGE="JavaScript">
function moveIt(){
  pTop=pTop+4*(Math.sin(pLeft/(2*Math.PI))); //go up
and down
  pLeft++;
  if (pLeft>360) {pLeft=0;} //reset after 360
degrees of sine
  document.layers["active"].top=pTop;
  document.layers["active"].left=pLeft;
  setTimeout ("moveIt()",75);
}
pLeft=0;
pTop=100; //initial settings
moveIt(); //start the action
</SCRIPT>
</BODY>
</HTML>
```

It's hard to show animation in a book, but at some point your screen should look like Figure 12.10.

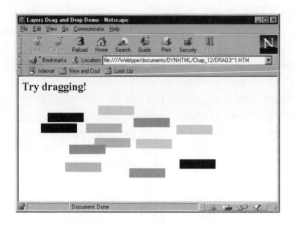

Figure 12.10 Sine curved block.

The layer will amble across your screen, moving up and down according to the mathematical rhythm that governs it.

Drag and Drop with Layers

We can use Netscape Navigator to let the user move layers around in much the same way that we moved images around with Internet Explorer in Chapter 7. We'll do some of the same things, but we'll implement them differently because of differences in the event model and the way we address layers. In Netscape, events don't bubble, but you can "capture" them at the window and document levels using the captureEvents() method. Once you've captured an event, you have a monopoly on it until you release it with releaseEvents(). The Netscape event object doesn't have properties to indicate the state of the mouse buttons, so we'll manage the drag and drop through the onmouseup and onmousedown events. In addition, we must determine which layer received the event in the first place, something that takes a bit of searching. We break this task into several functions. The whichLayer(x,y) function takes an X and Y location and returns the bottom layer at that location. The drag() function moves the brick with the mouse cursor and cancels any further processing of the operating system with regard to drag and drop. The endDrag() function turns off dragging; we'll use it later to figure out where the object was dropped. The beginDrag() function calls whichLayer to figure out which layer to move and starts the event capture that lets us drag the bricks. Altogether, it looks like this:

```
<HTML>
<HEAD><TITLE>Layers Drag and Drop
Demo</TITLE></HEAD>
<BODY BGCOLOR=#FFFFFF>
<SCRIPT LANGUAGE="JavaScript">
//the following functions implement drag and drop
function whichLayer(x,y){ //checks the position of
the layers
foundLayer=1001; //indicates nothing to move
for (i=11; i>-1; i—){
  layerCheck=document.layers[i];
  if (x>layerCheck.x && x<(layerCheck.x +
layerCheck.clip.width) && y>layerCheck.y &&
y<(layerCheck.y + layerCheck.clip.height)) {
    foundLayer=i; //a match - the one to drag!
    }
  }
return foundLayer;
}
function drag(e){
  inMotion.moveBy(e.pageX-oldX, e.pageY-oldY);
  oldX=e.pageX;
  oldY=e.pageY;
  return false;//remove this and the OS will try to
drag
```

```
}
function endDrag(e){
window.releaseEvents(Event.MOUSEMOVE);//ends
dragging
}
function beginDrag(e){
     layerDrag=whichLayer(e.pageX, e.pageY); //find
out which layer to move

     if (layerDrag!=1001) { //check to make sure the
cursor was on a brick
          inMotion=document.layers[layerDrag];
          oldX=e.pageX;
          oldY=e.pageY;

window.captureEvents(Event.MOUSEMOVE);//turn on
event capture for drag
     }
}
var oldX, oldY;
var inMotion=null;
//Event capturing information
window.captureEvents(Event.MOUSEDOWN|Event.MOUSEUP);
window.onmousedown=beginDrag;
window.onmousemove=drag;
window.onmouseup=endDrag;
window.offscreenbuffering=true; //for smoother
redraws
</SCRIPT>
<H2>Try dragging!</H2>
<LAYER TOP=100 LEFT=50><IMG SRC="black.gif"></LAYER>
<LAYER TOP=100 LEFT=50><IMG SRC="black.gif"></LAYER>
<LAYER TOP=100 LEFT=50><IMG SRC="black.gif"></LAYER>
<LAYER TOP=100 LEFT=150><IMG
SRC="bluegray.gif"></LAYER>
```

```
<LAYER TOP=100 LEFT=150><IMG
SRC="bluegray.gif"></LAYER>
<LAYER TOP=100 LEFT=150><IMG
SRC="bluegray.gif"></LAYER>
<LAYER TOP=100 LEFT=250><IMG
SRC="orange.gif"></LAYER>
<LAYER TOP=100 LEFT=250><IMG
SRC="orange.gif"></LAYER>
<LAYER TOP=100 LEFT=250><IMG
SRC="orange.gif"></LAYER>
<LAYER TOP=100 LEFT=350><IMG
SRC="green.gif"></LAYER>
<LAYER TOP=100 LEFT=350><IMG
SRC="green.gif"></LAYER>
<LAYER TOP=100 LEFT=350><IMG
SRC="green.gif"></LAYER>
</BODY></HTML>
```

Notice that we set up some critical initialization at the end of the <SCRIPT> tag. The oldX and oldY variables help us keep the mouse cursor positioned on the brick where it was at the start of the drag. The inMotion variable identifies the layer that we're moving. After the variables are defined, we tell the browser to pass all onmouseup and onmousedown events to the window object for processing, and we tell the window object which functions to call when those events arrive. We also tell it to use the drag() function to handle the onmousemove event; once the user has clicked the mouse button, all mouse movement events will be captured by the window object and the dragging will commence. Until then, nothing will happen.

The results are similar to the fun we had in Chapter 7 (see Figure 12.11).

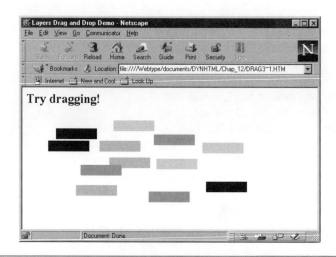

Figure 12.11 Bricks strewn about the screen.

The best part of this routine is that it can easily be converted into a drag-and-drop routine that has real results. The same whichLayer() function we use to determine which brick to move can also tell us where the object has landed. In fact, the ability to drop objects is the reason that the for loop in the whichLayer() function counts down to zero instead of up to 12. We've become accustomed to having the object that we're moving in the foreground and the object that we're dropping in the background. If the whichLayer() function counted up, it would return the object in the foreground—the same object we're moving. By making whichLayer() count down, we can drop objects and figure out where they landed.

To make this work, we add a few lines to the endDrag() and beginDrag() functions along with one layer and one variable. First, we add this line right before the other layers in the HTML:

```
<LAYER TOP=280 LEFT=400 HEIGHT=200 WIDTH=200
BGCOLOR="BROWN" NAME="trashcan"></LAYER>
```

We need the beginDrag() function to set a flag so that endDrag() can tell whether we were dragging something or someone's clicking on the trash can. We initialize the variable in the same area we initialized oldX and oldY:

```
var dragFlag=0;
```

Then we need to add a line to beginDrag() to set the flag to 1 when dragging commences and to make sure we aren't dragging the trash can around:

```
function beginDrag(e){
     layerDrag=whichLayer(e.pageX, e.pageY); //find
out which layer to move
     if (layerDrag!=1001 && layerDrag!=0) { //check
to make sure the cursor was on a brick and not the
trash can
          inMotion=document.layers[layerDrag];
          oldX=e.pageX;
          oldY=e.pageY;

window.captureEvents(Event.MOUSEMOVE);//turn on
event capture for drag
          dragFlag=1; //indicate dragging for
endDrag()
     }
}
```

When we release a brick, the endDrag() function checks to see whether the brick was dropped on the trash can or someplace else. Then endDrag() complains about the trash can if the user left the brick on top of that layer:

```
function endDrag(e){
if (dragFlag==1) { //were we dragging?
     window.releaseEvents(Event.MOUSEMOVE);//ends
dragging
     dropOff=whichLayer(e.pageX,e.pageY);
```

```
        if (dropOff==0) { alert('fire in the trash!');}
        dragFlag=0;}
    }
```

This program has a few interesting side effects. Once you've dropped the objects completely in the trash can, you can't get them out. If an edge is sticking out, you can still pull the brick away, but once it's surrounded it becomes immobile. The whichLayer() function always returns the trash can when you click anywhere inside that brown area, because the trash can is the furthest layer back. After you've lost a few bricks, the screen looks like Figure 12.12.

Figure 12.12 bricks in the trash can.

This simple trash can marks the start of a GUI interface. Drag and drop is at the core of many of the desktop functions. This means that it's possible to move from this example toward an environment that users have worked in before: the classic desktop interface. Once again, we've moved from HTML joyriding to development practicality.

Clipping: Windows On Layers

For our final layers example, we'll explore *clipping*: an easy way to show only a portion of a layer. Clipping is handy for animations or for showing the appropriate part of a layer in response to user needs. For example, you could put a set of graphics in one layer and use clipping to show only one at a time—a kind of layered radio button. Our example, which will demonstrate how clipping works, includes two layers. The back layer is fully visible and has a background GIF of horizontal black and white stripes. The front layer is visible only through a 50 × 50 pixel square but covers the same area with a GIF of vertical black and white stripes. The code includes buttons for moving the visible (clipping) area, changing the pattern:

```
<HTML>
<HEAD><TITLE>Clipping Example</TITLE></HEAD>
<BODY>
<SCRIPT>
function UpDown(direction){
movelayer=document.layers["FRONT"];
movelayer.clip.top+=direction;
movelayer.clip.bottom+=direction;
}
function LeftRight(direction){
movelayer=document.layers["FRONT"];
movelayer.clip.left+=direction;
movelayer.clip.right+=direction;
}
</SCRIPT>
<P><A HREF="javascript:UpDown(-4)">Go up</A></P>
```

```
<P><A HREF="javascript:UpDown(4)">Go down</A></P>
<P><A HREF="javascript:LeftRight(-4)">Go
left</A></P>
<P><A HREF="javascript:LeftRight(4)">Go
right</A></P>
<LAYER NAME="BACK" HEIGHT=300 WIDTH=150 TOP=0
LEFT=300 BACKGROUND="horiz.gif"></LAYER>
<LAYER NAME="FRONT" HEIGHT=300 WIDTH=150 TOP=0
LEFT=300 CLIP="50,50,100,100"
BACKGROUND="vert.gif"></LAYER>
</BODY>
</HTML>
```

When you first open the document, the screen looks like Figure 12.13.

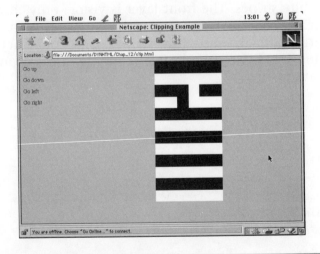

Figure 12.13 Clipping, original position.

The window on the vertical layer is tiny—just a strange disturbance on the field of horizontal stripes. But moving the window (by adjusting the clip properties of the FRONT layer) doesn't move the stripes; instead, it moves your window on to the stripes, which remain (invisibly, for the most part) in the same place the whole time (see Figure 12.14).

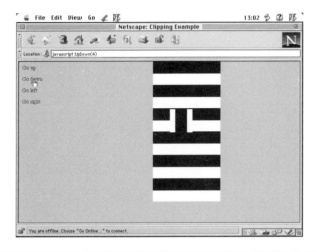

Figure 12.14 Clipping example after a few moves.

CHAPTER 13

Future Web Architectures

Dynamic HTML is the most powerful new Web technology to appear since Java, and it promises to revive HTML as the primary medium of Web expression. Combined with the new power of scripting languages, the clean structures of cascading style sheets, and the approaching possibility of XML, (eXtensible Markup Language), Dynamic HTML brings new life to Web documents and sites. These technologies are much more than a new coat of paint for the Web. The technologies we've begun to explore in this book will have a strong influence on the architecture—not just the interior design—of Web sites. When HTML first appeared, it brought a new style of presentation, one to which the world has barely begun to adjust. For most people, hypertext and hypermedia are distant cousins to print and broadcast media. They are strange new worlds that don't quite mesh with the way most people have been taught to consume information. And the medium is about to get stranger. For the rest of this chapter, we'll look at what some of these technologies may do to the hypertext world pioneered by the early HTML-centered Web.

Cascading Style Sheets: The Return of Structure

Of all these technologies, cascading style sheets has the strongest roots in print media. Designers are used to specifying type and photos with precision, expecting the results to be the same almost every time. A corporate annual report must look exactly the same to every stockholder. For many forms of information, presentation is as important as the content, and adjusting that presentation to the rough-hewn structures of Web pages was more of a chore than many designers cared to work with. When they had to, many people chose to re-create the kinds of typography and images they'd used effectively on paper—and buried the Web in slow graphics and confusing image maps.

HTML wasn't designed to support magazine layout, and many designers cringe even at the more-powerful tools of SGML, HTML's better-equipped relative. Although HTML provided useful tools for structuring documents, from a graphic designer's perspective it did little to support page layout. Precise control over em spacing, color, layering, dropped capitals, or even fonts wasn't considered critical until the Web became a commercial zone. Once that crossover began, Web design was often in the hands of marketing departments and advertising agencies who had never heard of CERN or even Mosaic but knew very well what Netscape was and knew that an audience was waiting for information.

The maze of formatting tags and the battles over their adoption may finally be coming to an end. Cascading style sheets give designers the control they want and the flexibility and reusability they need to manage large sites, at the same time returning to a much more structured document framework. As we saw in Chapter 2, cascading style sheets make the old tags usable again. An important aspect we barely touched on is the ability of cascading style sheets to unify the appearance of an entire site. Although we've used the style sheets extensively, we haven't used their cascades, which allow a central file, or even a series of central files, to direct the appearance of as many pages as you like. A designer can set basic corporate standards that will appear as the default on all pages built for a site; only a tiny piece of additional code needs to be placed in each document. Designers of individual pages can override the standards, but the point is that standard-setting tools are finally available. Whether or not you choose to use the scripting possibilities we've explored in this book, cascading style sheets can transform your sites and change the way you create HTML code.

XML

XML is only in its formative stages and doesn't appear in the current version of Internet Explorer or Netscape Communicator. XML has been touted as everything from do-it-yourself standards creation to the magic bullet that will end the browser wars, but XML probably won't solve all the world's problems. XML reflects the recognition that the set of tools HTML provides isn't up to every task and that creating new HTML extensions for every demand will complicate a system that's growing more complex at an alarming rate. Instead of trying to capture all the world's needs in one global superset of tags, XML offers designers the power to create local tags with tools already in use.

Like HTML, XML provides a subset of SGML. Whereas HTML offers a subset of tags, however, XML offers a subset of functionality, including the ability to create new document type definitions. A valid XML document will include a reference in the <!DOCTYPE> tag that specifies a DTD file that the browser will download and use to interpret the XML file. Existing HTML documents will remain compatible; if there aren't any XML specifications, the browser will assume that the page was written in HTML and will process it according to that DTD. Creating DTDs is not for the faint of heart, although the XML creators have pared back the more complex aspects of SGML DTD creation.

Using XML and creating DTDs are subjects for another book—or two or three. XML is probably for developers several steps beyond the level of skill needed to work with Dynamic HTML, but it promises to extend the capabilities of our browsers as far or further. XML should be programmable using the same tools and techniques as Dynamic HTML. Keep in mind, however, that XML is more like cascading style sheets than like Dynamic HTML. XML extends the basic structures of HTML rather than focus on programming pages.

For more information on XML, see the specifications at http://www.w3.org/pub/WWW/TR or the FAQ at http://www.ucc.ie/xml/.

Scripting Languages: Client-Side Programmability

We've used scripting extensively throughout this book without pausing to consider its effect on Web development. Scripts have been around for a few browser versions and have made a quiet entry when compared with the splash of Java or the marketing of ActiveX. Without the scripting languages, though, none of the rest would make much sense. Everything that wasn't a simple document would have to become a Java applet or some other kind of programming object, and for a brief period it seemed that the Web might be headed in that direction. Lightweight scripting languages have given life to once static documents, making Web pages into programmable interfaces.

JavaScript has come a long way from its origins as a browser manipulator and data validator, emerging as a powerful new programming tool in its own right. JavaScript now has a new open standard from the ECMA, (European Computer Manufacturers Association) endorsed by both Netscape and Microsoft. Similarly, VBScript has brought the power of Microsoft's Visual Basic environment to the world of Web pages, giving developers new control over the world of the browser. Without these tools, applying Dynamic HTML would be impossible.

Layers: The Promise of Encapsulation

For me, the most exciting feature of layers is the SRC attribute. Layers can be useful for manipulating data, but their greatest advantage from my perspective is that they provide a useful way to group information, whether as parts of a document or as separate files. It's easy to use layers to manipulate groups of elements, allowing developers to create large clusters of interacting elements without having to keep track of every piece. Like textRange objects, layers are blunt tools. They can make simple tasks more complicated, but they can also make the impossible easy.

Their status as mini documents both helps and hinders layers. It gives them more power and a level of independence from the main document structure, but it also can make addressing large numbers of layers unwieldy. It's easy to get lost when you're looking for a particular piece of a document that may appear in several different places. Event handling can get especially strange, because layers can capture events within their document space. The inflexibility of layers (especially that of ILAYERs) will probably ease over the next few releases, making this approach a promising way to gather the parts that the document object model is threatening to unleash.

Document Object Model: All the Parts, All the Time

Although Netscape's layers offer possibilities, they don't offer the revolution promised by Microsoft's blasting open the browser. By exposing every attribute of every element (or aiming to), Microsoft is transforming the Web landscape. After several years as static documents, Web pages are now granular and free to change at will. The documents that broke down traditional document structures are themselves breaking down and opening yet more new vistas. HTML was an adequate interface for reading information and perhaps for querying it, but the document object model makes it possible to create interfaces that do useful work on the client.

The ability to modify element properties means that programmers can now create interfaces that resemble the GUI operating system interfaces (Windows and the Macintosh) that users have worked with before—and to create new interfaces that go beyond them. Clicking on links is an important addition to these interfaces but by itself provides an incomplete model for user-computer interaction. Moving elements—and more important, letting the user move objects—means that it's now possible to do tasks with Web pages that used to be the realm of the desktop interface. This capability doesn't automatically lead to the development of Web-based spreadsheets, word processors, and presentation systems, but it makes their creation much easier and much more likely. Web page elements can now be linked to the power of Java applets and ActiveX controls, letting those powerful programming tools focus on program logic while the browser manages the interface and the presentation of individual elements.

The addition of the textRange object to the document object model is a double-edged sword. It gives Web pages nearly infinite flexibility, making it possible for programmers to create scripts that encapsulate tens or hundreds of similar pages into one compact codebase. It also opens up the possibility of using a Web interface to create real applications—most likely a word processor. Combined with scripts and an applet or ActiveX control to provide menus or a toolbar, the textRange object makes it easy to produce data-creation interfaces as well as data-entry and data-manipulation interfaces.

Data Binding

With the appearance of the data-binding extensions for HTML, it's now possible to create client database applications for the Web without needing to use applets or ActiveX controls to manage every request. Web pages can now perform some of the data processing that used to take place on the server, especially Web-specific tasks that already burdened servers undertook with CGI and other interfaces. Some data processing is now done in intranet Web applications, and HTML extensions should accelerate that trend by providing a simple, generic interface for Web database presentation, lifting most of that burden from the applet or control. The flexibility of Dynamic HTML means that the number of Web transactions per task should also decline, because more of the data manipulation and page rebuilding can take place within the browser.

Microsoft's announcement of JavaBean support for data binding should do a lot to ease the concerns of developers who don't want to get locked in to one company's technology, and it also makes it much more likely that standards bodies (the W3C in particular) will look favorably upon this announcement. Microsoft's extensions for data binding are reasonably intuitive, but then may face competition from other proposals. Still these extensions will serve as a catalyst to ensure that those standards are created soon.

The Future of the Interface

Whether or not the browser will become the primary interface remains to be seen, but both Netscape's Netcaster and Microsoft's shell integration are strong steps toward the widespread use of the browser for much more than surfing. Both companies needed a stronger foundation of scripting and scriptability than was available in the early versions of the Web, and both of them have found the tools they needed by making those earlier protocols more programmable. The advent of the scripting languages made this development possible, and the development of object models for making content programmable is a huge step toward more powerful (and interesting) interface design.

Perhaps the most important factor in my enthusiasm for Dynamic HTML is its simplicity. The only new thing it does is to expose the HTML elements to programming after the page has been downloaded. There are a few complex parts, such as textRanges, but for the most part changing a tag is as simple as changing a property in a visual programming environment such as Visual Basic or Delphi. Although HTML developers will need scripting skills to take advantage of this new technology, a more critical shortcoming is a lack of knowledge of the particlars of HTML tags.

Several roadblocks remain on the way to Dynamic HTML's acceptance. First, and most important, are the positions of Netscape and Microsoft. Apart from obvious conflicts in the way Netscape and Microsoft handle events, there are few apparent technical obstacles to prevent at least a partial adoption by Netscape of Microsoft's version of Dynamic HTML. Undoubtedly, there are dramatic differences in the way the browsers are built, but it's hard to imagine the need to use a different syntax for handling document objects and elements. As we saw in Chapter 12, layers make some of this functionality possible, but the advantages of making everything available seem to outweigh the advantages layers give you grouping objects. The main advantage of Internet Explorer is its fine granularity; anything and everything can be changed at any time. Netscape's advantage lies in the opposite direction; you can encapsulate objects in layers and work with groups rather than hordes of individual pieces. Layers will remain a point of contention for a while, although both Microsoft and Netscape have made comments about supporting layer functionality through the DIV tag, perhaps providing a middle ground for the two feuding companies. Whether or not they do it in a compatible way remains to be seen. The dramatic differences between the two companies' versions of event objects is a portent of potential problems, but maybe they will eventually be able to settle this.

With any luck, in a few months you'll be able to use the techniques I've illustrated in this book without regard to the conflict between Internet Explorer and Netscape. That hope is the main reason I've covered many of the differences and similarities between the browsers—I hope you'll be able to write vendor neutral Dynamic HTML code soon, and hope you'll try to make your information available to users of multiple browsers now.

The other roadblock to the adoption of any of these technologies is in the tools market. Most development environments, including Microsoft's own FrontPage, don't include support for cascading style sheets, much less tools for organizing and building scripts beyond a few simple shortcuts. For the immediate future, it looks as if Dynamic HTML will remain in the hands of those who handcraft most of their pages. This situation may not be a bad thing—it will keep a few painfully flashing pages off the web—but it stands in the way of HTML's becoming a full-fledged interface.

In the past five years, the Web has transformed the way people do business, creating a new field for designers and developers. This transformation has created new needs and new demands for better tools. Roadblocks rise and fall, but the Web keeps growing. Dynamic HTML, its variants, and strong supporting cast promise to shift our focus from pages to objects, breaking pages down into their components and making it easier for them to grow yet again. To create support for their new technologies at all levels of Web development, Netscape and Microsoft must settle their differences. Designers and programmers who ride the cutting edge may love the latest tools and wildest toys, but most Web developers are interested in presenting information to the widest possible audience. This potential market puts Netscape and Microsoft in the odd position of promoting divergent new technologies (to differentiate their products) while needing to find common ground to keep the market from fragmenting into pieces that can't communicate. The rapid growth of networks, including the Internet, is painfully dependent on standards. If users can share a network but can't communicate, the network's overall value diminishes tremendously. The days of hype are starting to fade, and people are hoping to get some real work done. That demands standards and not corporate duels, 'not invented here' attitudes, and deliberate incompatibility.

In conjunction with the new developments in HTML (cascading style sheets and XML), the new programmability of Web pages demands a new architecture for Web sites. Managing flexible content requires designers to re-examine the structures they've built. In a few years, the Web may no longer be recognizable as a distinct part of the computing world, as it takes over the interfaces we've known and blurs them into the network. Dynamic HTML is a critical part of integrating our computers into larger networks, providing a framework for collaborative applications and shared documents. For today, it's highly experimental, cutting-edge stuff. In a few years, Dynamic HTML will be the concrete in the foundation of a new world of computing applications.

The Fine Art of Detecting Browsers

The new browsers offer wonderful features, but the code for any of them seldom works for any other browser. What we need is a browser detection program we can count on. I've stitched together a simple detector that uses the navigator object to let you know whether the browser is Netscape ("NS"), Microsoft ("MS"), or other (??) and also report its version. The code is an amalgamation of various Microsoft and Netscape browser detection routines:

```
<HTML>
<HEAD><TITLE>Browser Sleuth</TITLE></HEAD>
<BODY>


<SCRIPT LANGUAGE="JavaScript">
<!—hide from old browsers
function whichBrowser(){
browser="??";
if (navigator.appName=="Netscape")
   {browser="NS";}
else
   {var msie=navigator.userAgent.indexOf("MSIE");
   if (msie!=0) {browser="MS";}
```

```
    }
return browser;
}
function whichVersion(browser) {
version=0;
if (browser=="NS")
{version=(parseInt(navigator.userAgent.substring(8,9
)));}
if (browser=="MS")
    {ua=navigator.userAgent
     msie=ua.indexOf("MSIE");
     version=(parseInt(ua.substring(msie+5,
ua.indexOf(".",msie))));
    }
return version;
}

browse=whichBrowser();
verse=whichVersion(browse);
alert(browse + " " + verse);
//end hide->
</SCRIPT>
This text gets seen on old browsers or on browsers
you don't use
window.location="http://yournewlocation" on.
</BODY>
</HTML>
```

This code is JavaScript (it must be JavaScript if you want
to detect Netscape). It gives you two handy functions.
The whichBrowser() function lets you know whether
you're on Netscape, Microsoft, or something else. The
whichVersion() function lets you know what version of
the program you're working on. When you have this
information, you can redirect the user to the appropriate
page. Ideally, the HTML in the body of this document

would be for older browsers (such as AOL and Mosaic), and you'd use the version information to redirect people with newer browsers to pages that took advantage of the added functionality. The comments for hiding the code are critical if you think that anyone with an old browser may be coming through. If you omit these comments, your script will adorn the top of the page.

APPENDIX B

Note on terminology

Dynamic HTML has opened up a hornet's nest of terminology. I've done my best to be consistent in using the following terminology throughout the book. Applying definitions that were originally created in the disparate worlds of SGML and object-oriented programming is a difficult task, and the distinctions can be obscure.

An *element* is a piece of a page defined by a complete HTML markup. Here are some examples:

```
<IMG SRC="img.gif">
<P>This is a paragraph</P>
<ILAYER>This is a layer</ILAYER>
```

Elements have *attributes*, such as the SRC in an element using the IMG tag, the TYPE in an element using the INPUT tag, or the STYLE or ID in any element. A *tag* is the piece of the HTML code that identifies the type of element; for example, IMG is the tag in the first example. Some tags are placeholders: DIV, for example, exists only to create subelements within a block of HTML.

When we refer to elements from within a script, we're addressing *objects*, which are representations of these elements that the browser uses to build the page. An *object* in this context is a way to address the element in the browser's scripting framework. Objects represent the attributes of the original element (and possibly other features as well) as *properties*. Any object that represents an IMG element will include an src property. Objects may also have *methods*, which can accept and return parameters. The main differences between the competing Netscape and Microsoft versions of Dynamic HTML lie in the particular objects each version allows you to address and modify.

Not all objects represent elements; many objects are built into the browser, and you can create others of your own. All objects are instantiations of more abstract programming *classes*, given life with specific data, memory addresses, and so on. Classes are to objects as tags are to elements, more or less: an abstract description of a group of items that behave similarly. Properties are to objects as attributes are to elements, providing the details of a particular case.

NOTE JavaScript and VBScript are not object-oriented languages in the formal sense represented by Java and C++. Instead, JavaScript and VBScript are fairly simple procedural languages with object-oriented features. Most important, they allow you to manipulate the objects created by the browser and the Web pages.

INDEX

Listings in *italic* are on topics most likely to change at press time. Check http://www.mispress.com/dynamichtml/ for the latest information.

A

Abstract Windowing Toolkit (AWT), 119
ActiveMovie control, 110-5
Active Server Pages (ASP) 246-247, 264
ActiveX controls, 13, 15, 26, 103-115, 221, 253
  and OBJECT tag, 107
  prebuilt controls, 107
Advanced Data Control (ADC), 246, 254, 263-9
AdvancedDataFactory, 264, 266
AdvancedDataSpace, 264-5
all (document.all) collection, 31, 65
anchor array, 30
animation
  with Paths control, 229-31
  with layers, 292-294
applets, 25, 103-4, 118-126
AREA tag, 156
artificial intelligence, 207
ASCII values, 94-5
attributes, 39, 321
authentication, 249, 266
AVI files, 110-5

B

Berners-Lee, Tim 18

BLINK tag, 41
bots, 9
browser detection, 317-9
bufferDepth property, 55
bytecodes, 116

C

cache, loading images into, 160
cancelBubble, 101, 134
captureEvents(), 101-2, 294-5
Cascading Style Sheets, 20-5, 33, 305, 314-5
  relation to style properties, 40
  layering, 203-6
  positioning, 46-55, 148-155
  properties, 56-60, 131
CERN, 17, 306
CGI (Common Gateway Interface), 6-9, 246, 311
character, 180
child layers, 277
Chr(), 94
CLASS tag 22, 135, 137
classes, 322
CLASSID, 108
clearTimeout(), 41
client-server computing, 245
client-side includes, 276-280
clipping, 301-3
COBOL, 117

CODEBASE, 108
collapse(), *181*
colorDepth property, 55
comic strip, 202-6, 288-92
comment tags, 12
commonParentElement(), *191*
compatibility, throughout
   and browser detection, 317-9
   with older browsers, 12, 133, 317-9
Component Object Model (COM), 104, 118, 122
concatenation, 14
container:positioned, 48
Content-Type, 8
cookies, 12
createRange(), *192*
createTextRange(), *173*, *175*
CSS – see Cascading Style Sheets
cursor, following, 146-148

D

databases, relational 241-245
data binding, 239-270, 311-2
   consumers and sources, 253
data hiding, 175, 202-206, 219, 280-92
Data Source Name (DSN), 248
data storage, 211-212
DATAFLD, 253-5, 261
DATAFORMATAS, 253, 255
DATASRC, 253-4, 261
DataURL, 256
DELETE (SQL), 244
Delphi, 106, 312

detail section (IDC), 251
digital signatures, 105, 117
Distributed COM (DCOM), 104, 265
DIV tag, 99, 131, 134, 137, 139, 211, 313
document object, 29-34, 61
   as dataset, 160-7
document object model, 29-34, 109-10, 310-11
Document Type Definition (DTD), 307-8
dragging 77, 78, 148, 152, 294-301
DSN – see Data Source Name
Dynamic Link Libraries (DLLs), 104

E

ECMAScript – see JavaScript
element, definition, 321
Eliza, *206-19*
encapsulation, 309-10, 313
events
   and ActiveX controls, 109-15
   bubbling (Microsoft model), 98-101, 141, 148, 171
   capturing (Netscape model), 102-3, 294
   models, 70-71
   objects, and conflicts between Netscape and Microsoft, 71-75
   parameters, 73
   properties, 72-3
   as properties of document object, 74

return values, 152
expand(), 181

F

fonts
  families, 22, 46
  size, 46
  style, 46
  weight, 46
forms
  processing, 6
  validation, 86-7, 89-90
  validation with ADC, 267-269
forms array, 30
frames, 28, 195-199
  frame object, 29
FrontPage extensions, 9
FrontPage 2.0, 252, 314
functions, 42

G

GUI (Graphical User Interface) interface, 169, 310

H

handleEvent(), 101-2
HEIGHT (attribute vs. style property), 48
history object, 29, 34
hres property, 55
HTML, history 18-20
htmlMatchCase, 182
htmlMatchWord, 182
htmlSelText, 174

htmlText, 174
HTTP, 2-4, 6-7, 11, 18, 265-6, 278
HTX – see Internet Database Connectivity

I

ID tag, 22, 135, 162-6
  dangers of duplicates, 139, 175
ILAYER tag 272-4, 276-280
images collection, 28, 30, 61-66
Internet Database Connectivity (IDC/HTX), 246-53
  documentation, 247
  fields, 251
  if...then, 252
  and static HTML, 253
Internet Information Server (IIS), 5, 246, 264
interpreter, Java, 117
image maps 155-160, 306
IMG elements, 65, 156
INSERT (SQL), 244
InStr(), 214
isEmbed(), 189

J

Java, 15, 25-26, 27, 103-4, 115-26, 305
  Beans, 125-6, 239, 254, 269, 312
  calling JavaScript from, 122-26
  exception handlers, 124
  and LiveConnect, 118-26

packages, 123
Virtual Machine, 116
Java Development Kit, 119,
125
JavaScript, 10-13, 34-5, 309,
322
and JScript, 10, 34-5
functions, 42-43
syntax, compared to
VBScript, 14, 34-5, 70-71,
114-5
JScript – see JavaScript
just-in-time compiler, 117

K

keys, 241-2
keywords, 211
kiosk applications 221, 235

L

LANGUAGE parameter, 44-
45, 70
LAYER tag, 272-4
layers
CSS, with zIndex, 49-54
Netscape, 54-55, 271-303
attributes, 273-4
collections, 274
clipping, 301-3
debugging, 271
encapsulation, 272
methods, 276
positioning, 272
properties, 275
tags, 272-4
left, 46
link array, 30
LiveConnect, 118-126

LiveScript – see JavaScript
location object, 29
logical tags, 19

M

MAP elements, 159
MARQUEE tag, 90-92, 253
MAYSCRIPT, 124
methods, 33, 34, 321
Microsoft Access, 241, 242
Mixer control, 238
mouse button, 77
move(), 180
moveAbove(), 285
moveEnd(), 180
moveNext(), 261
movePrevious(), 261
moveStart(), 180
Mr.Alienhead demo, 149

N

NAME attribute, 196, 198,
200
naming conventions, 65, 71,
135, 140, 145, 159-161,
284-5
navigator object, 29-30
NCompass, 106, 221
Netcaster, 312
newline (\n), 8
NOLAYER tag, 274

O

object model, 27-34, 321
syntax, 32

terminology, 28, 33, 321-22
Object Linking and Embedding (OLE), 104
OBJECT tag, 107-109
  parameters, 107-8
ODBC, see Open Database Connectivity
OLE DB, 265
onabort, 82
onafterupdate, 269
onbeforeupdate, 269
onblur, 85-6
onbounce, 91
onchange, 86-7
onclick, 75-6, 148
ondblclick, 76-7
ondragdrop, 96-7
onerror, 82-3
onfinish, 91-2
onfocus, 87-8
onhelp, 93
onkeydown, 93-4
onkeypress, 94-5
onkeyup, 95-6
onload, 83-4
onmousedown, 77-8, 154, 294
onmousemove, 78-9, 148
onmouseout, 35, 79-80, 143, 288
onmouseover, 35, 80-81, 143, 145, 149, 206, 288
onmouseup, 77, 81, 294
onmove, 97-8
onreadystatechange, 84
onreset, 88-9
onresize, 97-8
onrowenter, 269
onrowexit, 268
onselect, 89
onstart, 92
onsubmit, 89-90
onunload, 84-5
Open Database Connectivity (ODBC), 248-9, 264, 266
operating system, replacing with browser 169
OS/2 Warp and Java, 116
outlines, expandable, *127-31*, 132-41, 278-280

P

PARAM tag, 109
parentElement(), 187
parsing, 2, 6, 215
parseInt(), 154
pasteHTML(), 66, 175, 131
  glitches, 179, 208
  vs. changing text property, 178
paths control, 229-231
  parameters and Ticks, 231
Peer Web Services, 246
Perl, 6-9
Personal Web Server (Windows 95), 246
plug-ins, 25-26
pop-up menus, 141-145
position:absolute, 48
positioning, see cascading style sheets
properties, 33, 39, 321
psychotherapist, 206-19
puzzle, 160-7

Q

queries, database 242-4

R

rabbits, marshmallow, 63-65
range (parameter), 182
rangeFromElement(), 173, 175
rangeFromText(), 182
releaseEvents(), 101-2, 294
routeEvents(), 101-2

S

screen updates, problems,
    50-51, 54
script object, 30
SCRIPT tag, 71, 114
scripting tutorials, 31
scripts, see JavaScript and
    VBScript
    position in HTML, 45
search-and-replace function,
    182-187
security, 105
SELECT (SQL), 244
select(), 183
sentence, 181
Sequencer control, 235-237
server-side includes, 2, 4-5
setRange(), 181
setTimeout(), 41-42, 64, 293
SGML (Standard Generalized
    Markup Language), 19-20,
    306-8
shtml, 5
SiteBuilder network, 240
Smalltalk, 117
SPAN tag, 99
Sprite control, 238
SQL, see Structured Query
    Language
srcElement, 100, 140

startPainting(), 224
status bar, 88
stm, 5
stopPainting(), 224
story, 181
Structured Graphics Control,
    231-235
Structured Query Language,
    242-244
STYLE tag, 21
style sheets – see Cascading
    style sheets
subroutines, 42-43
substring(), 159
switchboard programming,
    140

T

tables, database, 241-244
tables, HTML 160-1
Tabular Data Control (TDC),
    212, 240, 255-63
    filtering, 259-60
    properties, 256-7
    reset(), 256
    sorting, 258-9
text files, delimited 255
textRange, 66-67, 169-193,
    219, 311, 312
    creating, 171-3
    and frames, 198
    and outlines, 128-131
    outside document object
        model, 170-2
    properties, 174
    set statement in VBScript,
        210
    testbed, 176
    units, 181

tickers, 91, 117
top, 46
transactions, database, 267-9
transitions 222-224
   available effects, 222
Trojan Horses, 117

U

UPDATE (SQL), 244
URL, manipulating, 29, 165-6
UseHeader, 256

V

validation, see form validation
verification, 105
VBScript, 13-14, 34-5, 221, 309, 322
   functions and subroutines, 42-43
   syntax, compared to JavaScript, 14, 34-5, 70-1, 114-5
vector graphics, 231-2
video, 110
Visual Basic, 104, 106, 312
Visual C++, 104, 106
visual filters, 225-9

available effects, 228-9
Visual InterDev, 247
Visual J++, 119
visual object, 55
vres property, 55
Visual Studio, 106, 247
   macros, 192

W

W3 Consortium, 20, 22, 32, 46, 102, 240, 308, 312
white space, 212
WIDTH (attribute vs. style property), 48
WIN32 API, 105
win.call (LiveConnect), 124
window object, 29
windows, managing multiple 195-6, 199-202
word, 181

X

XML, 20, 305,307-8, 315

Z

zIndex, 46

Please remember – all listings included in this book are available at http://www.mispress.com/dynamichtml/ .

Stay updated!
(and save yourself a lot of typing)

Dynamic HTML is unfortunately a field in rapid flux. What's true today will likely not be true tomorrow. To help you cope with the changing standards and revised architectures, we've set up a Web site to supplement this book. Visit **http://www.mispress.com/dynamichtml** to find the latest information on Dynamic HTML, updated to keep you current with the newest tools and techniques. If a topic in the index is in italics, you should check out the Web site before proceeding for updated information. Chapters 8 (text ranges) and 10 (multimedia effects) are especially in flux. Check the site for the latest information.

All of the example code complete with the fine original graphics used in the book, will be posted on the Web site. If you have any problems with an example, check the Web site for any corrections. Spare yourself the typos and get the latest code. All of these examples have been tested on the most current browsers from Netscape and Microsoft.